ABRAZANDO EL ESPÍRITU

AMERICAN CROSSROADS

Edited by Earl Lewis, George Lipsitz, George Sánchez, Dana Takagi, Laura Briggs, and Nikhil Pal Singh

Ana Elizabeth Rosas · *ABRAZANDO EL ESPÍRITU*

Bracero Families Confront the US-Mexico Border

UNIVERSITY OF CALIFORNIA PRESS

University of California Press, one of the most distinguished university presses in the United
States, enriches lives around the world by advancing scholarship in the humanities, social
sciences, and natural sciences. Its activities are supported by the UC Press Foundation and by
philanthropic contributions from individuals and institutions. For more information, visit
www.ucpress.edu.

University of California Press
Oakland, California

Library of Congress Cataloging-in-Publication Data

Rosas, Ana Elizabeth, 1978–
    Abrazando el espíritu : Bracero families confront the US-Mexico border / Ana Elizabeth
Rosas.
        pages   cm. — (American crossroads ; 40)
    Includes bibliographical references and index.
    ISBN 978-0-520-28266-7 (cloth : alk. paper) — ISBN 978-0-520-28267-4 (pbk. : alk. paper)
— ISBN 978-0-520-95865-4 (e-book)
    1. Foreign workers, Mexican—Family relationships—United States—History—20th
century.   2. Migrant agricultural laborers—Family relationships—United States—
History—20th century.   3. Mexicans—United States—Social conditions—20th
century.   4. Families—Mexico—Social conditions—20th century.   5. Immigrant
families—United States—Social conditions—20th century.   6. Mexico—Emigration and
immigration—Social aspects.   7. United States—Emigration and immigration—Social
aspects.   I. Title.
    HD8081.M6R66   2014
    305.8'6872073—dc23   2014010258

Manufactured in the United States of America

23   22   21   20   19   18   17   16   15   14
10   9   8   7   6   5   4   3   2   1

In keeping with a commitment to support environmentally responsible and sustainable
printing practices, UC Press has printed this book on Natures Natural, a fiber that contains
30% post-consumer waste and meets the minimum requirements of ANSI/NISO Z39.48–1992
(R 1997) (*Permanence of Paper*).

En memoria de mis abuelitas y abuelitos:
Francisca Ramirez Medina y Desiderio Ahumada Medina
Josefina Gomez Rosas y Manuel Ricardo Rosas

Para mi familia:
Francisco Rosas Gomez, Dolores Rosas Medina, y Abigail Rosas
Su cariño, ingenio, oraciones, y valor han hecho este libro una realidad

Para los de mi barrio:
Su ánimo y lucha iluminaron el camino

Para mis estudiantes de Chicana/o studies:
Nuestras conversaciónes y sus logros mantuvieron vigente la urgencia
de escribir con coraje y corazón

Para todas las familias inmigrante:
Nuestra lucha sigue

Para los que ya no estan
Para los que estan aqui
Y para los que vienen

For those who are no longer here
For those who are here
For those who are on their way

Calle 13, "PAL' NORTE" ("To the North"), *Residente o visitante,* 2007

CONTENTS

ILLUSTRATIONS

ACKNOWLEDGMENTS

This history would have never been written had it not been for Dr. George J. Sanchez's mentorship. Beginning in 1998 and to this very day, Dr. Sanchez has been a generous mentor to me, and the more I am a part of this profession the more I am convinced that he is one of the best mentors in the nation. Upon enrolling in his undergraduate course "The History of the Mexican American" at the University of Southern California (USC), I became inspired to research further a subject that was at best a fraction of what Dr. Sanchez shared with his students in this course and, over time, with the thousands of women and men participating in his many conferences, programs, workshops, and forums in support of a truly interdisciplinary and diverse education at this and countless campuses nationwide. His affording us the confidence, trust, and funding to pursue our own research with honesty, rigor, and heart at a campus in which this was a rarity for a first-generation working-class Mexican immigrant female undergraduate student like me transformed my thinking and in turn my world. Dr. Sanchez's brilliantly expansive investigation and teaching of the Chicana/o experience reaffirmed for me that becoming a Chicana historian was not only possible but worthwhile.

More concretely, since day one, Dr. Sanchez refused to give up on me or on what would become my publication of this history. With unparalleled high standards and humanity, he mentored me through my participation in USC's Ronald E. McNair Scholars Program; a cruel first year of graduate study at USC; USC's Ahmanson Foundation's Fellowship Program; USC's first dissertation workshop in the

Department of American Studies and Ethnicity; a Latina/o Studies Fellowship from the Smithsonian Institution's National Museum of American History; a Doctoral Fellowship from the Ford Foundation; and a fellowship from Stanford University's Bill Lane Center for the Study of the West. He provided extensive comments and editorial recommendations on what went on to become an award-winning dissertation; with his equally supportive wife, Debra Sanchez, he opened his family home to me when I was transitioning out of USC; and he was most persistent in my not allowing my perfectionist streak and voluminous research to delay my submission of this history for publication.

Years of working with me on my BA and doctorate in history did not discourage Dr. Sanchez from selflessly giving of his precious energy, time, and editorial wizardry to advance the publication of this book. Hence, it is with great respect that I detail his unwavering and meticulous efforts in support of my working in a profession as part of a larger struggle for a more just society that has immeasurably improved my life. I hope that if he reads this expression of my gratitude he understands why, even after more than fifteen years, I still call him "Dr. Sanchez" and not "George" as other colleagues do: it is my small way of honoring his commitment to my education. He will always be a person worthy of my utmost and wholehearted respect—a true *profesor,* as my late grandmother Francisca Medina Ramirez used to say.

Among the introductions that my participation in Dr. Sanchez's dissertation workshop made possible, none was as generative as my meeting to share and discuss my dissertation proposal with Dr. Vicki L. Ruiz. In 2003, when I first met Dr. Ruiz, she made sure that I left with a renewed confidence in the promise of pursuing a doctorate in history. Before this meeting, no other professor of women's history had treated my work with the respect with which Dr. Ruiz reviewed my dissertation proposal. Our working well together at this workshop and in continued correspondence resulted in her serving on my dissertation committee, acting as my faculty mentor for the University of California President's Postdoctoral Fellowship Program, and now being my chair and colleague as part of the University of California Irvine's (UCI) departments of Chicano-Latino studies and history. These stages of my career and her role within them have substantially strengthened my investigation and writing of this history. She has transformed each of these opportunities and interactions into invaluable projects from which I have been able to grasp what is possible when one writes from the heart. Throughout the last couple of years, her support of my publication of this book and my work at UCI have made evident just how much she believes in the promise of being generous with what we know.

Writing this book has also afforded me the honor of learning from Dr. George Lipsitz, who served as my Ford Foundation Postdoctoral Fellowship faculty mentor. I doubt that I will ever be able to repay him: his mentorship was only the beginning of his contribution to this history. After I completed the bulk of the research and a book draft that was deemed two books' worth of research and writing, Dr. Lipsitz's advice and editorial recommendations helped make my manuscript publishable and capable of undergoing the rigors of academic peer review. I appreciate his setting such a high standard for how to hold each other accountable while generously sharing what we know in our struggle for a more humane professoriate and society.

Philippa Levine and Pierrette Hondagneu-Sotelo also contributed to my investigation of this history. Each in her own way held me to the highest standard when reviewing my work and remained graciously steadfast in her friendship with me. Both continue to be fabulous role models for how to take a feminist perspective on several fronts with integrity. Maria Elena Martinez and Lon Kurashige were also helpful throughout the early stages of my pursuit of this history. Funding from the USC's Norman Topping Scholars Scholarship Program and Ahmanson Foundation Fellowship Program, the Ford Foundation's Doctoral Fellowship Program, the Smithsonian Institution, the Huntington, Texas Tech University's Formby Research Fellowship Program, Stanford University's Bill Lane Center for the Study of the West's Fellowship Program, the University of California President's Postdoctoral Fellowship Program, and the Ford Foundation's Postdoctoral Fellowship Program, as well as the archival research support of Polly Armstrong at Stanford University's Special Collections, made writing this history feasible and enabled me to complete what throughout the years became a broadly interdisciplinary investigation and interpretation of the rigors of the bracero family experience in the United States and Mexico. It is my hope that the result will help to fuel these institutions' investment in such worthwhile fellowship programs, as they are needed and effective. I cannot stress enough just how much they added to my investigation and writing of this history.

Crossing paths and learning from extraordinary scholars in our field of Chicana/o history has been one of the most enjoyable aspects of writing about the bracero family experience. Dr. Albert Camarillo has been most exemplary in his support of my writing of this history. His generously gracious collegiality and friendship and contributions to Chicana/o history have made him a wonderful source of support for me. Jose Alamillo, Milo M. Alvarez, Mike Amezcua, Gabriela Arredondo, Alexander Aviña, Geraldo L. Cadava, Miroslava Chavez Garcia, Lori Flores, David G. Garcia, Mario Garcia, Jerry B. Gonzalez, David G. Gutiérrez, Ramon Gutiérrez,

Felipe Hinojosa, Gerardo "Lalo" Licon, Gustavo Licon, Jorge Mariscal, Lorena Marquez, Veronica Matsuda Martinez, Jimmy Patino, Monica Perales, Stephen Pitti, Albert Rodriguez, and Alicia Schmidt Camacho have been most generous in sharing their incisive insights on the Chicana/o experience with me. The collegiality of Natalia Molina, Robin D. G. Kelley, Mae Ngai, Kelly Lytle Hernandez, Ruth Wilson Gilmore, John Mckiernan Gonzalez, Luis Alvarez, Tiya Miles, Suzanne Oboler, Elizabeth Escobedo, Shelley Fishkin, Marvette Perez, Steve Velasquez, Faith Ruffins, Peter Liebhold, Pete Daniel, Maria Eugenia Cotera, Mary C. Kelley, Regina Morantz Sanchez, Linda Gordon, Virginia Sanchez Korrol, Gaye Theresa Johnson, David A. Chang, and the late Clyde Woods at different stages of this undertaking also made for great breakthroughs when I shared this research at conferences, meetings, and symposia. Their own foundational research has helped me make my work urgent and viable.

Navigating the demands of interdisciplinary research has been a formative and fun dimension to my investigation of this history, in large part because of conversations shared with friends and scholars in ethnic studies. Stevie Ruiz has been a fabulous friend in steering me toward superb scholarship in this field of inquiry and discussing it with me. Desiree Campos Marquez, Christopher Jimenez y West, Ilda Jimenez y West, Mercedes Mendoza, Laura Gutiérrez, Elda Maria Roman, Adrian Felix, Mark Padoongpatt, Robert Eap, Daniel Gebler, Anne Choi, Karen Bowdre, Maria Elena Espinoza, Armando García, Genelle Gaudinez, Belinda Lum, Sharon Sekhon, Laura Fugikawa, and Roberto G. Gonzalez have been great people with whom to share energizing dialogue that stretches across academic fields, activist platforms, employment sectors, destinations, and generations of struggle.

Being among the few tenure track faculty members at UCI to work in departments that span this campus's School of Humanities and School of Social Sciences has afforded me the privilege of working alongside a diverse and talented group of colleagues throughout my writing of this history. In the Department of Chicano-Latino Studies, Belinda Campos, Anita Casavantes Bradford, Leo Chavez, Janet DeSipio, Louis DeSipio, Cynthia Feliciano, Raul Fernandez, Glenda Flores, Stella Ginez, Gilbert G. Gonzalez, Michael Montoya, Alejandro Morales, Ramon Muñoz, Lori Ramirez, and Vicki L. Ruiz have been most supportive. During the last couple of years, Debbie Michel, our department's administrative manager, has been resourceful and tireless in helping me organize our department's student-centered events, forums, showcases, and workshops. Always going the extra mile, Debbie has been instructive to my work as director of undergraduate studies, insisting (with humor and heart) that I not lose sight of the importance of bringing the hard-earned lessons of working with students and my neighborhood to everything I teach, facilitate, and write on campus.

Throughout the years colleagues in the Department of History have also been enthusiastic in their support of my writing of this book. I've benefited greatly from the collegiality of Sharon Block, Yong Chen, Bibi Do, Alice Fahs, Douglas Haynes, David Igler, Marcus Kanda, Lynn Mally, Jessica Millward, Rachel O'Toole, Jaime Rodriguez, Emily Rosenberg, Uli Strasser, Heidi Tinsman, and Jeff Wasserstrom. Robert "Bob" Moeller has been especially steadfast and generous in his counsel and support of my teaching and research and my commitment to South Central Los Angeles, California, and its influence on my interdisciplinary approach to the investigation of this history. Similarly Bridget Cooks, Catherine Benamou, Jennifer Chacon, Daniel Fabrega, Cristina Flores, Kevin Huie, Michelle Lee, Raslyn Rendon, Said Shokair, and Diego Vigil have been fabulous colleagues in the most important struggle that consistently brings us together: that of alerting our undergraduate and graduate students to the potential of taking their intellectual imaginary, identity, and rights seriously.

I owe incalculable gratitude to the undergraduate and graduate students of UCI. Throughout my research and writing, they have made this campus a source of productive work and good times. Each quarter, our learning together from Chicana/o history paved the way for conversations and collaborations in support of a more humane society that transformed my writing of this history into a truly generative act. Our collaborative engagement in thinking and acting historically—developing a historical understanding of our past and drawing on it to understand and act in the present in our homes and neighborhoods with a sense of personal accountability—has led to countless forums, lessons, presentations, film productions, live performances, poems, songs, reading groups, workshops, cards, memorable moments, bouts of laughter, and new insights that showed me the power of writing this history with *entrega, fé, coraje,* and *corazón,* and in the company of amazing intellectual allies in the making—*ustedes*—you. For this and all of the heartening hard work you have done and continue to do, *mil gracias:* Kendra Aguilar, Mariana Arcila, Mayra Arredondo, Joselyn Ayala, Edgar Barron, Nora Barron, Nicholas Bravo, Venecia Caldera, Alexandra Cazares, Rosalio Cedillo, Michelle Cifuentes, Karina Colina, Madelene De Arcos, Cynthia Florido, Erika Garcia, Daniel Gonzalez, Jennifer Gonzalez, Nancy Herrera, Komal Jain, Briana Jex, Jeffrey Jimenez, Siahara Jimenez, Jonathan Lopez, Melissa Madrigal, Nathalie Madrigal, Daisy Marin, Julissa Marin, Bryan Martinez, Ashley Medrano, Mayra Mejia, Evani Molina, Adriana Naranjo, Chad Ngo, Mark Ocegueda, Virginia Orozco, Jocelyn

Pedroza, Johanna Perez, Juily Phun, Karina Prada, Jessica Ramirez, Cristela Reyes, Maria Lourdes Reyes, Vanessa Reyes, Sadie Retana, Maribel Rodarte, Nancy Briyidt Rodriguez, Delmy Ruiz, Viviana Salazar, Vincent Sanchez, Salvador Solis, Anacany Torres, Karina Vasquez, Carmen Verdugo, and Omar Zepeda; on the UCI Multi-Disciplinary Design Program Team, Liliana Aguila, Megan Bonilla, Heyzel Chevez, Linett Chevez, Vileana de la Rosa, Anthony Delgado, Maritza Duran, Cristina Gonzales, Mayra Lopez, Jacqueline Orozco, and Jeanettte Reveles; in the UCI Reading and Honors Research Groups, Diana Aguirre, Irving Alejo, Blanca Anselmo, Andrew Araujo, Valente Ayala, Jennifer Botello, Jesus Camacho, German Castilla, Daisy "Delsy" Cedillo, Erica Cesena, Miguel Chavez, Ernesto Conde, Iliana Cruz, Sesar Galvez, Leana Gutierrez, Julissa Hamilton, Guadalupe Llamas, Jesus Macias, Jessica Muñoz, Jacqueline Navarro, Samantha Navarro, Pricila Novoa, Vishal Patel, Victoria Ramirez, Betsy Robles, Fatima Roman, Crystal Romero, Christopher Ruiz, Viviana Salazar, Cindy Salgado, Pablo Silva, Katie To, Elaine Torres, Ivan Torres, Melissa Valdez, Uriel Varela, Angelica Vazquez, and Gabriel Vidal; in the UCI Movimiento Estudiantil Chicana/o de Aztlán, Fatima Acuna, Gracie Arguelles, Patricia Cruz, Sandra Flores, Andrea Gaspar, Christopher Jimenez, Alejandro Muro, Franchesca Ocasio, Irais Rodriguez, and Laura Zavala; in the UCI Phi Lambda Rho Incorporated Sorority, Karina Camacho, Isabel Diaz, Denise Leon, Lisa Diane Padilla, and Erika Santacruz; and among the UCI Summer Undergraduate Research Program Fellows, Ivania Enriquez, Claudia Maravilla, Brenda Medina Hernandez, Mario Obando, Frank Ortega, and Yuridia Ramirez. Each of you is well on your way to making the field of Chicana/o studies that much more promising. Maritza Duran and Crystal Romero deserve my special wholehearted gratitude for having shared, with the utmost trust, their family histories and photographs with me. Mayra Arredondo and Brenda Medina Hernandez provided invaluable help with my transcription of several oral life histories and collection of important documents.

The University of California Press, and especially Dore Brown, Kim Hogeland, Elisabeth Magnus, Pamela Polk, and Niels Hooper, provided helpful information and feedback contributing to the publication of this history. Their attentiveness to every detail proved most helpful when working to turn this history into this book. I deeply value their efforts in support of a rigorously constructive consideration of the bracero family experience. It made for a more forceful consideration of the family formations at the center of this history.

The life histories I heard from residents in my home neighborhood of South Central Los Angeles have led me to make writing this history a cherished priority.

The day-to-day interactions in the 'hood that made these conversations possible and integral to my investigation and writing of this history have intensified my appreciation for the power of acting in solidarity with bracero families who have opened their hearts, family archives, and homes to me. Their histories and those of their families in San Martin de Hidalgo and Ameca, Jalisco, and in Acambaro, Guanajuato, Mexico, have shown me how much more becomes visible and urgent when we pause to listen to each other—particularly the obligation to see and write *con el alma.* For this life lesson and much more, I am grateful to have interviewed many families, among them *las familias* Cervantes, Duran, Frias, Guerra, Lopez, Magallanes, Manzo, Medina, Ramirez, Rios, Rodriguez, Romero, Rosas, Ruiz, Sanchez, Santander, and Torres. Their stories have augmented my long-standing admiration and respect for the confidence, *oraciones,* and resilience of my late extraordinary grandparents: Manuel Ricardo Rosas, Francisca Medina Ramirez, and Desiderio Ahumada Medina. *Los quiero mucho.* They are the heart of this history. Josefina Rosas Gomez, Maria Elena Medina, Ignacia Zarate Mandujano, Angelica Medina, Sandra Medina, Olga Ramirez, Alejandra Ramirez, Mariana Ramirez, Carmen Medina, Luis Medina, Armando Medina, Sergio Medina, Moises Medina, Blanca Medina, Cesario Rosas, Rosa Rosas, Miguel Rosas, Juventina Carlos Rosas, Bernardo Carlos, Manuel de Jesus Rosas, Maria Teresa Rodriguez, Maria Concepcion Ruiz, Magdaleno Ruiz, Leticia Nuño Zarate, Emma Solorzano, Ramona Frias, Salvador Frias, Sylvia Manzo, Maria Francisca Ordonez Torres, Veneranda Torres, Jesus Torres, Maria Graciela Garcia Guerra, Artemio Guerra de Leon, Sonia Torres, Miguel Torres, Esther Legaspi Delgadillo Sanchez, Catalina Ruiz, Antonio Ruiz, and Ramon Rea Ruiz have also given much to this history and me. I hope that in some small way this history meets their expectations and honors their spirited generosity and struggle.

Throughout the years, "catching up" or "taking a break" from my research and writing with Aracely Gomez, Yadira Cervantes, Esther Sanchez, Jazlyn Sanchez, Stevie Ruiz, Hector Ruiz, Oscar Cervantes, Bernardo Nuño, and Sandy Escobedo has elevated my appreciation for the restorative power of friendship. I thank each of them for the uniqueness of the ties and trust that connect us, often when we least expect it.

I especially and *con todo mi corazón* thank Ricardo Alvarez for sharing conversations and strolls that have made for countless debates, laughter, and promises; he is a most cherished person in my life. Always up for "good conversation and good times," he is someone whose acumen, humor, trust, honesty, and heart made him the ideal person to discuss the Mexican immigrant experience and this history with.

Our love has made a world of difference in my life and inspired me to prioritize writing about the promises of love framing important dimensions of this history.

My deepest gratitude and love are reserved for my parents, Dolores and Francisco Rosas Medina. Writing this history has made me realize more than ever that they are the nicest and strongest people I have the great fortune to know. They have done everything within their power to keep me optimistically determined about the responsibility and the promise of working as a Chicana historian, whether teaching or writing this history *con corazón* and making it accessible to our community and family. The devotion they instilled in me for La Virgen de Guadalupe, San Judas Tadeo, and *la divina misericordia* also allowed me to share a strong spiritual connection with them that transcended the isolation of writing and to take on years of hard work with inner peace. Always willing to go the distance on a moment's notice, they have never shied away from being there for me whenever I've needed them, and for that I am forever grateful. Our conversations, our enjoyment and analysis of soccer matches, and the songs we sang, especially Gerardo Reyes's "Sin Fortuna" and Vicente Fernandez's "Marioneta," have made everything I set out to do that much more personally meaningful and satisfying.

Last and as always never least, I owe the world to my sister and best friend, Abigail Rosas, a fabulous scholar in her own right in the field of American studies and ethnicity. She is the person that I automatically turn to. Whether we are troubleshooting computer problems, making our way through mazes of archives, or devoting time to our family, our neighborhood, or the field of Chicana/o studies, Abbie is the most generous person, who makes it all fun and doable. She is always honest in her assessment of my work, and her "keeping it real" has made everything I write that much more reflective of the concerns and questions that matter to us most. Tireless, funny, and "scary smart," she is a constant source of knowledge, laughter, and love. I feel privileged and blessed to learn from her own rigorous and insightful research and to have shared this important journey—the investigation, conceptualization, and writing of this history—with her. With our pets, Pimienta and Nuko, in tow, I look forward to our continuing to be there for each other as sisters and friends—unconditional allies in the struggle for social justice. ¡Sí se puede!

Introduction

Between 1942 and 1964, the governments of the United States and Mexico administered the Bracero Program, an initiative that brought "guest" workers from Mexico to labor in the farmlands of the western United States. In the scholarship about twentieth-century labor history, immigration history, and Chicana/o studies, the Bracero Program has been frequently studied and widely discussed, yet its full contours and consequences have been only partially comprehended. Studying the guest worker initiative from the top down, scholars have done excellent work delineating the particular policies and practices that governed the importation of Mexican laborers to the United States and how these left the workers vulnerable to racial hatred, violence, and systematic economic exploitation. Yet seen from this perspective, the workers themselves appear to be powerless pawns and passive victims.

Abrazando el Espíritu examines the Bracero Program from the bottom up. It presents a transnational narrative of the guest worker experience from the perspective of the Mexican families who endured and countered the hardships of separation and migration, of estrangement and exploitation. Without contradicting the traditional historical accounts that emphasize vulnerability and victimization, this book tells the story of the agency of Mexican people on both sides of the border, especially the ability of families to craft innovative strategies of solidarity and mutuality in the face of profound change and loss. The Bracero Program compelled husbands, sons, and fathers to leave their families and experience loneliness and hardships thousands of miles from home. Yet this very assault on family life also compelled mothers, daughters, and wives to take on new identities and responsibilities. In working to preserve traditional families, these women created nontraditional roles and relationships. The Bracero Program created transnational families as well as new transnational class and racial relations, and in the process also promoted a thorough transformation of gender relations inside Mexican families.

Like previous books on the Bracero Program, *Abraẓando el Espíritu* makes use of the kinds of social history evidence found in government documents, consular files, and the correspondence and personal papers of powerful administrators and legislators. Yet in order to reveal how the bracero experience looks from the bottom up, it draws as well on the evidence available in unofficial archives: in letters, diaries, photographs, musical recordings, plays, fashions, and oral history. These sources tell a story that complicates the dominant narrative. Without erasing the real suffering, sacrifice, and struggle that the Bracero Program imposed on Mexican workers, their families, and their communities, the people's own history of the Bracero Program also reveals a collective capacity to author and authorize survival strategies of imagination, innovation, and adaptation that have shaped the past and that persist powerfully in the present.[1] By tracing the evidence about the Bracero Program that emerges from family photographs, love letters, and popular songs and oral history interviews, we see that the guest worker program's economic and social consequences on the US side of the border were accompanied by equal or greater transformations inside Mexican villages, towns, and cities.

Many of those who talked with me used the phrase *abraẓando el espíritu* (literally "embracing the spirit") to describe the intensity of their emotional commitment to confronting the ongoing crises generated by the Bracero Program with their humanity intact. Though the US and Mexican governments did not describe the program as targeting, recruiting, or employing entire families, family members nevertheless faced its challenges together, acting resourcefully and humanely in support of each other and maintaining and deepening relationships complicated by separation and stress.

One point of entry for me into understanding the Bracero Program from the viewpoint of the working people most directly affected by it came in March 2010 when I had the privilege of interviewing and learning from Veneranda Torres.[2] Her account of her family's history would go on to be formative in helping me see how "embracing the spirit" emerged as a distinctly gendered women's response to the challenges posed by the guest worker program. Veneranda talked to me about daring to "*enfrentar y darse valor*" (confront [things] and embolden herself) in order to protect her family from becoming lost to each other across the US-Mexico border. Her phrasing illuminated the special care and urgency with which she undertook such important yet historically forgotten work.³ In this particular case, Veneranda deployed the technology of photography to craft an image that she hoped would help keep her family together despite the separation imposed on it by the Bracero Program. Five years into her husband Jesus Torres's bracero labor contract in 1963, Veneranda found it emotionally painful to continue to be separated from him, left behind in their Mexican hometown of Acambaro, Guanajuato. She appreciated that he made sacrifices by living apart from her and their three young children for six to nine months at a time to earn money to finance their family's welfare. Yet she longed for him to return. She pursued a plan that entailed working longer shifts in their family's store so that she could afford to purchase cloth, thread, and other items to adorn herself and the children to pose for a professional family portrait that she hoped would motivate Jesus to finally forfeit contract labor and rush home to settle permanently by their family's side.

Veneranda staged and sent this meticulously crafted family portrait to Jesus to confront and awaken him subtly to her longing for his return. She did not explicitly use her own words to urge him to permanently reunite with their family, crafting instead a visual image to appeal to him. She designed and sewed the exact same dress for herself and their daughter, Maria Francisca Ordoñez Torres, adorning the skirts of both dresses in a likeness of the face of a grandfather clock. These dresses showed that Veneranda and Maria were keeping track of their time apart. Veneranda lined up the children in a pose that left gaps between them to signal Jesus's absence from his rightful place within the family.

Throughout the Bracero Program's history, Mexican women, even those who were married, were systematically discouraged from sharing their feelings of longing and loss with their spouses. Program administrators and family members cautioned them against being explicit about the emotions they felt in long-distance marriages that stretched across the US-Mexico border. They were warned that women's desires for reunion could be interpreted as improperly challenging their migrant husbands' judgments and intentions. It took great courage and considerable ingenuity and labor for these women to express and share their feelings of loss and longing.

The Torres family portrait reveals some of the emotional issues confronting families during the bracero era. Thus it serves as a perfect cover illustration for the concerns in this book. The photograph provides a window into difficult decisions families faced in both countries.⁴ Veneranda used the portrait to express and share her feelings with Jesus. Her deft navigation of the expectations shaping gender relations between women and men captures the spirit of the bracero family confrontations that are at the center of the mid-twentieth-century Mexican immigrant family experience in Mexico and the United States. Upon receiving this family portrait, Jesus did not rush to Veneranda's side immediately, but he understood and embraced its spirit. It invigorated him to work tirelessly to ensure that ultimately they would reunite permanently when circumstances permitted. Despite this delay, Veneranda derived much peace of mind from having used this family portrait to share her love and hopes with Jesus and to assert and evoke the humanity of all family members.

The loss and longing created by the separations of the Bracero Program led to desires for personal reunions and family reunification. We have no reason to doubt Torres's sincere love for her husband or her desire to keep her family intact. Yet the program threatened women with material as well as emotional losses. The migration to the United States of male laborers compelled women and children in Mexico to enter the workforce as overworked and poorly paid unskilled employees. The conditions that divided families also created the preconditions for abandonment. Years apart could create chasms that estranged family members from one another. Husbands working in the United States could come to resent earning money that they could not spend but had to send home. Men thousands of miles from their families in Mexico might find new partners and form new families in the United States. Moreover, the workers who labored in the United States and their families could not even count on actually receiving the wages they earned. Employers, supervisors, and government officials in both countries understood that contract laborers had limited power and as a result viewed them as ripe for exploitation. Employers did not always pay workers their wages, and money sent home sometimes disappeared en route. Because remittances were sparse to begin with and might not even arrive, families of workers in the Bracero Program had to develop new ways of making money in their hometowns. This necessitated new social roles for women and children outside the home that they did not want to surrender once the guest workers returned home. Moreover, as de facto heads of households, Mexican women found themselves taking the lead in challenging the US and Mexican governments' conceptualization and implementation of the Bracero Program. Its abandonments of the Mexican immigrant family paved the way to women's emergence as an integral yet far too often conveniently forgotten and neglected historical force, defending their own interests and in the process raising the consciousness of their families and other women. For these women, the Bracero Program was a source of both stress *and* empowerment, a decisive factor leading them to shoulder new responsibilities and to express to their Mexican immigrant male relatives their aspirations, fears, and hopes. In the wake of newfound loneliness, their love, ingenuity, and determination enabled them to learn to act and function more independently. Traditional Mexican mores sometimes led women partners of guest workers to be looked down on in their communities, positioned as abandoned, disgraced, expendable, forgotten, immoral, and unwomanly. Yet these dismissals motivated them to assert themselves and voice their concerns with special care and caution for their own and their families' sake.

Those connected to the Bracero Program suffered emotional, physical, and financial turmoil as members of transnational families in a historical moment shaped by family separation across borders. The program was inaugurated on August 4, 1942, when the Mexican and US governments agreed to the importation but eventual repatriation of temporary Mexican immigrant contract laborers under the aegis of the Emergency Mexican Farm Labor Program. Mexican president Manuel Avila Camacho proposed that the agreement would transform allegedly racially inferior rural Mexican men like Jesus Torres into modern citizens by exposing them to US customs, skills, and work habits. Confident that after earning US wages and learning US methods and skills the men would return adequately prepared to invest and labor in Mexico and move the nation forward on the path toward technological sophistication and modernity, Avila Camacho overlooked this program's emotional, financial, and physical costs.[5]

The Bracero Program's vision of rural working-class progress did not automatically modernize Mexican immigrant families in Mexico and the United States, but it did disrupt their lives and cause them emotional pain and labor exploitation. This book studies that disruption and these confrontations, exploring the program's impact on families in Mexican rural towns, villages, and cities and in US agricultural labor camps and surrounding towns. Based on oral life histories of Mexican immigrant families and primary and secondary sources, this book documents the desires, resourcefulness, limitations, losses, and obligations of children, women, and men in families in both Mexico and the United States. Bracero Program conditions compelled them to work in both countries but made it difficult for them to thrive together in either country. Arduous, poorly compensated, temporary contract labor, periodic deportations, and restrictive gender norms complicated their negotiation of short- and long-term family separation and reunification.

The US and Mexican governments' enforcement of the Bracero Program weighed heavily on the hearts, minds, and shoulders of Mexican immigrant families, especially the women in them. The onset of the program intensified the prominence of the US-Mexico border in the lives of these families. The US and Mexican governments used the program to manage Mexicans' immigration to the United States and their subsequent settlement in ways that depended on the labor of their families and required extensive management of their families, laying the foundations for whole families to feel like braceros, as if they all worked in and for the United States. The US and Mexican governments' failure to recognize the burdens that the program directly or indirectly laid on the families left behind in Mexico explicitly fueled women's feelings of abandonment.

Scholarship on the Bracero Program has generally emphasized the experiences of men to the virtual exclusion of the experiences of children, the elderly, and women and the nature of transnational family formation. Yet Mexican men laboring as guest workers depended on the families they left behind. *Abrazando el Espíritu* focuses on transnational Mexican immigrant families' separation, cooperation, and reunification as foundational to understanding the changes the Bracero Program initiated—changes that set in motion a constant reconfiguration of the social meaning of the US-Mexico border that continues to this day. This book emphasizes the importance of gender in transnational Mexican immigrant family life—"the social and cultural ideals, practices, and displays of femininity and masculinity organizing and shaping opportunities, decisions, and relationships"—throughout the program's trajectory to demonstrate the US and Mexican governments' overdependence on the labor of entire Mexican immigrant families to finance and sustain the program.[6] I argue that the program's government-sanctioned family separation, cyclical temporary reunification, and resettlement under economically, racially, socially, culturally, and emotionally unequal terms compelled Mexican immigrant families, especially women, to lead a transnational, circuitous, and gendered immigrant family life that cautiously defied program ideals.

Family disruptions and confrontations and gender instability permeated the Bracero Program's activities. Since its inception, fears of promoting uncontrollable Mexican immigration to the United States and settlement there, as well as fears, in the United States, of Mexican immigrant women's reproductive potential, led the two countries' governments to recruit Mexican immigrant men exclusively and to manage their behavior as husbands, fathers, siblings, and sons in ways that rendered their families participants in the program as well, whether in Mexico or in the United States. Yet responsibility for financing entry into the program and managing its consequences fell on Mexican women, the elderly, and even children. This government-sanctioned family separation produced a complex continuum of transnational family anxiety, flexibility, and resilience on both sides of the US-Mexico border. It required overwhelmed families to *embrace the spirit* of making and implementing difficult decisions concerning their family situations, employment conditions, gender relations, and settlement in Mexico and the United States. The two countries' constant oscillation between sending and receiving status and downward shifts in the Mexican economy compelled an estimated 5.2 million Mexican men to separate from their families and participate in the program in anticipation of earning enough to invest in desirable life opportunities back home in Mexico.

After the Bracero Program's initial recruitment campaign, participating families soon recognized that modernizing the Mexican rural working class was not a governmental priority. Satisfying alleged US labor shortages and managing undocumented Mexican immigrant settlement was at the heart of the US and Mexican governments' program management. Both governments concentrated their energy on interrogating, bathing, delousing, and registering—in effect, dehumanizing—Mexican men to labor in the United States without ever informing them or their families of their destinations or the duration of their contracts.[7] Bracero dehumanization and segregation in contracting sites and agricultural labor camps limited the workers' interactions, physical mobility, visibility, and settlement, allowing the US government to depress wages and to repatriate the men upon their contract's expiration, denying them the right to organize and bargain for fair wages individually and collectively. Neither the US nor the Mexican government advocated or protected the interests of Mexican immigrant men or their families.

The Mexican government's failure to create competitive and desirable domestic employment opportunities among the rural working class and the US government's reluctance to address the ubiquity of Mexican immigrant exploitation in its agricultural industry made it difficult for Mexican immigrant families to reunite and settle in either country. Leading lives stretched across borders was often their only option. Transitioning into and out of temporary contract labor and into a combination of internal migrant and undocumented Mexican immigrant work arrangements throughout Mexico and the United States emerged as a popular alternate route for surviving a struggling Mexican economy and the tight controls over the US-Mexico border. After years of bracero, migrant, and undocumented immigrant labor, Mexican immigrant families often settled for long-distance family relationships or permanent family separation. The economic and emotional price they paid for the disruptions of their lives generated surplus profits for agribusiness in the United States by depressing workers' wages in the industry and subsidized the costs of foodstuffs for US consumers, who could buy products at lower prices because of the exploitation of Mexican labor.

Mexican immigrant men's pursuit of work in two countries was at the heart of an extraordinarily charged transnational family process. Manipulative public exercises of power through border enforcement and deportations intensified Mexican families' alienation, exploitation, and dispersal. The Mexican and US governments' commitment to controlling Mexican immigrant labor and settlement escalated over the years, resulting in widely publicized border enforcement campaigns, Operation Wetback, the Internal Security Act, and the Walter-McCarran Act.[8] Both governments' commitment to obfuscating the US agricultural industry's insatiable demand for vulnerable Mexican immigrant labor and a worsening Mexican economy challenged Mexican families to devise creative new ways of belonging in Mexico and the United States in protection of their interests.

By investigating the Bracero Program experience in Mexico and the United States as a key component of an as yet largely unwritten transnational and gendered Mexican immigrant family history, this book does not conform neatly to the traditional linear teleology generally used to frame and investigate immigration to the United States, which posits a linear progression from immigrant settlement to inclusion in US society and full citizenship. The US government used program labor agreements to deny braceros and undocumented Mexican immigrants this trajectory. Both governments and the families left behind depended on Mexican immigrant remittances to prevent the disintegration of employment, entrepreneurial, and social networks. These conditions render this immigrant family experience qualitatively different from that of earlier waves of transatlantic immigrants' relationships with the United States and with their countries of origin.[9] Despite transatlantic immigrants' very real labor exploitation, emotional turmoil, and racial discrimination, eventual improvements in their class, ethnic, race, and labor relations in the United States weakened their accountability and ties to their sending countries. The immigration process for mid-twentieth-century Mexican immigrants, however, was very different. The Bracero Program's cyclical nature and costs required Mexican immigrants to remain connected to their sending Mexican rural towns and villages. Transnational family labor and business agreements financing their program participation or undocumented immigration entailed developing and financing transnational economic and social networks that required their temporary return and continued economic investment in their places of origin. Economic and familial ties to their sending towns and villages limited workers' ability to reenter and resettle permanently in the United States. Thus Mexican immigrants confronted obstacles to permanent settlement in the United States and Mexico that were different from, and far more complicated than, those that previous immigrants to the United States had experienced.

Immigration required those who left and those who stayed behind to confront what Matthew Frye Jacobson calls the "weight of departure and absence."[10] Lured by increased earning potential and armed with a sense of caution shaped by conversations prior to migration in Mexican rural towns and villages, bracero workers were still not fully prepared to face what Michael Kearney and Roger Rouse describe as the simultaneous transnationalization of Mexican immigrants and the Mexican rural towns and villages from which they migrated.[11] These changes would mature into what Douglas Massey argues are the building blocks of post-1965 Mexican immigration to the United States: "interpersonal, institutional, and economic incorporation [into the United States] through Mexican immigrant ties with each other and the United States resulting from their social interaction, membership, employment, and consumption patterns."[12]

Abrazando el Espíritu builds on the importance and diversity of approaches that braceros and especially entire bracero families used to confront the program's gendered and transnational costs throughout their departure from Mexico, their contract duration, their undocumented immigration, their temporary or permanent return to Mexico, and, for some, their undocumented permanent settlement in the United States. This history's consideration of family relationships and networks that made braceros' plans for progress transnationally intricate, emotionally arduous, and financially feasible illustrates how families left behind played a decisive role and devised strategies of their own to facilitate braceros' transition into and out of this program and their families' lives. Yet it is also important to avoid overemphasizing the power of Mexican immigrant families' appropriation of Bracero Program conditions, support networks, purchase of US products, and investment in transnational business agreements, property, and educational programs. These strategies and expenditures provided Mexican immigrant families with incentives to remain committed to their transnational family and their economic relationships with it, and to persevere through difficult situations, but did not protect them against alienation in US and Mexican society. The Bracero Program and restrictive immigration policies targeting ethnic Mexicans—like the Internal Security Act, the Walter-McCarran Act, and Operation Wetback—escalated class, ethnic, and racial tensions among and between braceros, undocumented Mexican immigrants, longtime Mexican immigrants of varying legal statuses, and Mexican Americans, all of whom competed for employment in the US agricultural industry. The US government's aggressive pursuit of deportable aliens of ethnic Mexican background fueled varying levels of intolerance toward bracero and undocumented Mexican immigrants, even among Mexican Americans and longtime Mexican immigrants.[13] Mexican American community service organizations coordinated naturalization workshops, programs in English-language acquisition, voter registration drives, and labor union organization to facilitate US citizenship and longtime residence in the United States. They generally excluded braceros and undocumented Mexican immigrants from these efforts, restricting their interactions with them to employment situations, occasional chats in social settings, and seasonal public outreach efforts. Mexican Americans worried that identifying and interacting with braceros and undocumented Mexican immigrants would diminish their right to claim their fundamental Americanness. Overwhelmed, they too often lost sight of and became unsympathetic to the plight of braceros and undocumented Mexican immigrants in the United States and Mexico.

Nonetheless, and unlike many histories of the Mexican American experience, *Abrazando el Espíritu* expands on the transnational resonance of such alienation among Mexican immigrant families left behind in Mexico. The alienation migrant workers experienced in the United States paralleled similar tensions among and between Mexican rural elite and working-class families in Mexican society. The struggle against dehumanizing class tensions among and within Mexican immigrant families who had been left behind escalated in accordance with worsening US class, ethnic, and racial tensions, revealing the transnationality of both the workers' vulnerability and their resilience. Like Mexican Americans, Mexican rural elite families developed a subset of discourses and initiatives to solidify class stratification and to protect their economic and social interests throughout the Bracero Program's duration. They appropriated state funds for their own ends, controlling Mexican immigrant families' education, investments, and labor to their advantage. The rural Mexican elite took advantage of Mexican immigrants' alienation in the United States to implement consistently exploitative transnational economic practices governing emotionally and financially vulnerable families in Mexican society. Ethnic Mexican families in Mexico and the United States did not generally respond to the call of Mexican American labor activist Ernesto Galarza to organize transnational labor unions and organizations that could advance a collective struggle for ethnic Mexican equality and progress in Mexico and the United States. Selective inclusion, exploitation, and the Immigration and Naturalization Service's arbitrary interrogation, apprehension, and deportation of ethnic Mexicans made it extremely difficult for Mexican immigrants of varying immigration statuses to cooperate with Mexican Americans and Mexican citizens.[14]

Rethinking the Bracero Program requires a reassessment of the cognitive mapping of Mexican American lives. Rather than restrict itself to the history of the Bracero Program in US agricultural towns, *Abrazando el Espíritu* encompasses sending Mexican rural towns such as San Martin de Hidalgo and Ameca, Jalisco, and

Acambaro, Guanajuato, to trace the continuities and diversity of the program's impact across the Mexican countryside and among Mexican states hardest hit by this program's implementation. San Martin de Hidalgo looms largest for me, as it was the Mexican rural town that best lent itself to investigating the local relationship to the program; it was also a part of Jalisco, which emerged as the second-largest sending Mexican state, rendering it a most valuable location for understanding the mid-twentieth-century Mexican immigrant family experience in Mexico and the United States.[15] The program's configuration in receiving US cities and agricultural towns throughout the state of California is also at the center of this transnational family history, and this study culminates with an exploration of the simultaneous acceleration of San Martin de Hidalgo's transnationalization and the transnational, cyclical, and multidirectional intensity of Mexican immigrant families' alienation, flexibility, and resilience in California throughout the program's trajectory. The relationship between program conditions, familial ties, transportation routes, and other long-standing economic and social networks connecting families and these locations demonstrates that the Mexican and US governments used transnational discourses on border enforcement and rural working-class Mexican inferiority, family, womanhood, and progress to manage Mexican immigration and settlement. This history reveals that the Mexican and US governments were often far more aggressive in their management of Mexican children, the elderly, and women in Mexico than in their management of Mexican immigrant men and the US-Mexico border. The program's dependence on their flexibility, labor, and sacrifice was critical to its longevity, leaving very limited room for families left behind to create desirable life opportunities of their own.

Each site's management of Mexican immigration and settlement informed the confrontation of Mexican immigrant children, women, and men with government priorities concerning the Bracero Program, elucidating the local class, ethnic, and gender politics shaping their sense of belonging, physical mobility, and family. San Martin de Hidalgo serves as the most prominent sending rural town from which to historicize the changes and continuities of this Mexican immigrant family experience. Located ninety miles south of Guadalajara, the largest city in the state of Jalisco, this town was connected to transportation routes spanning the entire Mexican countryside and leading to the US-Mexico border, a location that facilitated an uncontrollable movement of Mexican immigrants to and from the United States. Like other sending Mexican rural towns and villages throughout the Mexican states of Campeche, Guanajuato, Mazatlan, Distrito Federal, Michoacán, Monterrey, Oaxaca, Sonora, and Zacatecas, this town's local government, elite middle class, and struggling rural working class financed and sustained participation in the Bracero Program by developing intricate transnational social and economic networks. Despite an influx in undocumented Mexican immigration, the Mexican and US governments remained committed to screening and contracting Mexican men in program selection centers in Mexico, Distrito Federal, Empalme, Sonora, San Ysidro, Baja California, and Ciudad Juarez. Unprepared to process thousands of Mexican immigrant men, these sites increasingly expanded their management of Mexican immigration to the United States by strictly managing town residents and abandoned, financially desperate Mexican immigrant women who journeyed to these sites in search of employment. Maintaining a public semblance of border control to appease government concerns about the program, the work at these sites entailed managing Mexican children, women, and men under increasingly dehumanizing terms.

The US state of California is also critical to understanding the evolution of the dehumanization shaping the intimate contours of this transnational immigrant family experience. This state emerged as one of the few destinations in which the Mexican and US governments invested themselves aggressively to develop a permanent labor camp culture that would facilitate the temporary employment, repatriation, and deportation of vulnerable Mexican immigrant men.[16] The US government firmly believed that by perfecting US contractors' management of braceros' and undocumented Mexican immigrants' interaction, labor, mobility, and visibility it would offset US residents' anxiety and opposition to the Bracero Program.

As in other US states that benefited from the employment of braceros, the agricultural labor camps in California were populated by immigrant and US-born ethnic Italian, Portuguese, Filipino, African American, and Mexican families dependent on the harvesting of lettuce, strawberries, cherries, grapes, and garlic. Vehement opposition to recently arrived Mexican immigrants performing and competing for jobs at dramatically lower wages intensified class, ethnic, and racial tension among longtime residents, braceros, and recently arrived undocumented Mexican immigrants throughout US agricultural towns nationwide. The US government's development of internal program management models did not quell US residents' and workers' opposition but intensified Mexican immigrant men's commitment to transnational family, economic, and social networks as a way to advance their families' visions of progress.

Hence, and in accordance with George J. Sanchez's conceptualization of negotiations of change in an earlier generation of Mexican American working-class families, I argue that these families demonstrate that Mexican government officials' and families' transition into the program stemmed, not from a fixed set of customs, but from a process influenced by the selective borrowing, retention, and creation of distinct cultural forms of accommodation, resistance, and transformation of individual and collective identities.[17] Fleshing out the transnational and gendered dimensions of the mid-twentieth-century Mexican immigrant experience in Mexico and the United States through an examination of discourses, policies, and labor administration as these played out among Mexican government officials, rural elite middle-class families, and working-class families of varying immigration statuses expands our understanding of the Bracero Program's costs and limitations. The program disrupted families and did not automatically result in their desirable resettlement, but it was an indispensable source of revenue for national and local Mexican governments, the US agricultural industry, and Mexican elite, middle-class, and rural working-class families alike. For Mexicans with relatives serving as guest workers, selective appropriation and violation of program conditions to avoid jeopardizing their immigrant relatives' contract renewal or undocumented immigrant labor entailed carefully coordinated resistance.

Ethnic Mexican families' oral life histories and personal archives inform and shape the mapping and scope of this book. They reveal the context and human spirit that gave meaning to these families' disruption, ingenuity, resistance, and resilience in confronting the US-Mexico border. Without their interpretations of the transnational and gendered exigencies of the reopening of the border, it would be difficult to understand or find primary or secondary sources that would bring their family experience to life. Only after I had collected and studied their recollections and records did integral yet overlooked dimensions of this experience surface. These families' oral life histories uncovered the generative research potential of overlooked yet enduring musical recordings, correspondence, conversations, films, and photographs that registered the underestimated emotional range of emerging gendered and transnational subjectivities as these children, women, and men confronted and awakened each other to the rigors of the separation of their families across the US-Mexico border. A close reading of their personal perspectives and documents magnifies their assertion of what Alicia Schmidt Camacho conceptualizes as migrant melancholia, "an emergent mode of migrant subjectivity that contests the dehumanizing effects of border crossing."[18] This combination of sources makes most obvious the problems with official accounts of this experience that ignore the impact of repatriation, instead collapsing this history into misleading and racially infused one-dimensional and episodic accounts and categories. Learning more about this experience, and specifically the transnational and gendered costs of belonging in Mexico and the United States, requires taking seriously what Vicki L. Ruiz frames as the historian's task: "providing spaces for people to express their thoughts and feelings in their words and on their own terms."[19]

Taking this task to heart was the driving force behind this historical attempt to take up what historian Robin D. G. Kelley describes as "stepping into the complicated maze of experience that renders 'ordinary' folks so extraordinarily multifaceted, diverse, and complicated."[20] After I had researched extensively the arbitrary repatriation of an estimated three hundred thousand US citizens and immigrants of ethnic Mexican background in Los Angeles, and thought introspectively about my own family's transition into the United States, I became interested in the immigration and gender politics shaping the World War II and post–World War II Mexican immigrant experience.[21] I wondered how families who had recently witnessed the Mexican and US governments' reckless disruption of thousands of ethnic Mexican families interpreted and negotiated the reopening of the US-Mexico border via the Bracero Program. My search for records revealing the anxiety associated with Mexican immigration to and from the United States, and more specifically with separation from one's family after the turmoil of repatriation experienced under similarly alienating and uncertain terms, led me to San Martin de Hidalgo and ultimately to the investigation and writing of this book.

Abrazando el Espíritu consists of three parts. Part 1 examines the emergencies shaping the promotion and implementation of the Bracero Program in Mexico and the United States. Chapter 1 centers on the importance of dynamics in the sending Mexican rural towns and villages for understanding divergent visions of rural Mexican working-class progress. Chapter 2 explores how repatriation and government policies on both sides of the border shaped workers' efforts to respond to the program resourcefully and responsibly. Workers' estimation of the program's benefits and costs—as well as of rural, working-class families' desires and financial vulnerability, and the effects of their being viewed as inferior in both countries—converged and intensified their decision not to embrace the program automatically but to warn against the idealization of the United States and the program in Mexico and the United States. Chapter 3 examines the underestimated pressures on Mexican immigrant families struggling to benefit from the US and Mexican governments' management of intimate aspects of their transnational family life in both countries.

Part 2 captures the love and longing that defined Mexican immigrant families' confrontations with the emotional rigors of the Bracero Program and family disruption over time. Chapter 4 explores the censorship of these families' correspondence as they struggled with the program's separation of their families across the US-Mexico border for indefinite periods of time. Chapter 5 explores the emotional configuration of the program. It portrays the undocumented emotional work of women and men coping with their longing for each other. Chapter 6 explores the resourceful use of photographs to maintain loving relationships and a sense of self-worth across the US-Mexico border.

Part 3 centers on the decisive measures that energized and emboldened children, women, and men to respond resourcefully to the abandonment, estrangement, and negligence that occurred as a result of the US and Mexican governments. A struggling Mexican economy, Bracero Program conditions, and agricultural labor camp management often did not leave much money left over for bracero and undocumented Mexican immigrants to finance their families' welfare. Severe forms of family disruption compelled struggling women to assume head of household obligations on their own under extremely gendered and precarious terms, forcing them to spend much time away from their children. Mexican immigrant relatives' failure to return or to write and send remittances regularly motivated financially vulnerable female heads of household and their children to undertake important emotional work on behalf and in support of their families. Chapter 7 delineates the emergence of women's efforts toward establishing healthier and financially feasible transitions into less emotionally exhausting family situations through their forging and sharing of restorative conversations, interactions, and sites. Chapter 8 illuminates the unique accountability shouldered by children entrusted to sustain their parents' program participation. It focuses on the silencing and public invisibility and visibility that these children endured for the sake of their families. The ninth and final chapter of this history considers the precariousness of undocumented Mexican immigration—and how it ultimately emboldened Mexican and Mexican American women in Mexico and the United States to ask difficult questions and to launch investigations that would promote their best interests in the long term. Finally, this history concludes with an epilogue that examines the generative potential of embracing the spirit of this history to understand our relationship to it.

By reconceptualizing the Bracero Program experience as a transnational immigrant family experience of disruption, this history focuses on Mexican immigrant families' confrontation of the US-Mexico border. It assesses how they embraced the spirit of sacrifice, ingenuity, and resilience. It illuminates the human consequences of contract labor in Mexico and the United States. By following the lead of American studies scholar George Lipsitz, who urges historians to "investigate how people live in the world, down to the most localized, personal, and intimate issues, imagination, and desire," we can resist collapsing our approach to Mexican immigration and settlement into neat state-manufactured categories, labor agreements, and periodizations of immigrant life that do not account for the emotional costs and disruption that immigration policy inflicts on children, women, and men across borders.[22] Without acknowledging or learning from a long-standing, interconnected, and relational transnational history of Mexican immigrant ebbs and flows to and from the United States, historians, politicians, and voters risk an erroneously dangerous and inhumane conceptualization of these matters. That misunderstanding can only extend into this new century our dehumanized treatment of Mexican immigrant children, women, and men as expendable and homogeneous.

My scholarly interest in the Bracero Program has personal motivations and ramifications. My grandparents and other women and men of their generation have shared with me their recollections and reflections on the reopened border's impact on their lives. They have been extremely thoughtful and generous in their candor and detailed explanations. They opened their family archives and gave me tours of important locations. They welcomed me into their homes to feel and familiarize myself with their life histories. My attention to them also awakened memories and promoted reflections. My willingness to apply for research grants, schedule archival research around their schedules, read extensively on the subject, visit them on multiple occasions outside the scope of research, and carefully coordinate our oral life history interview sessions encouraged these women and men to expound on the intimate dimensions of their confrontations with difficult family situations. They insisted that if I wanted to learn more about US history I should not lose sight of Mexico. Their recollections of the pervasive presence of the US-Mexico border in their lives and their constant anxiety concerning the disintegration of their families, and now the potential loss of their generation's history, motivated them to reflect on the severity of the circumstances shaping their decisions and opportunities. After years of extensive research, during which many of them have now passed away, I am convinced that the program left an indelible mark on them and on my own family, bequeathing timeless and hard-earned lessons that for the most part they had not previously put into words. In this book, I attempt to describe and analyze those lessons.[23]

PART ONE · EMERGENCIES

CHAPTER ONE · Bracero Recruitment in
the Mexican Countryside,
1942–1947

On August 7, 1942, Gabino Preciado, president of the rural town of San Martin de Hidalgo, Jalisco, faced an unenviable challenge. Mexican president Manuel Avila Camacho had ordered him to embrace the spirit behind the recruitment of the townsmen into the Mexican Emergency Farm Labor Program, more commonly known as the Bracero Program.[1] With the repatriation of three hundred thousand Mexican American and Mexican immigrant children, women, and men during the 1930s still fresh in their minds, unskilled rural Mexican men would be asked to immigrate to the United States in pursuit of Avila Camacho's vision of national progress.

Avila Camacho's vision went beyond strengthening ties to the United States in a time of war. He believed firmly that unskilled rural Mexican men were an inferior race who could acquire the qualities, skills, and wages necessary for Mexico to advance socially and technologically only by being exposed to elements of more developed countries like the United States.[2] He believed the program suited unskilled rural Mexican men perfectly. According to this racial logic, rural Mexican men's mastery and implementation of US agricultural methods and skills "improved the character of [the Mexican] people, advancing Mexico's social and technological development."[3] Temporary US contract labor would modernize them and, upon their return, indirectly influence generations of men throughout the Mexican countryside.

This chapter considers Bracero Program recruitment, focusing on San Martin de Hidalgo's appropriation and translation of Avila Camacho's vision. In doing so, it enriches historical interpretations that have overlooked how rural towns throughout

Mexico embraced the program's enactment, reinforcement, and redefinition of concepts of race, gender, and national and personal advancement.[4] The Bracero Program exacerbated racial and gender inequality in Mexico as well as in the United States. Reduced to an intellectually, culturally, and socially inferior race worthy of exploitation in Mexico and the United States, unskilled rural Mexican families countered the program's logic with strategies to realize their own visions of advancement in Mexico and the United States. Yet rural Mexican men's visions consistently took women's labor for granted and preserved gender and race inequality, just as the vision of Mexican president Avila Camacho did.

FEDERAL VISIONS, LOCAL IMPLEMENTATION

Avila Camacho entrusted rural Mexican town and village presidents throughout the states of Jalisco, Michoacán, Sonora, Veracruz, and Zacatecas to recruit an estimated seventy-five thousand men for the Bracero Program. He issued a confidential mandate to them, announcing that the Mexican and US governments had agreed to the program after months of negotiation. Under its terms the US government would import Mexican men to build and repair railroads and harvest crops throughout the United States for three- to six-month contract periods. Contracted men, who would be known as braceros, would be exempt from the usual immigration requirements, such as literacy tests, head taxes, and other admission fees. In addition, they would be exempt from military service and protected from social discrimination. The US government guaranteed employment for at least 75 percent of their contract period at the "prevailing wage rate," as well as housing, meals, and transportation to and from the United States. Once their contracts expired, they would be required to return to Mexico. Both governments agreed to compensate fairly and to penalize program violations.[5]

Avila Camacho emphasized that braceros would return with something to show for their time in the United States. The program required the US government to withhold 10 percent of braceros' semimonthly earnings. These funds were to be deposited into a rural savings fund, then transferred to Mexico's Agricultural Credit Bank, and would be redeemable upon the braceros' return. Avila Camacho imagined that with these savings braceros would purchase agricultural equipment to plant and harvest plots of land efficiently and profitably and in this way would apply the program's knowledge, skills, and wages to help Mexico achieve economic, social, and technological progress.

The president of San Martin de Hidalgo, Gabino Preciado, received Avila Camacho's mandate. Rural Mexican town and village presidents like Preciado were charged with recruiting men carefully and selectively. In the mandate they were cautioned against promoting the benefits of the program too aggressively. US grower associations administering the program were not too committed to the terms of the program and had never been obligated to provide such guarantees for US domestic workers. Even as the program stipulated that braceros would not be contracted to displace US domestic workers, that they would not serve as strikebreakers in labor disputes, and that they would work for the "prevailing wage" or the current average wage paid by the piece or by the hour to US domestic workers for the same job in the same region of the United States, the program actually facilitated administrative violation of these very conditions. The braceros were to be warned that US government officials, instead of conducting independent surveys of regional wages, would survey US grower associations and then accept their responses without investigating the accuracy of their claims. This process would depress wages, as grower associations would mobilize into regional associations that collectively set the regional wage far below the accepted wage for the tasks in question. US domestic workers would then refuse to work for such wages, making grower associations eligible for program contracts. Such covert and carefully planned program violations had the potential to go unnoticed and to confine braceros to exploitative and unprofitable employment. Preciado was among the presidents advised to consider that this program would not automatically promote braceros' economic advancement and that it was in their interest to avoid promising more than the program could deliver in their local recruitment efforts. This would prevent the promotion of an unreliable process with improper incentives that could lead to a return migration reminiscent of repatriation.

The government officials of Mexican rural towns were asked to specifically target for recruitment experienced agricultural laborers with wives and children because their family obligations would motivate these workers to accept the offer and to comply with government-sanctioned return schedules. The Mexican government speculated that single men would be more likely to skip out or to continue to work after their contract's expiration.

Preciado was also urged to promote the program as crucial to the war against the Axis powers and participation in it as what Avila Camacho called a "manly act of loyalty to country and progress."[6] Braceros' labor promised to strengthen wartime US-Mexico efforts and relations, since it would prevent US labor shortages. It would also lay the material foundation for braceros' own advancement, since upon their return US training and savings for equipment and supplies would raise their earning potential by allowing them to grow and harvest crops more efficiently and skillfully.

Rural town and village presidents were instructed to paper their respective communities with promotional materials offering local men these inducements.

After carefully assessing the program, Preciado concluded that it was a risky yet crucial first step toward exposing San Martin de Hidalgo's men to the United States. He too was confident that men's mastery of US skills and earning of US wages would prove a welcome change from town life at home. Ironically, contracted men would perform work similar to what they had always done, namely unskilled and poorly paid manual agricultural labor, hence the term *bracero*—literally "arm man." Preciado realized that despite the Bracero Program's promise, town families could participate only by paying for transportation to this program's selection center in the nation's capital: Mexico, Distrito Federal.[7] Indeed, the transportation cost for each prospective bracero was an estimated 150 pesos, roughly the equivalent of four months of a typical unskilled town family's earnings. This made the town's unskilled rural working class, those most in need of new economic opportunities, ineligible. In San Martin de Hidalgo, only middle-class men could afford such recruitment fees. Their temporary absence would drain the town's economy and resources, doubling unemployment among the unskilled rural working class. Preciado needed the middle class's investment and purchasing power to keep businesses open and employment opportunities intact. His administration could not afford to lose middle-class families to immigration without a plan in place. This local assessment did not conform to Avila Camacho's vision or to the financial interest of Preciado's administration.

Even worse, participating families were required to pay for the public notarization of letters confirming the men's moral and physical eligibility to work in the United States and their financial ability to afford transportation to the program's selection center. After careful deliberation, Preciado strategically decided to enlist the town's middle-class families to finance rural working-class men's participation. By developing and facilitating a local discourse and financial agreements that went beyond Avila Camacho's mandate, he laid the foundations for a deceptive yet comprehensive local appropriation and translation of the program. Securing middle- and working-class families' participation would prevent further unemployment and complete disinvestment in the town. This required conveying a narrowly defined set of identities, roles, and values that would mobilize the town's women, children, and men to act collectively for the town's advancement.

To recruit these families effectively, Preciado aggressively pursued a local discourse on program conditions and incentives that would resonate among middle-class families. Convincing successful entrepreneurs, teachers, and professionals to immigrate to a country that had recently repatriated town families and to undertake physically demanding labor in agriculture and railroad construction was difficult. Like other Mexican rural town presidents, Preciado speculated that the Bracero Program's conditions and terms could potentially advance braceros and, in turn, towns economically if the town's vision of advancement centered on women, children, and men working collectively across borders. Certainly, temporary US wages and training were preferable to unemployment. He promoted a vision of family progress through program participation to enlist families to weather the hardships that the program would involve. But casting participation as a means of rising out of poverty would offend middle-class families and draw unwanted attention to class differences, fueling existing town hostility between the middle and working classes.

Like Avila Camacho, Mexican rural town presidents idealized the contract labor that participants would undertake and the opportunities that would be available to them on their return. In doing so, they were complicit in his failure to protect prospective braceros and their families from exploitation and the hardships of family separation. Neither developed employment opportunities that accommodated short-term family separation or facilitated returning braceros' transition out of contract labor into profitable long-term settlement in Mexico. In San Martin de Hidalgo, Preciado recruited middle-class families by presenting the program as an excellent opportunity brimming with potential for middle-class entrepreneurs. Middle-class braceros were expected to return and invest their earnings into an already profitable business or trade. As for working-class families that were financially dependent on male laborers, their program participation and return would involve paying existing family debt, fulfilling recruitment loan agreements, and creating employment opportunities within and outside agricultural labor on their own.

Like Avila Camacho's vision, the vision developed by local officials did not prevent overwhelming debt and exploitation from occurring. According to Mexican government officials, only legal access to US skills and wages could make profitable long-term settlement patterns throughout the Mexican countryside possible. Families interested in economic betterment had no other choice but to struggle collectively and across borders. It was men's responsibility to work as contract laborers while their families patiently worked and waited behind.

COMMUNITY FORUMS
AND THE LOCAL GENDER SCRIPT

To deflect attention from international, national, and local negligence and to fulfill recruitment quotas, Mexican rural town presidents developed a local script that appealed strategically to middle-class families and excluded working-class families. Confident that the news of potentially earning an estimated sixty pesos for eight hours of agricultural labor in the United States—the equivalent of three weeks' worth of a local agricultural laborer's wages—would spread widely throughout their respective towns, Preciado, like many other Mexican rural town presidents, did not bother to recruit the town's working class because he simply assumed that working-poor men would add their names quickly to the list and because he feared that active recruitment of families from different class backgrounds with the same rhetoric would lessen middle-class families' support and enlistment. The middle class were needed as contract laborers and, ever more urgently, as lenders to others. Their willingness to lend large sums of money toward the recruitment fees of the working poor would ensure the participation of those most in need of economic betterment, a recruitment goal that fulfilled Avila Camacho's vision.

On August 10, 1942, Consuelo Alvarez, a middle-class town resident, helped her husband Jesus bake orders of sourdough bread, *pan dulce* (sweet bread), and cakes before rushing off to walk her children to school and attend a town forum on the Bracero Program on her family's behalf.[8] She sat alongside fellow bakers, barbers, cooks, doctors, merchants, seamstresses, tailors, and other enterprising married and single middle-class women and men, but she noticed that agricultural laborers were absent. Men in attendance were given handbills announcing the Mexican and US governments' demand for their *"brazos, lealtad y hombría"* (arms, loyalty, and manhood)—essentially calling upon them to separate from their families in order to build and repair railroads and harvest crops throughout the United States.

Consuelo read her older brother's copy because this document was not distributed to women. Despite the history of US repatriation and the fact that most in attendance had struggled to maintain their own businesses or trades to avoid this line of work, most of these families did not object to performing railroad or agricultural contract labor in the United States. Consuelo and other forum attendees were receptive to earning US wages. As she would later recall, at the time the Bracero Program had struck her as a sound investment of energy and money. San Martin de Hidalgo families believed that they stood to earn a healthy profit, especially if they did not have to take out a loan in order to enlist.

Preciado's decision to recruit middle-class families caught middle-class interest, while reconceptualizing the Bracero Program as a sound business venture. The program was thus promoted as a sound investment of energy, money, and time among middle-class families, and worthy of men of moral and physical strength. Discussions of Avila Camacho's racial logic were replaced by characterizations of program participation as a loyal and responsible assertion of the masculinity of middle-class men, effacing the stigma of contract agricultural labor. Moreover, Preciado assured middle-class men that by serving their country they would improve their ability to provide for themselves and their families.

Notions of traditional masculinity and femininity also influenced Preciado's recruitment of middle-class women. Regular town hall meetings were already restrictively gendered, family-oriented events. During these meetings, women were prevented from expressing concerns and opinions beyond suggesting future meeting dates and times to organize town events that did not conflict with their household chores. Often they were restricted to hosting and organizing town fund-raisers and festivals after a town committee composed of men had settled on the events. Women's accommodation to the Bracero Program's conditions did not initially include increased decision making or purchasing power. Their potential empowerment through their adaptations to program conditions was overshadowed by discussions that neglected women's concerns regarding power relations within and outside their households, businesses, and trades.[9]

Convinced that women were often the driving force behind men's success, program officials encouraged women to adapt to the program's conditions, particularly family separation, by appreciating the long-term advantages of US wages. Without ever acknowledging potential changes in the decision-making roles in families and businesses, officials recruited entire families to support and participate in the Bracero Program. They assumed that men were entitled to control and demand women's labor and flexibility, so they urged women to work, under the direction of their male relatives, in already promising family businesses that male recruits would be leaving behind. Exaggerating the financial benefits and the brevity of their male relatives' absence was meant to efface doubts about how these families would manage to adjust emotionally and financially.

Throughout the Mexican countryside women were directed to accommodate their male relatives' participation in the Bracero Program by continuing to excel in their caretaking and homemaking while contributing to the preservation of town businesses. They were cautioned, however, that independent attempts to expand their resources or increase their earning power might actually jeopardize their families' long-term financial potential as well as their marriage and other family relationships. The increase in their family's earning potential that the Bracero Program would provide would automatically improve their quality of life. Participation would afford these families the luxury of expanding their businesses' personnel and purchase of equipment, demanding less of their labor and time.

It is important to stress that even before the Bracero Program middle-class women in San Martin de Hidalgo were responsible for much of their respective families' success and that middle-class female heads of household embraced their families' businesses or trades as their occupation. Their occupational skills and responsibilities also suggest deep involvement in their family's livelihoods. Laboring in support of bracero relatives was promoted as women's obligation to family and nation and as in their interest. Such a narrow conceptualization of middle-class women's interests and roles, however, overshadowed their own concerns and vision of economic betterment.

The gendered overtones of the Bracero Program's presentation did not escape the women. The biased approach made Consuelo want to walk out of the program's town forum. During this meeting she had been denied the privilege of asking questions and being treated as a businessperson. Consuelo reacted with bitter frustration: she had thought of nothing else than how an increase in her family's earnings would allow them to purchase a few acres of land to add a dining area to their bakery. They would expand their menu and clientele and finally be able to run a *lonchería* and *cenaduría* (an eatery that served lunch and dinner). They had already built large brick ovens, as well as an aluminum counter with wooden stools to accommodate customers craving coffee, cocoa, milk, or tea with their *pan dulce*. Her family's participation would finance the expansion of their business and would double their clientele and profits. In the end, such plans made her decide to overlook the town government's dismissal of her distinctly gendered concerns.

The promise of US wages also inspired Emilia Lozano to accommodate her husband's participation by agreeing to work longer hours cutting women's and children's hair to preserve their clientele.[10] Her husband was a barber with a strong town following but in desperate need of new chairs, equipment, and the US dollars that could finance such expenses. The couple also anticipated making a fair profit from loan agreements. Emilia's plans were widely shared, since she intended to dedicate herself to working longer hours to preserve the family business. Her husband's participation in the Bracero Program might also make US beauty trends financially accessible for the business. Emilia was confident that their investment in US equipment and styles would expand their already strong following into neighboring towns.

These women's plans and visions were compatible with the Mexican government's visions of family cooperation and progress, but they also reflect profound familiarity with and interest in contract labor and its relationship to US consumer and labor trends. Emilia and many other women believed that emulation and application of US styles would improve how they worked and catered to their customers. Middle-class families often knew about US equipment, products, and trends not only from some family members' previous experiences in the United States but also from subscriptions to US catalogs and magazines. Further, middle-class women's own idealized imaginings of the benefits of legal access to US wages drove their support and their male relatives' enlistment in the program.

Focusing on middle-class women's aspirations in relationship to their male relatives' Bracero Program participation, decision making, and earnings, the Mexican government's promotion of the program was meant to inspire and nurture women's commitment to their male relatives' participation in ways that were publicly compatible with local gender norms. Women were to labor for the sake of the entire family and encourage others by example. Developing their own visions of progress outside this framework of collective family labor was publicly discouraged.

Preciado's recruitment strategy achieved its desired effect. Upon returning to their businesses, trades, and neighborhoods, middle-class families encouraged working-class families to join the Bracero Program. Middle-class men overlooked class differences that had often separated them from the working class to describe and promote program participation as a feat worthy of strong and responsible men. They replaced Avila Camacho's racial logic with their own translation of this program's sacrifices and benefits. Moreover, middle-class families in San Martin de Hidalgo recruited working-class families into the program after agreeing to finance their loans. Prospective working-class braceros borrowed an estimated 250 pesos from middle-class families at a monthly interest rate of 8 pesos. Middle-class families aggressively pursued loan revenues as well as enlistment.

REPATRIATES' INTERVENTION

By August 18, 1942, many of this town's men, both middle-class entrepreneurs and poor agricultural laborers, had enlisted in the Bracero Program. Nonetheless, it had not been a smooth process. This was not the first time that this town's men had been lured to the United States. Between March 1920 and April 1928, midwestern and western US railroad and steel industries had contracted townsmen nationwide. The Mexican government's recruitment efforts did not allay an older immigrant generation's concern for the future of the working poor and inexperienced working class, a widely ignored yet receptive pool of prospective braceros. This older generation believed that immigration to the United States "was not a way to get to know the world."[11] Their own immigration histories informed their distrust of the US and Mexican governments and, more urgently, this program's conditions. Such sentiments inspired them to take a different approach to recruitment.

This older generation, composed of former immigrants to and repatriates from the United States, warned working-class men that Preciado had not promoted the Bracero Program among them, that he did not want to be accountable for working-class men in desperate need of creating profitable life opportunities through the program. They explained that Preciado had personally recruited older heads of middle-class families and strategically sidestepped recruiting working-class families in order to avoid future accusations of deception and fraud. The targeted younger generation's future during and after program participation was highly suspect. High-interest loans and potentially exploitative employment conditions were a losing combination. Moreover, repatriates claimed that the Mexican government knew it would take very little convincing to lure thousands of working-class and inexperienced men to journey to the United States in pursuit of earning higher wages. They insisted that the Mexican and US governments were taking advantage of recruits' poor educations, limited life opportunities, and low wages to enlist them in an unprofitable and unhealthy mode of life.[12]

Repatriates' intense distrust of the program, coupled with their immigration histories, made them advise young would-be braceros who were working class to participate responsibly, using their participation to transition into profitable long-term settlement with their families. This older generation of immigrants pointed out that a contract would not translate automatically into such a settlement: careful planning would be necessary for dealing with family separation, increased debt, and tense ethnic, gender, race, and class relations.

Upon learning of the Bracero Program, many young prospective braceros sought out repatriates, who held meetings in the privacy of their homes, offices, and neighborhoods to discuss immigrant life in the United States with them and their families and to offer testimonials and advice on contract labor's short- and long-term implications. Repatriates remembered setting out for the United States without foreknowledge of US employment conditions and politics. Acting as concerned parents and town residents, they circulated what they considered important advice to demystify the Mexican government's idealization of the Bracero Program's conditions, because the working class "deserved better."[13] Repatriates' advice attracted and resonated with concerned grandparents, parents, partners, and children left behind.

Repatriates knew that the opportunity to earn US wages was not something working-class men and their families could afford to refuse. Local employment opportunities were scarce and poorly paid, and families were overwhelmed by debt.

Working-class prospective braceros were pursuing contract labor to pay off existing family debt. These families struggled with exploitative sharecropping, an inadequate educational system, poor health care, and histories of poor life opportunities. Most town men had begun working as agricultural laborers at ages as young as eight. They were not educated, did not own land, and did not have mastery of a trade to transition easily out of contract labor. It was important that they manage their participation strategically: uninformed pursuit of contract labor would potentially trap them in exorbitant debt and dependence on contract labor as a permanent way of life.

Although these private and group conversations between the older and younger generation of immigrants often excluded women, concerned grandmothers and mothers often collaborated to organize such meetings out of concern for their families' welfare. The resulting conversations emerged as vehicles for women to express their advice and concerns indirectly. Maria Elena Medina remembers that she and other concerned women recruited repatriates to advise potential braceros about "keeping their own financial records, writing down departure and return dates, and obtaining their contractors' names." They entrusted repatriates to speak for them, to "say what we [women] had to keep to ourselves." Medina explained, "We could not become overcome with worry. We had to arm everyone with knowledge before letting them go."[14]

Repatriates encouraged prospective braceros to avoid drinking, gambling, and overspending and to master a work pace that was compatible with labor demands but also with their staying healthy. Concerned grandmothers and mothers considered such advice empowering. It was often the first time that transitioning into and out of contract labor, as well as reaching adulthood, had been discussed with these young men. Repatriates' advice and testimonials echoed parents' concerns and emerged as a meaningful form of expressing their own anxiety.

Concerned female relatives also invited repatriates to bring generations of male relatives together to accept and support the Bracero Program participation of younger male relatives. To ease tensions between disapproving grandparents and parents and their sons and sons-in-law, former repatriates met and spoke with these men. Older and younger male relatives often disagreed on whether program participation was affordable and worthwhile. Older male relatives feared that the program's conditions would result in their sons' permanent, reckless bachelorhood and exorbitant debt. Repatriates and concerned female relatives took comfort in helping male relatives settle on the terms of their family's separation through in-depth discussion of the program's implications for young men's transition into adulthood. Older relatives demanded that young men assure them that they would act responsibly throughout their contract period and upon their return.

Other grandparents and parents agreed that they needed US wages desperately but opposed contract labor because they worried that their younger relatives would become transient men. These men feared that their sons' unsupervised transition into adulthood would distract and prevent them from building homes and raising families. Bringing their male relatives together for productive conversations to discuss the conditions that were compatible with family harmony comforted grandmothers and mothers, even if it entailed their exclusion.

Neighborhood meetings that women attended often addressed some of women's fears without drawing attention to any particular women's concerns or to their respective husbands' shortcomings. Women did not assert their own emotional and financial needs, concerns, or doubts at these meetings. This would have reflected poorly on them, their marriages, and their husbands. Instead, they utilized these forums to express their support of measures that might prevent male relatives' neglect and permanent family separation. Women prepared *aguas frescas* (drinks), coffee, entrées, *leña* (firewood), and pastries and set up tables and chairs to cater to families attending what other town residents assumed were birthday celebrations. Fearful of drawing unwanted government attention, women coordinated these meetings carefully. Maria Teresa Rodriguez had never been to the United States, so her husband "did not take her concerns or advice seriously."[15] Moreover, he doubted that as his wife she would ever support their temporary separation. Confident that this neighborhood meeting would finally address her concerns and that these would resonate with the concerns of other neighborhood couples, she helped organize it.

Neighborhood meetings appealed to women and men because they believed that lessons learned from lived experience were empowering and that it was their responsibility to equip themselves with the firsthand knowledge of repatriates. Families in attendance listened attentively and elaborated on repatriates' advice by drawing attention to contract labor's implications for their reputations and livelihoods. Men's failure to complete their contracts would be viewed back home as irresponsible conduct, ruining their reputation in town as well as their future prospects. Through these meetings, women also came to understand that their own collaboration with the Bracero Program would have to follow gender norms. Town respectability and collateral were contingent not only on men's successful contract completion but on women's management of a household, property, business, or trade under honorable conditions that did not include interacting with and catering to men who were not relatives.

Repatriates' approachability and receptiveness enhanced their credibility and popularity among working-class women. They set a positive example. Repatriates strove to incorporate women into these conversations by asking and addressing their questions concerning family separation. This prevented the emergence of power struggles between women and men. Often by the conclusion of these meetings, women's collaboration, coordination, and participation in setting up the meetings were determined to be socially responsible acts on behalf of their families and neighborhood. The women's tactful approach prevented power struggles between women and men from surfacing but also deflected attention away from women's successful community leadership in what were really acts of protest against local and national neglect. Women's organizing of these meetings and participation in them marked the utmost boundary of male relatives' tolerance toward women's leadership, which always had to be portrayed as a form of caretaking. In all other matters, women were expected to follow their male relatives' direction. Nonetheless, the meetings marked the beginning of collaborations between repatriates, working-poor women, and young men committed to their own visions of personal advancement.

Repatriates' outreach to braceros and their families went beyond informal meetings. Preciado relied on former repatriates like Manuel Ricardo Rosas in skilled employment sectors to administer a critical phase in prospective braceros' recruitment. Program administrators required letters of recommendation and formal written agreements financing loans from middle-class families to pay Bracero Program recruitment fees. To facilitate this process, Preciado enlisted Rosas and the entire town's skilled employees to write and issue program loan agreements and letters attesting to prospective braceros' strong work ethic and moral character. They felt that if braceros got fired and needed new employment or faced persecution or arrest, these papers would help protect them, since they to a certain extent documented that the men in question were not aimless wanderers but reputable citizens in their home country with solid work histories who had proven themselves worthy of initial admission into the United States. Rosas wrote letters of recommendation, but not before offering, with the help of former coworkers and repatriates, a few words of advice.[16]

Rosas and other repatriates told prospective braceros to tape their documents onto a sturdy separate sheet of paper, write their home address on this sheet, and fold it into sixteen squares so that they could easily carry the documentation with them at all times, as the repatriates had done previously when working in the United States (figure 1). Once they crossed the US-Mexico border, different rules would

FIGURE 1.

Manuel Ricardo Rosas's personal documentation of his US
immigration and employment records (front side), 1932.

apply. Mexican immigrant men were discriminated against, questioned, and deported with nothing but the clothes on their backs. It was their responsibility to carry documents confirming their legality and to keep their families informed about their assigned destination. This older generation advised them to understand that foreigners would not care "who you were nor who you must return to eventually."[17]

It was risky for the repatriates to make these recommendations to prospective braceros. Very few town residents had the courage to discuss publicly anything other than loan agreements and the promise of US wages. Prospective braceros and their families signing loan agreements without assurance of a contract or information on the Bracero Program's terms had to accept that they were making an important decision without much knowledge about its ramifications. Repatriates' and skilled employees' concerns emboldened the prospective braceros to assert their distrust. By acknowledging that crossing the US-Mexico border involved learning to negotiate language barriers, working under strict management, and enduring the violation of contract terms, social exclusion, and racial discrimination and exploitation, the older generation was doing a great service to those who would follow.

Repatriates' and women's ingenuity in negotiating the program's emotional demands evidenced their commitment to family and their careful negotiation of gender norms. Repatriates aggressively tried to instill accountability, goal setting, and an obligation to family in working-poor men and their families in order to prepare for their transition through contract labor and long-distance family relationships. Their efforts do not imply that working-poor men would otherwise idealize contract labor or be incapable of judging the program for themselves. Rather, they illustrate how an older and younger generation came together to pursue progress through immigration and develop an alternative discourse to program recruitment, one that in some ways confronted the racial logic of contract labor.

WORKING-CLASS VISIONS
OF PROGRESS AND THE MASS APPEAL
OF EMIGRATION

Working-poor prospective braceros were at a crossroads. They were unaware of Avila Camacho's vision for their betterment. The Bracero Program's unfolding confirmed that they would continue to inhabit a distinct and inferior racial category unless they transitioned successfully into and then out of contract labor. Throughout the history of San Martin de Hidalgo, working-class men had been restricted to poorly paid, unskilled agricultural labor and had been discriminated against on account of their lack of education, income, and property. In light of repatriates' stories, they realized that contract labor would also require negotiating racially discriminatory conditions and attitudes concerning their ability, background, labor, and rights, as well as gendered expectations concerning their emotional relationships, settlement, and success in the United States. Contextualizing contract labor, and more specifically the opportunity to earn and return with enough collateral to liquidate debt and enter into other trades, motivated them to pursue a delicate balance between being racialized—treated as expendable, illiterate, vulnerable, and unskilled laborers—and overcoming such racism and discrimination as determined and informed, goal-oriented men.

The town's working-class prospective braceros began this process by articulating their own visions of progress. They appropriated Bracero Program discourses to strengthen their resolve. These visions were contingent on taking advantage of town resources already in place in addition to recognizing and utilizing emerging trends. Like middle-class families, working-class prospective braceros asserted that access to US wages would strengthen their earning potential. They were confident that plans centered on the firsthand knowledge of repatriates and their own visions of economic advancement would enable them to eventually make the transition into desirable long-term settlement.

The plans of young working-class prospective braceros usually consisted of borrowing money from relatives or middle-class families to go toward their recruitment fees, learning skills and trades in the United States, then returning home to use them. Carlos Rodriguez, for example, was determined to learn how to fix automobiles so he could earn enough to buy his own. Realizing that very few working-class families in town owned or could afford automobiles, he envisioned that working in the United States would make this skill set and vehicles accessible to him as he became middle class and serviced that community's fleet of cars. After all, older immigrants had hailed the United States as "the automobile mecca of the world."[18] Although Rodriguez's goal was compatible with Avila Camacho's vision, it implied transcending poorly paid agricultural labor. Young prospective braceros clearly had their own visions of what the program could provide.

Jose Ramirez planned that after working as a bracero in the United States he would have enough money to purchase an automobile and build a newsstand.[19] Demand among town residents for the latest editions of international, national, and surrounding town newspapers, as well as comic books and magazines, had increased with news of the program. The town's thirst for information regarding the United States was growing, and Ramirez was confident that his US wages would also facilitate his purchase of a radio and large loudspeakers to air broadcasts of news and other popular programming and his sale of the most popular publications. He also envisioned selling sweets and other homemade treats to offset the cost of gasoline as he made his way to and from Guadalajara and the surrounding towns to pick up subscriptions. Confident that access to US technology, trends, and wages would lay the foundations for prosperous settlement, he signed a program loan agreement to pursue a contract. He was determined to transcend poverty in Mexico and the United States.

Meetings between generations of immigrants and men's plans for the future laid the foundations for a bracero culture that centered on the importance of transitioning out of the program by becoming informed and having clear goals. Nonetheless, the town's miscalculation of the program's mass appeal, as well as its economic and social impact, forced families to reconsider program conditions. Desperate for US wages and unable to obtain or afford loans to pay for program recruitment fees, many Mexican working-class men instead journeyed to the United States as undocumented Mexican immigrants. Mexican government town officials were unprepared to deal with this phenomenon. Both contract and undocumented immigration transformed families' plans for progress into a transnational struggle over local development that took advantage of working-class children, women, and men left behind to labor.

Preciado did not attempt to manage the adaptation of the town and its families to the absence of these men. Those left behind were on their own. The volatile combination of labor shortages, overworked women, and streets teeming with children plagued rural towns and villages throughout Mexico. San Martin de Hidalgo was no exception. This town's adaptation to contract and undocumented immigrant labor was complicated by the racial, class, and gender characteristics that the middle class perceived in this town's working class, as well as by the middle class's distinct vision of how families could better themselves: a model of investing US wages in their own businesses that applied more to middle-class than to working-class families.

The Mexican nation's preoccupation with national consumer patterns and trends among the urban middle class deflected attention and funds away from rural towns and villages confronting an unstable local economy and strained social relations. The Bracero Program's impact on rural, working-class families left behind was not a national priority. Instead, national authorities prided themselves on fulfilling program recruitment quotas successfully and on mobilizing urban middle-class families to invest aggressively in US-manufactured apparel, equipment, and trends in emulation of a modern way of living and working. The families' exposure to different customs was restricted to their purchase of US consumer styles and trends, reducing Avila Camacho's vision of economic development to an efficient model for managing Mexican men's immigration to the United States.

The Bracero Program's mobilization confronted middle-class town families with labor shortages and led to the unskilled working class laboring longer shifts for lower wages. Women and men struggled to keep up with demands on their labor and time. Orders for apparel, dairy products, dry goods, meats, vegetables, and other products were late most of the time, and wages declined significantly. Members of middle-class families worked fifteen-hour shifts to fill large orders or juggle several trades. The working poor worked thirteen-hour shifts to earn an estimated three pesos a day.[20] This roughly equaled one hour's wages in poorly paid unskilled US agricultural labor. Excessive pressure on town families' energy, time, and resources included children, especially among the working poor. School-age children missed days of instruction to help relatives with household chores and trades. Such demands on child labor and time resulted in the expulsion of elementary and middle school students on account of poor attendance and health.

Six months into the Bracero Program, working-class braceros acknowledged that their quality of life had not improved and that it would likely become worse on both sides of the US-Mexico border. Additionally, undocumented Mexican immigrant men began to emigrate, increasing the number of families left in Mexico to compete for poorly paid unskilled jobs. Working-class braceros understood that they urgently needed uninterrupted access to US wages despite the dehumanization and dislocation they were experiencing. It was important for them to convey the similarities between their own individual circumstances and their families' adaptation to long-term separation if they were to renew their families' confidence, resourcefulness, and trust, as they and their families engaged in a transnational struggle to make possible the braceros' eventual return.

LESSONS LEARNED

The immigration histories of working-class braceros reveal that their experience of long-term family separation and discretionary return was informed by lessons they learned before even setting foot in the United States. Their descriptions of program selection convey that becoming a bracero entailed undergoing dehumanizing, racially infused eligibility processes: Artemio Guerra de Leon, for example, recalled that he and other men had waited three hours in the nude to undergo program selection.[21] "Braceros often dwelled on the dehumanizing treatment involved in selection and processing when they were trying to convince their families that it was better to secure continuing, uninterrupted US employment, either legally (through renewals or special-immigrant contracts that were difficult to secure) or illegally, after their Bracero Program contracts had expired, and thus to endure long-term family separation, than to return to Mexico again and again to undergo the expense and humiliation of repeated program contracting.

To counter lingering widespread idealization of the Bracero Program back in Mexico, braceros who returned told others about intra- and interethnic tensions in the agricultural labor camps. Ramon Rea Rios shared that his father had told him, "We were not welcomed by anybody, white, black, other Mexican immigrants, or Mexican Americans. They saw us as competition."[22] Rea Rios explained, "It was stressful to keep all the divisions in my head [remember all the unwritten segregation rules] when working, trying to get some sleep, and bathing."[23] Their dehumanization and dislocation often led braceros to distrust one another and separate into regional groupings. All the divisiveness, braceros told their families, made contract labor emotionally as well as physically draining. Braceros wanted to convince their families that the interethnic hostility they confronted was similar to the demeaning treatment that their wives and children were receiving from the middle-class families that employed them. They hoped that this would convince their families that they were making sacrifices and were desperate to transition out of contract labor.

Middle-class braceros also wrote their families to justify their contract renewal. Arturo Buendia told his family that although he had "worked hard to prove that he was good enough to deserve braceros' approval" and earn US wages, he could not return.[24] He had not earned enough to expand his hometown business. Middle-class braceros also renewed their contracts and appealed to their families in ways similar to those used by working-class braceros.

Working-class braceros' stories of their lives in the United States did not lessen their families' anxiety and fears. Instead, families became disillusioned by their bracero relatives' willingness to continue to follow in the course articulated by the Mexican government. Though braceros described missing their families and feeling overworked and financially strapped, they continued to enlist their relatives' support as laborers. Families often resented braceros' requests that they continue to labor under existing conditions without addressing their individual concerns or needs as citizens, laborers, and relatives. Their immigration stories, long-term family separation, and discretionary return reminded families that their bracero relatives controlled their labor in Mexico from afar.

Eight months into the Bracero Program, families throughout Mexican rural towns like San Martin de Hidalgo were working sixteen-hour shifts for less than fifteen pesos a week, terms that reflect a drop in wages and an escalation in exploitation.[25] Additionally, middle-class families took advantage of what they considered had become the increasingly desperate situation of working-class bracero families by hiring family members to work for them under exploitative conditions. Punctual payment of Bracero Program loan agreement conditions left working-class bracero families with very little left over. Middle-class families realized that working-class families, even with their male relatives earning US wages, were unable to pay for much-needed winter clothing, nutritious meals, and adequate health care for their children.

In accordance with Mexican rural town gender norms, female relatives did not oppose, in public or in writing, their bracero relatives' proposals for long-term separation and discretionary return. They did not bring up the continued deterioration of their quality and standard of living. Weary of their bracero relatives returning without enough money to liquidate their program loan agreements, female relatives assumed instinctively that "their access to uninterrupted wages in either country was better than unemployment and unpaid program loan agreements."[26] Families settled for, at best, receiving remittances to finance program loan payments and complement their increasingly lower wages. They were convinced that if their previous efforts had not elicited much more than promises and remittances toward liquidating their program loan agreements, they could not do much more to inspire a different and more profitable response.

Instead, the wives of working-class braceros recorded remittance receipts carefully and, after paying their monthly loan installments, deposited leftover funds in their family savings account. Their husband's and children's sacrifices made them uncomfortable, and they feared braceros returning with only the clothes on their backs, demanding accurate records of how their earnings had been spent. When received, bracero letters convinced women that their male relatives were in denial about the hardships their families were experiencing back home. They took comfort at least in financing the liquidation of their program-loan agreement and, despite their situation, made it a priority to try to create better life opportunities for their children.

By 1945, working-class bracero families had learned that such a priority was no longer a central component of their bracero relatives' vision for family betterment. Even after the town's working-class braceros had completed a contract or two, they told their families that their plans continued to require their families' support as laborers and endurance of long-term separation. Braceros' failure to finance their children's enrollment in quality education, repair their homes, purchase land, begin businesses or trades, or enter into agricultural labor under more profitable conditions confirmed that they were unable to immediately better their families' financial position by transitioning into desirable long-term settlement.

Working-class braceros continued to depend on but often overlook the sacrifices of overworked working-class children, women, and older men as caretakers, laborers, and citizens. Yet they developed and financed a local bus-transit system to provide and nurture the profitable mobility of young men between fifteen and nineteen years of age. Returning braceros were committed to providing these young men—too young to secure Bracero Program contracts or pursue undocumented entry into the United States and too poor to enroll in local schools—with supervised internal mobility that could improve their quality of life and standard of living. Returning working-class braceros considered this generation of young men, usually their sons and siblings, worthy of financial investment. They realized that the young men's life opportunities, like their own, were limited by racially charged exploitation to poorly paid agricultural work and other forms of unskilled labor. Nonetheless, bracero relatives were confident that by obtaining transportation to and from surrounding towns and Guadalajara, Jalisco—one of the largest cities their town's home state—these young men would gain employment, skills, and wages that would prevent their entry into Bracero Program loan agreements, contract labor, and undocumented entry into the United States. Working-class braceros were committed to providing young men without families of their own and unbound by program loan agreements the mobility to thrive outside both the Bracero Program and the limited local employment opportunities.

Despite this benefit to the town's youth, other town residents refused to endorse the Bracero Program. Their assessment of the emergencies facing the US and Mexican governments led them to argue that the program was not in fact the most desirable, sound, or humane approach to dealing with the US government's alleged need for a labor surplus of Mexican-immigrant contract laborers; indeed, the program was bound to make an already unmanageable situation worse. Subsequent events would bear them out.

CHAPTER TWO · The Bracero Program as
a Permanent State of
Emergency

The Bracero Program was initially named the Emergency Farm Labor Program, and it was announced as a measure to address a temporary state of emergency, namely US shortages of agricultural crops and labor.[1] But in fact the program itself created a permanent state of emergency for people of Mexican descent in both Mexico and the United States. This chapter shows how neither the US nor the Mexican government officials entrusted to implement the program wanted to acknowledge this reality. It draws on assessments of the program by Mexican men, as well as a report by the US Department of Labor's Children's Bureau, to reveal emergency conditions that the US and Mexican governments neglected for their convenience and for the sake of promoting the US agricultural industry's need for a labor surplus.

SILENCING BRACEROS

The US and Mexican governments were negligent in protecting the rights and dignity of immigrant workers and their families. As labor activist Ernesto Galarza explained in his personal papers, the Bracero Program had been presented to recruits and to US and Mexican society as an honorable emergency wartime program, based on friendship between allied nations, that braceros should embrace in the spirit of transnational patriotism, even at their own and their families' expense.[2] As Galarza recalled the rhetoric of the US and Mexican governments, "On the present conditions of emergency, patriotism must be imposed with preference to any other consideration. America is in danger. Mexico is in danger. Therefore, no effort is too small and no risks should be disdained. The workers, the farmers, the professionals, the press, the industrial and commercial classes, all must gather around the glorious banner of friendship."[3]

Because of this indoctrination, braceros who met with exploitation and injustice that neither government attempted to remedy felt pressured to keep their true assessment of the program and its consequences to themselves. As a result, they felt deeply alienated and kept an unbearable silence. They themselves took on responsibility for the program as the government did not. In Galarza's words, "Before they leave Mexico, they are told that they are 'soldiers of the soil' whose job it is to help produce the food needed to defeat the Axis, that idleness or bad behavior will not be condoned, and that they will receive no sympathy in Mexico if they are repatriated for misconduct. As long as this attitude continues, hemispheric solidarity is strengthened at the expense of the bracero."[4]

Nevertheless, some Mexican citizens were bold enough to speak out about the program and assess for themselves its repercussions for the families who participated in it. In 1942, Manuel Ricardo Rosas, the repatriate in San Martin de Hidalgo whose efforts to prepare prospective braceros for life in the United States we described in chapter 1, told his family and friends that the US and Mexican governments had failed to recognize that the emotional turmoil of consecutive repatriation and now the beginnings of the Bracero Program had created a permanent state of emergency for families throughout the Mexican countryside.[5] From 1929 through 1939 these governments had refused to admit the burdens on Mexican children and women caused by the abrupt repatriation of an estimated three hundred thousand Mexican American and Mexican immigrant children, women, and men from the United States to Mexico. Now the governments were not acknowledging the emotional and material costs incurred by the new wave of recruitment of Mexican immigrant men who were leaving their families in Mexico to labor for one to nine months at a time in the United States.[6] In Rosas's estimation, the persistent lack of adequate protections or specific information concerning braceros' citizenship rights and destinations had the makings of a dangerously permanent state for children, women, and men that was exacerbated by these governments' reluctance to acknowledge or take responsibility for it.

Rosas and other former repatriates in San Martin de Hidalgo frankly assessed the effects of unceasing migration of desperate, emotionally exhausted, hardworking, ill-prepared, impoverished, and poorly treated undocumented Mexican immigrants of all ages to the United States and their failure to thrive on either side of the

US-Mexico border.[7] Rosas in particular took a daringly transnational approach to raising his own family and alerting others about how best to face this often over-looked reality.

PARENTING TOWARD AN INFORMED FUTURE

Rosas's emotional investment in protecting his children from the hardships of the permanent state of emergency in the Mexican countryside inspired him to instruct them not to idealize the United States. His own experience and continued exposure to the US and Mexican governments' racialized mistreatment of Mexican children, women, and men as inferior to whites informed his decision to instill in his children the habit of questioning migration to and labor in the United States as an avenue toward a promising future. Like Veneranda Torres, Rosas staged and used photo-graphic family portraits to craft and share a transnational family history with his children that would discourage them from migrating to the United States for work and would instead encourage them to settle permanently in Mexico. His own fam-ily's documentation of their history in the form of personally meaningful family portraits had given him courage when before and during his labor in the United States he had been required to answer personal questions from government officials or employers, and when he had to cope with being repatriated to San Martin de Hidalgo with only the clothes on his back.

Manuel understood the resourcefulness of his own parents, Jose and Agapita Rosas (figure 2), in acting upon the anxiety they felt when he chose to labor for years in the United States. They urged him to view their family portraits before his 1925 departure as a way of instilling in him an unforgettable sense of himself and his relationship to his family. The spirit of these photographs revealed that whatever the outcome of his migration to the United States, he had the potential and the fam-ily support to thrive in Mexico. Reflecting upon his parents' way of being support-ive, Manuel understood that they wanted to make sure that he did not underestimate the moral character, education, work ethic, and relationships at his disposal, should he need to recover and rebuild from the emotional toll of migration.

The portraits from his family history that helped Manuel most were those of his parents Jose and Agapita celebrating their marriage and of himself after completing his first year of college in Mexico City (figure 3), a portrait he used to process his application for legal authorization to labor in the steel industry of Chicago. While laboring thirteen-hour workdays in the snow-covered windy city, he was comforted by these images of his parents wearing elegant attire as they posed together and of

FIGURE 2.

Jose Manuel Rosas and Agapita Rodriguez de Rosas, 1925.

himself wearing one of his favorite three-piece suits that he had been able to purchase after saving his wages from delivering merchandise throughout the Mexican
countryside. So empowered, he did not doubt his emotional and physical ability
to complete an arduous employment schedule for a poor wage of at most twenty
cents an hour, or to give up on his larger goal of eventually earning and saving
enough US wages to return to his family and thrive—ideally wearing the suit he
had worn to take the self-portrait used to process his government-issued documents.
He could fondly recollect his parents' refinement, moral character, and marriage
and his own education, work ethic, and personal sacrifice to purchase and wear suits
that had made his completion of demanding employment and school schedules

FIGURE 3.
Manuel Ricardo Rosas, 1929.

before his departure to the United States worthwhile. This eased the emotional and physical burden of laboring under conditions that in 1932 resulted in severe injuries to his hands and his resulting repatriation to Mexico. Hardly anybody, least of all the Mexican and US governments, objected to employment conditions that overexposed Mexican immigrant workers to on-the-job injuries. It was more convenient to repatriate physically compromised men back to Mexico than to investigate and address their susceptibility to physical injury and other dangers while they were on the job in the United States.

During his time in the United States, Rosas had to travel on foot, bicycle, and train. He helped construct and maintain railroads in inclement weather for poor wages. When he was injured, he recovered in a US hospital where medical personnel refused to provide him with adequate information concerning his hands' injury. He returned to San Martin de Hidalgo in a railroad boxcar without restrooms, seats, or windows alongside at least two hundred other repatriated children, women, and men. Yet these experiences did not demoralize him completely because he embraced the optimistic spirit that had made each of the moments featured in his family's portraits possible. Focusing on what he had been able to share with his family and on what he had achieved in his employment history and a year of a college education at a time when most Mexican immigrant men had barely completed an elementary education motivated Rosas to endure the emotional and physical suffering that labor in the United States entailed. The qualities that his parents had instilled in him informed Rosas's spirited resistance against being treated as a disposable, illiterate, and undesirable Mexican immigrant. Each of the portraits his family had shared with him fueled his determination to overcome such hardships and to dedicate himself to finding employment opportunities and relationships that would not make him unrecognizably foreign to himself and his family.

These photographs helped keep Rosas from idealizing or settling in the United States under terms that would make his relationships, education, and other types of experience in Mexico irrelevant. Denied desirable employment opportunities, transportation, housing, and relationships, Rosas found it difficult to excel in the United States as a man who had completed one year of college, had once wore tailored suits on special occasions, had assisted business owners in their management of their enterprises, and had benefited from the support of dedicated and ambitious parents. The toil and invisibility of physically demanding and poorly paid US railroad construction had not afforded him opportunities to capitalize on his command of the English language, his college education, or what his college professors and employers had indicated was his gift for communicating well with others in person and in writing. Fortunately, these were qualities that his family photographs made readily accessible to him wherever he found himself.

Throughout his seven-year stint in the United States, Rosas had at best been able to labor alongside fellow Mexican immigrant men who, like himself, were losing sight of their identity, talents, and potential. All his work in the United States had amounted to his being able to finance only the medical expenses he had incurred there. The alienating experience of living as a man of Mexican descent in the United States made Rosas feel that who he had become in the United States failed to resemble the person he was raised and wanted to be. His family photographs emboldened him to remember that his failed migration was not the entirety of his lived experience and should not continue to define his identity and goals. A humble lifestyle was not new or foreign to him. Laboring tirelessly alongside his parents to keep their grocery store and other shops thriving throughout his adolescence and until his migration to the United States had already exposed him to working long hours. Nonetheless, being reduced to a "dirty Mexican" as he labored, traveled, or ate a diner meal in the United States made his experiences of working and socializing with his family and friends under far more personally satisfying conditions seem distant and foreign.

The disjunction between the photographs his parents had given him and the alienation he experienced as a migrant worker highlighted for Rosas that the United States was not receptive to who he was and wanted to become as part of his larger vision of a fulfilling day-to-day life and promising future. This introspectively and defiantly honest assessment of what had proven most restorative to him as he transitioned out of his own failed migration to the United States and into a new life back in Mexico led him to organize photographs of his children into a transnational family history in an informed attempt at inspiring them to take heart in what they had been able to achieve together—without having to experience firsthand the alienation of struggling to migrate and labor in the United States.

A TRANSNATIONAL FAMILY HISTORY

On his return, Rosas took on the lifelong project of crafting, collecting, sharing, and preserving a transnational history of the family for his children. Rather than overburden his wife, Josefina Gomez Rosas, with additional work, he first financed family portrait sessions in professional photography studios and eventually took photographs of the children himself. He wanted to give his children images that would show them that, even in the most challenging moments, thriving in Mexico was possible and preferable to migrating to and laboring in a foreign land.

One of the most personally meaningful photographs framing Rosas's transnational family history showed his children posing together after the family had completed the renovation of their home in 1955 (figure 4). Thirteen years into the Bracero Program, he enlisted a professional photographer to take this picture of his three eldest children—Cesario, Juventina, and Manuel Rosas Gomez—at ages eight, five, and seven, respectively, posing in front of a photo studio's painted landscape modeled after their town's plaza. The image shows that the family had

FIGURE 4.
Studio portrait of Cesario Rosas, Juventina Rosas, and
Manuel Rosas Jr., 1955.

saved enough to pay for not only a professional portrait but household fixtures and
to begin living under improved conditions that would include decorating their
home's freshly painted living room walls with this photograph. At a time when most
of their extended family and friends were pooling their earnings in support of
relatives laboring under the Bracero Program, the photo provided the children with
an enduring reminder of their parents' dedicated commitment to permanent settlement in Mexico.

This photograph was the first photograph of them together, as well as the most difficult to pay for. Manuel was determined that it would feature his children wearing new overalls and dresses, shoes, and impeccably ironed shirts—all purchases that confirmed his ability to simultaneously provide for them and complete recent additions and fixtures to their family home without having to join the Bracero Program. Financing these expenditures with their mother's support was meant to convey to the children that sharing their day-to-day life, working alongside and for those who meant most to them, could help them resourcefully forge a personally fulfilling future without their having to cross the US-Mexico border. Commemorating how the children had helped their parents raise and sell livestock and make cheese and other dairy products, and how the family's combined labor had provided them with a home and with portraits that would become formative to the children's upbringing, was meant to instill in their children a desire to pursue a future together without the separations required by immigration. Not allowing the Mexican and US governments' promotion of the promise of US wages to obscure the potential of working with one's children by one's side, Rosas used this photograph to write a responsibly defiant transnational family history.

In July 1956, photographs of their daughters Juventina at age six and Abigail Rosas at age five in rooms where Manuel and Josefina had made difficult decisions concerning their family's future were used to provide these children with glimpses of their influence during challenging moments in their family's history. During the summer of 1957, Juventina insisted on being at Manuel's side as much as possible, especially when her father was hard at work writing letters for the wives and parents of braceros who had not returned. She had such a calming and helpful presence that he failed to recognize how difficult this work was for a six-year-old child to understand or experience. The pain endured by these families had to a varying degree seeped into every family household. It was unavoidable. Sharing this important work with his daughter at such a young and impressionable age became his way of guiding her through the pain of the family separation she had encountered when interacting with relatives and friends. Sharing with her yet another form of responding to the permanent state of emergency facing fellow families throughout the Mexican countryside was Manuel's way of preparing his daughter to respond to such pain responsibly.

Beyond providing Manuel with an extra envelope, a pen, a sheet of paper, or a glass of water as he wrote letters on behalf of women and men in search of answers from their bracero relatives, Juventina was instrumental to his not giving up on writing these letters altogether. He suspected that the US and Mexican governments could be intercepting these letters, for families often told him that despite their not having received any letters in response from their bracero relatives it was emotionally comforting to write them anyway. His daughter's presence reaffirmed for him the importance of dedicating hours to writing letters twice weekly on behalf of families requesting information or providing updates on the status of ongoing family affairs. He never charged a fee for this service, although his family could have financially benefited from that or from his laboring at their family store instead of writing these letters. Juventina's mature presence during what felt more like counseling sessions of sorts—as these women and men came to their home's indoor patio overwhelmed by sadness and doubt—influenced Manuel to dedicate himself to helping these families pose important questions or share helpful information with their absent bracero relatives. His daughter's constant and considerate presence made it difficult for him to ignore the most promising result of writing these letters: the likelihood that those who would benefit most from these letters were the children whose parents and other Mexican immigrants were separated from them on the other side of the border. Making an effort to reach out to bracero relatives could at some point materialize into response letters containing emotionally reassuring information.

The family's photograph of Juventina wearing one of her favorite dresses and posing in their household's indoor patio where she helped Manuel write these letters was meant to reflect the diversity of ways in which their family had come together. It marked as well their support of each other in efforts to assist other families weathering the permanent state of emergency that the Mexican and US governments continued to ignore, even years into the Bracero Program (figure 5). A candid portrait not staged or posed before her father's desk or in his company reinforced that from the time Juventina was very young her labor crossed borders and was valued by the family. Rosas similarly took and used photographs of his youngest daughter Abigail to make clear to his children that they had been raised to actively participate in their family's work and that this orientation toward family life had been foundational to their welfare.

Abigail's closeness with Manuel and Josefina made her family-supporting work easy to document. From the age of five, she had been interested in helping them with their organization of receipts and other accounting tasks that kept her at her parents' side as they drew up their weekly budget. Rather than discourage her or exclude her from this undertaking, they welcomed her initial efforts to organize into neat stacks their expense receipts, written requests for merchandise, and payment stubs for customers paying for their milk and cheese products as part of their installment plan.

FIGURE 5.
Juventina Rosas in the Rosas family's home patio, 1957.

Even though Abigail did not understand the specific details or issues framing Manuel and Josefina's discussions of their family's financial future, her willingness to carefully help them organize documents that were a part of this conversation, and eventually to learn how to maintain meticulous records of their expenditures and revenue, made her among the most reliable of their children. She would emerge as the most dedicated to ensuring that their business was being administered properly. At her extremely young age, her presence during these evening meetings also prevented them from arguing over their differences regarding maximizing their business revenue. Out of concern for her, they tried to avoid disagreements. This

FIGURE 6.
Studio portrait of Abigail Rosas, 1957.

attitude often worked to Josefina's benefit. It left Manuel with no other choice than to discuss their family's business affairs with a receptive attitude toward her insights, concerns, and recommendations. Throughout the years, their daughter's continued participation in these conversations would prove an important example of the positive impact of sharing as much as possible with each other.

The photograph of Abigail before the chair in which she rested while Manuel and Josefina organized their family's finances, often well into the wee hours, records her influence on their careful management of delicate and important family investments (figure 6). Decisions made during these meetings had a strong bearing on the family's ability to finance living together in Mexico. Hence, taking this photograph of their daughter in a room that their children grew up in, and specifically the space where important family conversations occurred, signaled that, irrespective of their age, the children's proactive participation under their parents' supervision was valued. This photograph documents the children taking active interest in affairs that could foreshadow their interests as adults. Manuel's decision to use this photograph of Abigail to celebrate what he anticipated would mark her introduction to the demands of running a business was his way of classifying the children's every gesture toward being a part of this process as invaluable, as well as formative, to their own personal interests and goals. He intuited that their daughter had gravitated to them most when they were handling business receipts and discussing business-related issues because even at such a young age she was personally intrigued by the exchange and purposefulness of receipts and money, as well as the different people that money management would draw to their business. Without their having to encourage Abigail, her persistence at proactively participating in these meetings would only grow.

All this does not mean that Rosas took and displayed these photographs on the family's living room walls solely to instruct the children on the importance of defying repatriation, the Bracero Program, and the intensification of undocumented Mexican immigration to the United States. Rather, he used these and a series of other photographs that included those of their sons celebrating their completion of a hard day's work or sharing a good time together inside and outside their home to hold conversations with them that centered on their attitude toward their future. Throughout their transition into and out of the different stages of their lives and as women and men coming into their own, he used these photographs to portray their alternatives in Mexico and the United States as worthy of careful consideration, a defiantly responsible response to the continued underestimation and racialized mistreatment of people of Mexican descent in Mexico and the United States.

When the children were making decisions concerning their education, their employment, their romantic relationships, and especially their location of permanent settlement, Manuel would use these photographs to encourage them to reflect on the hardships and resilience behind each picture. The photographs reflected what a determined pursuit of their goals could make possible without migration to the United States. It was Manuel's way of at least stressing to his children that even in the most challenging of circumstances much could be and had been achieved in Mexico. Thus these photographs became an integral component of Manuel and Josefina's parenting.

By the summer of 1976, thirty-four years after the Bracero Program's inception, Manuel's transnational sensibilities toward raising his children became especially evident. His documentation and discussion of the transnational context framing their family's history, coupled with their own assessment of the alienation endured by family and friends laboring in the United States, motivated all but two of their

FIGURE 7.
Abigail Rosas and Josefina Rosas Gomez celebrating Abigail's
graduation from her trade school program in accounting, 1972.

eight children to permanently settle in either San Martin de Hidalgo or Guadalajara.
Their informed consideration of the stakes involved in attempting to make a life in
the United States, as well as their pursuit of college or trade school education, paved
the way for a variety of careers: Cesario ran his own candy shop in San Martin de
Hidalgo, Manuel Junior entered a series of businesses that combined the distribution
and purchase of food products throughout Guadalajara, Miguel became involved
in the production and distribution of textiles, Jesus thrived as a managing supervisor in the transportation of chemicals, Juventina dedicated herself to perfecting her
skills as a seamstress and raising her family, and Abigail continued to excel as a savvy
and enterprising businesswoman until she tragically died in a car accident at the age
of thirty-eight (figure 7). Only Gerardo and Francisco opted to defy their father's
counsel and, in some ways, their transnational family history: in search of their
future, they migrated to San Antonio, Texas, and Los Angeles respectively.

His sons' decision to pursue their future in the United States was a source of great
emotional pain for Manuel. Wary of losing them to the alienation of laboring in the
United States, he would write them regularly to ensure that at least he knew the
details of their whereabouts. Although he reminded them to learn from the history

FIGURE 8.
Abigail Rosas, Manuel Ricardo Rosas's grandaughter, 1984.

of Mexican and US governments' border enforcement and immigration policies, Francisco found it too much information to deal with. His decision not to follow in his older siblings' footsteps by getting an education or working in San Martin de Hidalgo or Guadalajara led him to pursue what not only his father but most of his brothers and sisters, except for Abigail, dismissed as a reckless course of action.

Having little in the way of savings and only an elementary education, Francisco ignored most of the family's disapproval and counsel against going to the United States as an undocumented Mexican immigrant. Confident that in time he would earn sufficient US wages to determine whether he should settle in Mexico or the United States, and that in this way he would finally make a responsible decision, he set out for the United States anyway. In 1984, eight years after migrating to the United States, Francisco would take and use a photograph of his youngest daughter, Abigail Rosas, in his attempt to honor the lessons his father had worked so hard to instill in him as well as to assert his own defiantly responsible choice to seek his future in the United States (figure 8). He recognized the permanent state of emergency that his father had described and that he had experienced since childhood. As an adult and parent in the United States he used this photograph of his daughter, which had been years in the making, to communicate to his father that even in the United States he had not forgotten the value of continuing to document, share, and derive inner strength from their family's transnational history.

Francisco began to come into his own after laboring as an undocumented Mexican immigrant for a year. He had endured firsthand the pressure of working in a furniture company without even a three-minute break in a nine-hour work shift. He learned to take comfort in his earnings, which made it possible to support himself and a family of his own. In 1977, after returning briefly to San Martin de Hidalgo, Francisco married Dolores Graciela Rosas Medina and a year later reunited with her in Los Angeles. Afraid to risk giving birth to their first child while crossing the US-Mexico border, she had postponed her migration to the United States. Once together, Francisco and his wife worked for five consecutive years assembling furniture and sorting used clothing, as well as catering food for friends hosting family celebrations of baptisms, birthdays, weddings, and wedding anniversaries. Working long hours and pooling their earnings made it possible for them to save enough to purchase their first home in Guadalajara, Jalisco, Mexico, and to take and send a photograph of their daughter to Francisco's parents as a way of continuing Manuel's writing of their family's transnational history. The photograph recorded Francisco's transition into what he anticipated to be a promising future—in ways that met some of his father's expectations.

It was not a coincidence that Francisco took and shared a photograph of his daughter, Abigail, wearing a beautiful dress to celebrate her first birthday and posing in the living room of their apartment. In this space, he and his wife met with women and men to settle the details of their catering needs, as well as to set up play areas for Abigail. Manuel's example of taking and sharing photographs that documented his children's influence on him, in rooms where especially meaningful interactions had taken place, influenced Francisco's commemoration of this important transition and effectively shaped his own family's history. The living room's use both for negotiating the terms of their catering services and for interacting closely with their infant child made it the ideal space to take a photograph of her as they celebrated her birthday and their purchase of a home of their own in Mexico. Earning enough to raise a family as well as purchase a family home in which Francisco and his family would be able to settle should the alienation they experienced as undocumented Mexican immigrants in the United States become too unbearable or result in their deportation was meant to ease Manuel's anxiety concerning some aspects of Francisco's future. It was intended to resonate as a defiantly responsible reaction to the Mexican and US governments' management of immigration, as having this home in place allowed him and his wife to feel that unless they were deported they could choose for themselves whether to remain in the United States or return to Mexico. Thinking and acting to maximize what was accessible in both countries was Francisco's way of making amends toward his father and family of origin, while responding with his own family's welfare very much in his mind and heart.

The photograph of Francisco's daughter Abigail resembles the childhood portraits of his older sisters, Juventina and Abigail, in rooms where their parents had completed important tasks supporting families who faced the challenges of the permanent state of emergency that migration policies had created. The resemblance was meant to reflect that Francisco had indeed learned from and valued recording family history and had the transnational sensibilities of his father. This photograph brought Manuel to tears. He was relieved and overjoyed to learn that despite his anxiety concerning his son and his family's exposure to the alienation of life in the United States, his son had not idealized such day-to-day hardship but rather had responded to it as best he could, and with a sensibility tempered by his hard-earned experience and his own family's journey. Manuel respected Francisco's cautious approach to migration with the worst-case scenario in mind as a promising first step toward making other transitions as he forged his permanent settlement.

Despite the power of this photograph and its transnational transmission—it had enabled Francisco and Manuel, father and son separated by the US-Mexico border, to reconnect with each other on far more harmonious terms—Francisco was silent for many years about the Bracero Program and its enduring influence on him. This photograph may have made it easier for Manuel to accept his son's migration to the United States, but the issue remained painfully delicate. Francisco ultimately did not get to share much more time with his father. In 1985, the elder suffered a fatal stroke. Francisco never quite forgave himself that he had been away for years and had returned only for his father's funeral, with the result that he found it hard to discuss with his own children his decision to ultimately settle permanently in the United States.

I know this because Francisco Rosas is my father. It was his unwillingness throughout my childhood to answer why, unlike my friends, I could not visit my grandparents, aunts, or uncles on weekends or holidays that would later inform my historical investigation of the emotional depth and range of the transnational configuration of our family—most importantly, the enduring silence. The most my father brought himself to share with me was that if I wanted to understand why he had migrated to the United States but our extended family had not I would first need to learn more about and from my grandfather, whom my mother lovingly remembered and referred to as Don Manuel. My father's spirited efforts in support of my attempts to do so—through my visiting and listening to our extended family and, in Mexico, through his and my grandfather's documentation of our transnational family history—paved the way to my learning more about and from my grandfather through the stories behind each of the photographs my grandfather had carefully organized into stacks of photo albums.

When in the comfort of their family homes, in each other's company, or on their own, Manuel and other Mexicans of his generation dared to draw on their own immigrant experiences to identify the Bracero Program as the cause of a state of emergency for families of Mexican descent and varying legal status still recovering from the earlier dislocations of repatriation. Ultimately, that situation led to a permanent state of emergency for all families of Mexican descent. The program persuaded financially vulnerable Mexican families to endure separation in anticipation of receiving US wages, but those wages, earned under inhumane conditions, ended up being too low, in most cases, to allow the family ever to successfully reunite either in Mexico or in the United States. Manuel was among those who diagnosed and confronted the governmental neglect of enduring and ongoing family turmoil as a permanent state of emergency in large part born out of the governments' enforcement of the US-Mexico border. He leveraged this awareness to raise his own family in the Mexican countryside without idealizing the United States.

THE REAL EMERGENCY

Historians have been reluctant to investigate the full implications of the Bracero Program for children, women, and men of Mexican descent.[8] Because the program followed on the heels of the massive repatriation of the 1930s, it extended the state of emergency that repatriation had begun, but historians have resisted seeing the program in this context. Instead, they have presented it solely as a wartime program intended to provide US agriculture with Mexican immigrant contract laborers to replace male and female citizens of Anglo, African, and Mexican descent who had left the fields to work in factories in US cities or to join the military.[9]

The crises unfolding simultaneously with the Bracero Program that have attracted the most attention from historians have been the indignities endured by *pachucas* and *pachucos,* the young Mexican American women and men who spoke a hybrid English-Spanish slang dialect, wore zoot suits, and tried to assert a personally meaningful style, forge friendships, and create a day-to-day social life and world.[10] In the Sleepy Lagoon incident, twenty-four Mexican American *pachuco* youths were arrested and charged with having beaten Jose Diaz to death, and despite insufficient evidence nine of them were convicted of murder (their convictions would later be reversed). They were mistreated while held in custody, denied due process during their legal proceedings, and inflammatorily portrayed in newspaper coverage. Hysteria over the murder led to a police roundup of six hundred zoot suiters, as well as the Zoot Suit Riots, in which servicemen and civilians attacked young Mexican American women and men while they were frequenting theaters, riding streetcars, and walking along the streets of downtown areas in Los Angeles and outlying neighborhoods.

Such injustices are important, but they reflect a more general reluctance on the part of the US government to protect its citizens because of their class, racial, and ethnic background and gender identities. The government neglected the state of emergency among people of Mexican descent while wholeheartedly serving the interest of agriculture, which it positioned as undergoing a real and consequential emergency. Similarly, historians have been hesitant to consider that around the same time as the Bracero Program inflicted hardship and separation on Mexican families, the internment of children, women, and men of Japanese descent in camps as a result of the December 7, 1941, bombing of Pearl Harbor similarly disrupted and tore apart Japanese American families within the United States. In a time of war, both were moves by the US government to assert and enforce its national security and its borders. The US government ignored the citizenship status of many Japanese American children, women, and men in order to address what it deemed a true emergency—containing this population's alleged threat to US national security.[11]

In the case of Mexicans and Mexican Americans, reports by the US Department of Labor's Children's Bureau show that the US government's pursuit of border enforcement measures often violated the rights of the very people it had been established to protect.[12] This agency documented for the US government a most urgent and real emergency, and its report asserted a transnational, humane perspective. But it could not compete with the American Farm Bureau Federation, the Vegetable Growers Association of America, the Amalgamated Sugar Company, the National Cotton Council, and other US agricultural interest groups that successfully persuaded the government to import a surplus of Mexican immigrant contract laborers to harvest much-needed crops as cheaply as possible.

THE MIGRATION OF THE CHILD CITIZEN

In April 1943, the Children's Bureau appealed to the US government to reconsider its continuation of the Bracero Program. The agency worried that the program, after being in place for eight consecutive months without any discussion of when it would end, had expanded to the point that the labor being imported was far greater than the wartime need. Although it did not describe the situation as a permanent state of emergency, it dared to point out that the implementation of the program hinged on the US and Mexican governments' separation of families of Mexican descent across the US-Mexico border at a time when the bureau was still struggling with the family dislocation caused by repatriation.[13]

In 1941, the problems attendant on repatriation had energized the agency to publish the first of a three-year series of reports, entitled *The Children's Bureau and Problems of the Spanish Speaking Minority Groups,* that extensively documented the US government's reluctance to consider the crisis already occurring—that of US citizen children as young as twelve years old crossing daily into the United States from Mexican border towns to labor in support of their parents in Mexico.[14] Because the bureau was entrusted with investigating and managing cases in which children were found laboring under unlawful conditions and terms in the United States, it identified and helped these children transition out of illegal work and into healthy family situations in the United States. Upon learning that US citizen children of recently repatriated Mexican immigrant parents were laboring as babysitters, maids, and shoeshine boys and girls in Mexico and the United States, this agency expressed its concern at the government's reluctance to acknowledge the situation as an emergency highly worthy of its attention and resources.

In the 1941 report the Children's Bureau had tried to appeal to the government by describing the lengths to which the most cooperative US elementary and middle schools throughout Arizona, California, Texas, and Nevada were going to accommodate US-born children aged five to sixteen, of recent repatriates into their schools. Noticing that they were without parents and at best accompanied by guardians who explained that their repatriated parents had not been able to finance these children's education in Mexico, the school administrators and teachers welcomed the students without requiring them or their guardians to submit the forms required for school enrollment. In Nogales, Arizona, school administrators' concern over "these children having drifted back to the United States, particularly older children, living from hand to mouth, and some having barely found sleeping space with friends or relatives and getting their living by fair and foul means—shining shoes, peddling, begging, and stealing," informed their decision to be as accommodating to these students as possible.[15] They deemed it the least they could do to keep the children from entering into lives of petty crime. The school administrators and the social workers heading the bureau had the disconcerting sense that the US government was not doing enough for these children as US citizens caught in a situation that their parents had not been able to protect them from. They argued that even under the best of circumstances these children still needed the US government to do more to care for them and their families.

Some US school administrators were, out of their own volition and concern for the welfare of these displaced children, doing their best to confront the ongoing consequences of repatriation. By identifying those administrators, the Children's Bureau report portrayed to the US government the accountability that those exposed to the plight of these students on a day-to-day basis had been moved to assume. The bureau devoted much of its report to describing the involvement of repatriated parents of Mexican descent in the lives of their children as posing a serious challenge to their handling of these children's cases. These parents were in such desperate emotional and financial straits that they would enter the country as undocumented immigrants to drop their children off in their child welfare department offices and ask that the staff look after their "American born 'orphan' children."[16] In Santa Cruz, Arizona, the greatest number of child welfare cases were US citizens who had been dropped off by their repatriated parents on the understanding that their being US citizens entitled them to social agencies' care. They feared that without any money or employment in Mexico they could not afford to be their parents for much longer. The feeble physical state of these children had moved social workers at these offices to accept custody of them as orphans so that they could pursue placing them in foster homes throughout the United States.

The bureau explicitly described what repatriated US citizen children had been doing in the United States, before being taken into its custody, to financially support their repatriated parents and siblings in Mexico. It used its report of repatriated children's activities to warn the US government that the new separations of the Bracero Program would similarly result in the migration of undocumented Mexican immigrant children from Mexico in search of their bracero fathers to the United States.

Repatriated twelve-year-old girl US citizens were reported as being taken into the bureau's custody after being found laboring as child caretakers, housemaids, and waitresses in the United States. Upon being interrogated in the processing of their case, these children admitted to laboring in order to send remittances to their repatriated parents and siblings in Mexico, and some had sought out the assistance of the bureau as a result of the exploitation endured at the hands of their US employers. One child, whose name was not provided, was described as laboring to support her nine-, six-, and five-year-old repatriated siblings in Mexico. Being the oldest child, and born in the United States, she was able to enter into the country to labor on their behalf. The department used these cases to emphasize for the US government the ongoing movement of US citizen children of Mexican descent, whose numbers, they feared, would increase if the program continued. New child laborers might migrate with the assistance of other children already doing so, then be exploited, and ultimately end up in the overburdened department's custody. The Children's Bureau tried its best to illustrate simultaneously that repatriated US child citizens were in desperate need of departmental services and that the department was unable to undertake more cases that might result from the US government's mismanagement of the border.

In anticipation of persuading the government to reconsider its pursuit of the Bracero Program's agricultural labor as the only emergency worthy of policy attention, the bureau report stressed that repatriated US child citizens were in emotional pain. It asserted that the US government had miscalculated in its implementation of repatriation and warned of the Bracero Program's impact on US citizen children and Mexican children, who would find themselves crossing paths with prospective braceros, undocumented Mexican immigrant men, and children who like themselves were journeying across the border in desperate search of US wages to support their families. It feared that their mutual and personal investment in providing for their families financially would lead more children to pick up bad habits from Mexican immigrant men and older children. According to the department's case records, US repatriation had resulted in a situation where US citizen children were "looking for things to take home" by stealing and committing other petty crimes for their families.[17]

Concluding its report with a thorough account of a case that had resulted in the death of a fourteen-year-old repatriated US citizen child in Nogales, Arizona, the bureau noted that the consequences of government enforcement of the border in the form of the Bracero Program could be fatal for the most vulnerable of populations. In this case, a repatriated father had asked his fourteen-year-old repatriated US citizen child to beg and "to work at anything he could find work in," resulting in the "child hauling garbage from a truck instead of going to school, jumping off the truck, the child falling under the wheels, and later dying as a result of his injuries."[18] Essentially, the US government had yet to develop a policy or program that could resolve or prevent the already dire and sometimes fatal consequences of repatriation and the Bracero Program.

In its efforts to acquire help in managing its caseload of repatriated US citizen children, the bureau requested that the government approve its efforts to locate these children in Mexico. This way, their repatriated parents could be afforded the choice of requesting their assistance in the raising of their children. The bureau guessed that these parents would prefer for their children to benefit from a stable family's care and an education in the United States rather than to starve, commit crimes, or migrate under dangerous conditions to and from the United States, even if this meant forfeiture of their parental rights. The bureau did not suggest reversing these parents' repatriation or allowing them to live with their children in the United States. Instead, it focused on what it considered best for the emotional and physical welfare of the children under its supervision. It did not advocate for any consideration of these children's parents and instead settled for urging the US government to do more to serve American children whose lives it had destabilized in unforeseen ways by repatriating their parents to Mexico—including going into the Mexican interior to find them and ensure that they had access to a childhood that did not center on laboring as an adult in Mexico or the United States.

The US government did not, however, approve of the bureau's expansion of its efforts to include locating and serving US citizen children of repatriated parents of Mexican descent in Mexico. The government also did not use the bureau's report when noting the potential drawbacks of continuing the Bracero Program. Instead, it carefully filed this report as part of its correspondence regarding the program with national departments under its administration. However, the report shows that at least one US department recognized the continuing emergency of destabilized and divided families that the US government had created and had neglected to address. The inadequate response to this report shows the US government's reluctance to hold itself accountable for the effects of its immigration measures and programs, even on its own citizens.

On November 13, 1948, the *Los Angeles Times* reported that thousands of braceros had been held in virtual slavery when working in the United States.[19] A group of them had been laboring for months without pay, hidden inside a packing plant and rarely afforded an opportunity to socialize with anyone but each other. They were locked inside barracks when asleep and restricted to their place of employment when awake. Such violation of their Bracero Program employment conditions had made them the subject of this news story, but nothing was done about it. Six years into the program, the US and Mexican governments' accountability for protecting children, women, and men continued to be, at best, dismal.

The US government was more concerned with shutting down El Escritorio Publico el Minutito ("The Quick Minute" Notary Public). Located in Mexicali, Baja California, Mexico, this notary public's office was derailing the US and

Mexican governments' management of the Bracero Program. It dared to print and circulate flyers that offered prospective undocumented Mexican immigrants the "blanks for the necessary immigration documents, so that they obtain documentation needed to get an immigration visa even if the interested parties do not have in their possession a certificate of their Mexican military training or have been excluded from the United States before." This public notary office advertised that "no matter how difficult the immigration [situation] and red tape is, we can do it" and boasted that their fees were "fabulously low, $80 to $90 for each immigrant." It boldly advertised, "If you need any help to work, we can get it for you: mechanics, expert chauffeurs, specialized farm workers, servants, cooks, and any other kind of employee you may need. Some of them already have appointments to the consulate for their visa," which struck the US and Mexican governments as posing a challenge to their control over the routing of braceros and undocumented Mexican immigrants at their discretion.[20] These offers made the US government, with the assistance of the Mexican government, respond aggressively in prosecuting this notary office for knowingly violating US immigration laws.[21] Their response reveals that in the eyes of the government this affront, unlike the actual social emergencies occurring at the time, constituted an emergency warranting immediate prosecution.

It was this kind of awareness of the US and Mexican governments' penchant for neglecting the new and long-standing interconnected emergencies shaping Mexican immigrant family life in Mexico and the United States that made Desiderio Ahumada Medina decide against becoming a bracero.[22] Instead, he used his training as a police officer in Mexico City at the age of twenty-one and his business license in San Martin de Hidalgo to apply and obtain a Mexican tourist visa to travel throughout the United States (figure 9). He would travel throughout California, Arizona, and Texas, purchasing clothing items, sewing machines, and other household items to sell to the wives of braceros left behind in the Mexican countryside. His frank assessment that one should not rely on either the US or the Mexican government to protect one's citizenship rights or to provide one with opportunities or fair employment conditions motivated him to use whatever he had been able to achieve to establish the legal right to cross the US-Mexico border under terms that did not overexpose him or his family to labor exploitation and family dislocation in Mexico or the United States. He deemed it a most resourceful response to having witnessed the repatriation of his closest friends—among them, Manuel Rosas.

Desiderio and Manuel's conversations on the racialized mistreatment that characterized the experience of Mexican immigrants—bracero or nonbracero,

FIGURE 9.
Desiderio Ahumada Medina's police academy graduation
portrait, 1950.

documented or undocumented—emboldened them to respond resourcefully to
what was in their estimation a most unfair permanent state of emergency. Desiderio
would buy and sell household goods for five consecutive years until he was able to
establish a thriving family business in the distribution and vending of grains and
other animal food products used to raise livestock throughout San Martin de
Hidalgo. Having exchanged with Manuel his thoughts on the risks of becoming

invested in the United States, Desiderio had never taken seriously the idea of permanently settling in the United States. He did not trust that he could hold on to anything or that anything could be truly his in the United States.[23] Experience with the program would lead many other braceros to eventually come to the same conclusion.

CHAPTER THREE

Special Immigration and the
Management of the Mexican
Family, 1949–1959

On August 30, 1949, after harvesting lettuce and strawberries, Renato Sandoval and
130 fellow braceros did not retire to their labor camp barracks. Determined to propose a solution to their grievances, they stood in four straight lines outside the office
of John Bowen and Montgomery Reynolds. They were silently, patiently awaiting
the return of the two men, contractors of a modest bracero labor camp in Tulare,
California.[1] These braceros had broken labor camp rules, since they were not
allowed to enter or assemble in this area. Seven years into the Bracero Program and
emboldened by their need to transition out of contract labor to financially better
themselves and their families, they took a calculated risk.

Upon their arrival, assembly organizer Saul Urbino and five other braceros
stepped forward from this human barricade to greet Bowen and Reynolds cordially.
Sandoval and others stood patiently waiting. Bowen supervised them closely, but
this was the first time they had approached Reynolds. After explaining that he had
been designated the assembled braceros' representative, Urbino proposed a change
in Sandoval's bracero contract. Bowen and Reynolds listened carefully. Urbino
urged them to contract Sandoval to provide much-needed camp services along with
harvesting crops, citing his eligibility and the advantages of this arrangement.
Before and after harvesting crops, Sandoval already routinely helped their inexperienced cook prepare and distribute nutritious and tasty meals, as well as repairing
their barracks' clogged drains, broken doors, and windows; cutting their hair; mending their *chalecos* (vests), *gabanes* (warm overcoats), and other work clothes; and

cleaning their barracks on his own. His labor had improved their diet, living environment, and personal hygiene and, in turn, their work performance.

Sandoval's fellow braceros provided Bowen and Reynolds with documentation in support of their proposal. They provided letters of recommendation once used to determine Sandoval's Bracero Program eligibility to confirm his experience as an agricultural laborer, barber, cook, and tailor, and they included his program contract renewal statements to substantiate his exemplary completion of previous contracts. They did their best to convey to their employers that Sandoval's labor camp services would dramatically reduce the time each spent cleaning and repairing their assigned barrack and commuting to and from town to obtain services that Sandoval would now efficiently provide. Contracting Sandoval to work mornings harvesting crops and afternoons providing labor camp maintenance and services would improve their collective earning potential. Doing labor camp chores and obtaining outside services required an estimated fifteen hours a week of their time to complete, time that they considered better spent working the fields.

After accepting these supporting documents, Bowen and Reynolds asked braceros to return to their barracks. They reassured them that they would consider their proposal carefully and would not penalize them for making it but warned them against doing so again in the future. In deliberating on the proposal, Bowen and Reynolds focused on tensions with town residents and displaced domestic agricultural laborers. Tulare residents did not want braceros and undocumented Mexican immigrant agricultural laborers to dine, gather, shop, go to movies, or attend weekend variety shows in the local marketplace. They considered Mexican agricultural laborers racially "inferior single men and unworthy of enjoying or interacting in family-oriented venues catering to town resident families on weekends."[2] Like contractors, families often set weekends aside to drive into and enjoy the marketplace. Escalating tensions compelled Bowen and Reynolds to accept the braceros' proposal and use supporting documents to recontract Sandoval as a special immigrant.

Special-immigrant status entitled Sandoval to form part of a workforce initially composed of exemplary and skilled contract agricultural laborers, cooks, buyers of town goods, entertainers, labor camp managers, and maintenance personnel to manage bracero labor, mobility, and interaction in labor camps and surrounding towns throughout the United States. Bracero and special-immigrant contracts were similar.[3] Special immigrants were guaranteed employment in agricultural labor and skilled trades for 75 percent of their contract period, a minimum hourly wage of fifty cents, labor camp housing, optional food services, protection of their social equality, transportation to and from their labor camp barracks, and transportation to their designated program selection center upon their contract's completion. Their eligibility was contingent on contractors' assessment of their employment history, physical fitness, and moral eligibility. Nonetheless, and unlike regular braceros, special immigrants were required to provide documentation of their responsible management of family obligations and investment in Mexico to remain morally eligible for this status. Contractors used moral eligibility standards to convey that, although they undertook increasingly uninterrupted nine- to eleven-month contracts, special immigrants were legally contracted agricultural laborers performing multiple services for extended contract periods. Documenting special immigrants' commitment to long-distance family relationships and investment in Mexican property, business, or trade to determine their moral eligibility offset governmental anxiety concerning special-immigrant US settlement. Moral eligibility was determined to be the most efficient tool for instilling among special immigrants an awareness of the temporariness of their immigration and labor.

The special-immigrant policy had been instituted that year by Immigration and Naturalization Service (INS) commissioner Joseph M. Swing. This provision entitled program contractors to legally recruit, at their own discretion, a compliant, efficient, and skilled Mexican immigrant workforce to manage and cater to braceros. Swing firmly believed that contractors needed a special-immigrant workforce to contain bracero mobility; reduce interaction between braceros and US domestic agricultural laborers or other town residents; and diminish bracero visibility. This arrangement would create and enforce borders throughout US labor camps and their surrounding communities without violating bracero contract terms. Reducing US residents' and displaced domestic agricultural laborers' anxiety concerning bracero settlement and INS border management was the impetus behind this new provision.[4]

SPECIAL IMMIGRANTS AND THE MOVEMENT OF THEIR FAMILIES TO THE UNITED STATES

The Mexican and US governments endorsed Swing's special-immigration plan. Each government was certain that this provision would improve bracero management throughout the United States. For the US government, hiring special immigrants to cater to braceros as barbers, cooks, buyers of goods, entertainers, tailors, labor camp managers, and maintenance personnel would reduce racial tension by reducing interracial contact.[5] The Mexican government was willing to overlook this racially motivated rationale because it supported the legalization of discretionary contract renewal in the United States rather than at stations along the border. It approved this provision out of a desperate need for Mexican immigrant remittances. In its estimation, this new immigration status meant longer, profitable contracts for Mexican immigrant men who would capably manage and cater to fellow immigrant men. Special immigrants' remittances would bolster local economies nationwide in Mexico.

Braceros tended to be unfamiliar with formal governmental rationales for special immigration but expressed mixed reactions to its implementation. Often they approved of special immigrants providing much-needed labor camp services. Still, resentment between braceros and special immigrants became widespread. Contractors pitted braceros and special immigrants against one another to coerce them into increasingly restrictive conditions. Special immigration fueled intraethnic tension in bracero labor camps and surrounding towns throughout the United States.[6]

However, when Bowen and Reynolds summoned Sandoval to recontract him as an exemplary and skilled contract laborer worthy of special-immigrant status, fellow braceros were supportive and anticipated an improvement in their conditions. They were unfamiliar with Sandoval's special-immigrant status. Motivated by their need to work more hours performing agricultural labor to earn more wages, they had collaborated to propose a modification to Sandoval's contract to improve their work performance without considering its implications for his contract terms. After they got what they had asked for, fellow braceros did not ask questions or express concern over Sandoval's status, nor did Sandoval express his concerns. He signed his special-immigrant contract and took comfort in laboring to improve the bracero labor camp environment. His new contract entailed working three hours harvesting crops and seven hours preparing and distributing meals, cleaning labor camps, repairing labor camp barracks, cutting hair, mending work clothes, and traveling into town to do shopping, using long lists recorded one night prior.

Sandoval followed instructions without opposing fellow braceros' restriction to their labor camp barracks. Three weeks into his special-immigrant contract, the travel of fellow braceros into the town's marketplace was restricted to weekday, bimonthly, four-hour trips. Contractors had developed travel schedules to reduce the number of agricultural laborers traveling into Tulare's marketplace to an estimated three hundred men on any given weekday and had scheduled special-immigrant entertainment to coincide with their travel time. They were prohibited from traveling downtown on weekends at all. Only special immigrants traveled into this area outside their designated travel schedule, to conduct errands. Weekends were reserved for town residents only. The restrictive travel schedules allowed contractors to manage bracero interaction with town residents. They "diminished contract laborers' mobility and public visibility to the days of the week with the lowest town-resident activity."[7]

The negative racialization of contract laborers motivated local Tulare business owners and salespeople to discriminate against them. Town barbers denied them equitable customer service, making them wait alongside twenty or more braceros for hours at a time to cut their hair. Moreover, they were forced to sit on muddy stools instead of the chairs used to seat other customers, and they had to accept a hairstyle not of their choosing. Department stores, restaurants, and shops set unreasonably high prices to discourage them from entering.

Sandoval's exposure to such discrimination motivated him to take his special-immigrant contract seriously. He diligently performed multiple tasks in support of fellow braceros. Although his labor reduced fellow braceros' access to Tulare's marketplace, he gave them quality services that provided an alternative to alienating marketplace customer service. Although he spent most of his workday completing tasks traditionally performed by women, Sandoval used the amount of work required and the quality of work performed for hundreds of Mexican immigrant men to offset his labor's emasculating potential.

In August 1952, after Sandoval had worked as a special immigrant for three consecutive years, his efficient labor camp maintenance and services compelled his employers to request that he be allowed to work with his wife and child by his side. His special-immigrant contract terms required family labor and reunification. Anticipating an estimated 526,000 undocumented Mexican immigrants throughout the US-Mexico border region, contractors needed a different special-immigrant workforce in place to manage their agricultural workforce's labor, mobility, and visibility without jeopardizing their contracting privilege.[8] The US government had become wary of braceros becoming independent and skipping out on their Bracero Program contract to travel throughout the United States in search of increasingly higher US wages. To ease this anxiety, contractors enabled special immigrants' families to join them and undertake contracts of their own—though men without families of their own were still able to obtain special-immigrant contracts.

There are no records of how many special-immigrant men were joined by their families, but we know that throughout the ten-year history of the special-immigration program an estimated 15,201 special-immigrant men were reported as working without their families by their side.[9] Probably numbers of special-immigrant families were low, but their contract conditions rendered them selectively visible. Fearful of losing his special-immigrant status, Sandoval complied with his employers' request: he could not afford to forgo US wages. A family contract would allow his relatives to conveniently manage his labor, mobility, and visibility. Sandoval's wife and son, Aurora and Roberto Sandoval, joined him in the United States, but the transition was difficult. Renato, Aurora, and Roberto had been unable to reunite before, but their family earnings had allowed them to purchase land, build a home, and buy three sewing machines so that Aurora could sell women's apparel from the comfort of their home in Guadalajara, Jalisco. It was difficult to convince her to leave behind what had taken years to build. Nonetheless, neither of them could afford to jeopardize Sandoval's special-immigrant status and earnings, since he had financed the bulk of their belongings and investments with this labor and money.

Special-immigrant family status was challenging and did not protect families from exploitation. All family members eighteen years or older were issued a contract guaranteeing employment for 75 percent of their contract period, housing, transportation to and from labor camps, transportation to program selection centers after their contract completion, and protection of their social equality, but an hourly wage rate was not part of the contracts[10] Special-immigrant family members were often women and young daughters and sons considered unworthy of fair wages. Under the best of circumstances, contractors paid them at their discretion. Special-immigrant families were required to pool their wages in order to finance their expenses. Moreover, their reunification was deceptive. Male special-immigrant family members labored away from their families for weeks and months at a time, while their families labored in different labor camps and surrounding towns. Special-immigrant women and children were contracted to clean labor camp interiors and exteriors, clean and operate restaurants and shops catering to Mexican agricultural laborers, harvest crops, prepare labor camp meals, and clean contractors' homes and care for their children. Special-immigrant families had to be flexible and were considered members of a workforce and not independent families.

US governmental scrutiny of Bracero Program management placed a high priority on using program selection centers to thoroughly document eligibility for special-immigration status and curb undocumented Mexican immigration to the United States. Before approving Sandoval's and other immigrant families' application for special-immigrant status, INS program selection center officials required proof of their previous US employment contracts, adequate earning potential to support dependent family members, and remittance receipts to prove their commitment to their family. The Sandovals' special-immigrant family status parted them under conditions similar to their previous family separation. Aurora had to work for the Reynolds family, cleaning their homes and caring for their children and grandchildren for seventeen hours a day, seven days a week. Roberto forfeited access to an academic education to help his father harvest crops, repair labor camps, and transport braceros to and from their labor camp barracks.

The Sandoval family came together on Sundays to prepare and host large labor camp picnics. Their interaction was consistently work related. Special-immigrant families organized and catered these gatherings to reduce bracero travel into surrounding town sectors. Contractors did not oppose special-immigrant women's interaction with large groups of braceros and undocumented Mexican agricultural laborers. Their similar racial background and their respective husbands' participation in these events made them the most obvious candidates for preparing and distributing meals at these gatherings. They did not express reservations concerning the implications for these women's honor and respectability. Among contractors, contracted Mexican immigrant women and men were the same. Neither the US nor the Mexican government considered their contract labor a family sacrifice. Their attention centered on the family's ability to earn US wages together that would eventually allow them to resettle in Mexico.

RESTRICTING MOBILITY AND MANAGING BRACEROS IN THE UNITED STATES

The creation of a flexible special-immigrant workforce illuminates how important it was to Bracero Program employers and US government officials to keep braceros and undocumented agricultural laborers contained in labor camp barracks and away from US residents. Using the documents and oral life histories of these special immigrants, this chapter examines special immigration in Mexico and the United States to portray the relationship between border management and labor camp culture and the investment of both the US and the Mexican governments in perfecting their internal management of Mexican immigration without overwhelming their resources. Focusing on Tulare, California, and San Martin de Hidalgo, Jalisco—both rural towns caught up in special immigration—it explores the local internal politics and the transnational repercussions of the special-immigration program and its management. Analyzing the impact of special immigrants on their families and on other contract laborers requires investigating the impact of race and gender on immigration and labor. It is important to understand that contractors' interpretation and enforcement of contract terms did not conform to governmental visions of management and fairness.

By focusing on the transnational implications of special immigration, this chapter expands on Mae Ngai's description of special immigration as a "system that privileged exploiting individual special immigrants' labor, making their healthy and full participation in US society impossible."[11] This passage describes the provision's exploitative aspects in the United States but does not cover Mexico, where special immigrants' family members who had been left behind were held to onerous conditions by local Mexican governments' interpretation and enforcement of the provision's moral-eligibility standards. Like special immigrants in the United States, female relatives in Mexico had to conform to increasingly restrictive labor management and intensive scrutiny in hopes of attaining a higher quality of life that was increasingly showing itself to be out of reach.

Tulare, California, is an important location for understanding special immigration as a means of internally managing Mexican immigration. Bracero Program contractors in this rural center were among the most organized in developing a special-immigrant model for insulating Mexican immigrants within bracero labor camps and their surrounding towns. This model involved employing special-immigrant labor camp managers and maintenance personnel and excluding undocumented immigrants from taking on these roles. Special immigrants like Sandoval were maintenance personnel, contracted to maintain labor camps up to Bracero Program standards, provide camp services, and conduct outside errands to reduce bracero travel to and interaction in surrounding towns. Other special immigrants were camp managers who supervised braceros' labor, mobility, visibility, and interaction inside camp barracks and in the fields.

Despite its incentives, opposition to the special-immigration program was widespread. Braceros, domestic agricultural laborers, and labor activists opposed the exploitative coercion of some special immigrants into year-round contracts. Labor activist Ernesto Galarza protested that special immigration "lowered the validity of bracero recruitment and selection already in place. It was the driving force behind the recruitment of a larger and far more vulnerable pool of immigrant labor."[12] He claimed that the potential for these contracts to be renewed was especially damaging in that it kept contracted and prospective special immigrants from challenging this program's management. Moreover, special immigrants who served as labor camp managers had to exhibit an exemplary work ethic and full compliance with program contractors. They were required not only to maintain an accelerated work pace but to demand it as well from the braceros and undocumented immigrant laborers working under them—a conflict of loyalties that exposed them to antagonism from other braceros and made their jobs increasingly difficult.

Contractors were indifferent to labor camp tensions. They simply assumed that racial similarity, shared language, and a shared lack of citizenship status would enable braceros and their special-immigrant managers to work well together and that their contract conditions would obligate them to do so. The incentive of contract renewal motivated special-immigrant managers to train and manage braceros and undocumented Mexican immigrant laborers far more efficiently than US domestic agricultural managers who did not live in labor camp barracks. Even so, the most efficient special-immigrant managers feared losing their status and were strict in their management of both field labor and camp barrack life. They enforced strict curfews and monitored bracero interaction and pastimes to prevent the escalation of existing tensions, especially destructive alcoholism and gambling after work hours. They also were required to maintain detailed records of production levels of individual braceros to document their wages and account for overall bracero production. Managing braceros soon became a full-time duty in itself.

Gustavo Juarez, a former special-immigrant manager, shared with Ernesto Galarza that establishing a cooperative and productive labor camp environment did not have to include the adoption of alienating management strategies. When his contractors gave him binoculars to monitor braceros from a distance, he refused to use them, in the belief that a management strategy that "did not include spying or using surveillance equipment was a far more efficient way of monitoring bracero labor."[13] He claimed that he benefited most from establishing cooperation with braceros based on mutual trust, providing them with an opportunity to labor under less supervision for a few hours of their workday, and timing work breaks adequately. Distributing pamphlets detailing contract terms and labor camp rules, even when these were translated into Spanish, was not as helpful as assembling braceros and undocumented Mexican immigrant laborers to explain the rules. Special-immigrant managers tried to strike a balance between complying with management concerns and gaining the trust of braceros.

Before beginning a workweek, special-immigrant managers assembled braceros and undocumented Mexican immigrant laborers and announced pay scales and schedules to prevent tension from surfacing. A clear and detailed announcement of these prevented confusion, reduced anxiety, and enabled braceros and others to focus on their work more than on their remuneration. Assured punctual payment of due wages set the right tone to beginning and managing an arduous work schedule. According to the special-immigrant manager Agustin Martinez, an advance warning that their attendance and productivity were being recorded and that their wages would reflect their actual hours worked helped inform braceros and others "how things really worked."[14]

Special-immigrant managers throughout labor camps in Tulare, California, prioritized establishing good communication with the men under their management. Bracero complaints or low productivity levels exposed them to contractor questioning, possible termination, and deportation. Yet special-immigrant managers were rarely reassigned: more typically they were deported, or resentment, shame, and bracero criticism discouraged them from continuing to work in labor camps at all, in which case they returned to Mexico or settled for *trabajando de mojado* (working as a "wetback" or undocumented Mexican immigrant) in other employment sectors. Contract conditions for special-immigrant managers were often far more challenging than those for other braceros, even though they all earned the same wage of fifty cents an hour: contractor scrutiny pressured special-immigrant managers into exhausting work schedules, and they were held to increasingly high standards of accountability. Although such pressures were draining, employment conditions in Mexico compelled them to continue with labor camp management, since "they had little choice but to complete their contract."[15]

Beginning in August 1950, special-immigrant managers were required to monitor bracero interaction inside labor camp barracks after work hours and on weekends. Setting a positive example and enforcing orderly conduct was their responsibility. Bracero weekend activities were attracting national attention, so the supervision that some special-immigrant managers had already been providing on their own was no longer optional. Poorly supervised bracero weekend activities had resulted in an increase in bracero-on-bracero crime. An unreported number of undocumented Mexican laborers across the nation had undergone medical treatment for wounds received in labor camp fights. Expanding labor camp management to include after-work hours and weekends intensified special-immigrant managers' alienation from their fellow immigrants. Contractors scrutinized their ability to enforce discipline, compelling them to act with "much more caution. One could not stay late playing cards or drinking. Everyone else would follow suit. It was a distinct way of living and working."[16]

In an effort to prevent the escalation of existing tensions into physical fights, contractors advised braceros to avoid abusing alcohol and reckless gambling. A combination of drinking and gambling accounted for much of reported bracero violence. Nonetheless, they were not entitled to ban either activity. Contractors feared that boredom would make tensions worse or would push braceros to develop weekend activities that involved town-resident interaction. They preferred placing the burden of managing these issues on special-immigrant managers. The accounts of special-immigrant managers in Tulare, California, demonstrate that determining when and how to intervene to prevent or de-escalate conflict was one of the most challenging aspects of managing braceros after work hours and on weekends. It was difficult to gauge to what extent special-immigrant managers were able to befriend fellow braceros, since in general braceros resented being managed and surveilled around the clock. This model of labor camp management did not allow for healthy camaraderie between special-immigrant managers and other braceros.

MORALITY AND MANAGEMENT OF SPECIAL IMMIGRANTS' FAMILIES IN MEXICO

When special-immigrant status was first instituted, town families in Mexico pursued it aggressively because it increased the likelihood that immigrant men could get their contracts renewed for periods of up to ten to twelve months, thereby keeping much-needed employment to provide for their families. It also assured town merchants and lenders that special-immigrant families would be able to make timely payments on their debts. Over time, however, these families' struggle no longer centered on raising themselves economically but on preserving what little they had been able to establish. And even this became increasingly difficult as local Mexican government officials used special immigration to enforce lengthy separation of family members and their own model of family enterprise on the female relatives left behind.[17]

Special-immigrant status became invaluable in San Martin de Hidalgo. Special immigrants' ability to labor and earn US wages for uninterrupted and extended periods of time provided them with the collateral to adjust agreements with town lenders regarding their original Bracero Program loans and to enter into reasonable new agreements for loans to finance annual business, property, and trade fees. Eight months into the second special-immigration contract cycle, this town's special immigrants had sent their families an average of $285 that could go toward purchasing land, building and repairing homes, investing in family businesses and trades, and making loan payments.[18] Their increasing expenditures and investments confirmed to INS and program contractors their commitment to long-distance family relationships and Mexican settlement. The families of other braceros and undocumented Mexican immigrants, however, were placed at a disadvantage in getting loans at good rates, and their male relatives' failure to achieve special-immigrant status was viewed as reflecting poorly on their earning potential and work ethic. These attitudes back in braceros' hometowns kept special immigrants compliant with contract conditions.

Town officials and lenders assumed that special-immigrant status was accessible and desirable. However, they underestimated not only the overall scarcity of special-immigrant status but also its demands in terms of labor and family separation: after completing an average of five contract cycles of ten to eleven months, special immigrants had typically barely begun to purchase land, build or repair homes, or invest in family businesses or trades. Aware of the limited number of special-immigrant contracts issued, neither the Mexican nor the US government publicly circulated information on special immigration among residents in Mexico or the United States. Instead, both governments required INS officials, program contractors, and Mexican rural town and village government officials to collaborate to select and contract the most eligible applicants. And because both governments were anxious to prevent special immigrants from permanently settling in the United States, their definition of eligibility emphasized having a family and investments in Mexico. Developing and enforcing local criteria that conformed to this broad national standard became the local officials' responsibility. Further, it became the task of local officials to vet the supporting documents that families submitted, given that forgeries of such documents had been suspected and overextended INS and Bracero Program contractors did not have the resources to scrutinize them.

In the beginning of the special-immigrant program, San Martin de Hidalgo's town government officials monitored families' receipt of remittances and women's careful management of them. Special immigrants returned to their families for two-week periods to request family letters and government-issued supporting documents to confirm their commitment to long-distance family relationships and eventual Mexican settlement. Typically, they went to the town's municipal government office—accompanied by their wives—to have town officials document the legitimacy of their remittance receipts and their wives' careful remittance management. This process required these men to answer broad questions concerning their expenditures and how these related to their plans for settlement. Women, despite their labor and decision making, were not questioned on these matters. Town officials feared that asking wives about expenditures, investments, and plans would emasculate their male relatives. Even though women conducted and kept careful records of these transactions, government officials ignored their experience and knowledge.

At about two years into the special-immigrant program, town officials, though still monitoring remittances, shifted to making families' successful investment in the town's economy the primary factor determining men's moral eligibility for special-immigrant status. An increase in female-managed businesses had piqued town officials' interest: aware that working-class women had labored in such businesses without incentives or formal documentation of their participation throughout the town's history, town officials now decided to use special-immigrant moral eligibility standards to require women to get business licenses and pay fees. The shift impelled special-immigrant families to invest earnings and remittances in establishing and expanding businesses, whether they could afford to or not; officials simply assumed that special-immigrant families did not have other pressing financial needs.[19] Men's moral eligibility for continuing special-immigrant status now depended on the successful management of a business, property, or trade by their families back in Mexico, and determination of that success depended on the business's annual earnings and annual payment of business license fees.[20] Failure to pay the license fee meant loss of license renewal for the following year and shutdown of the business. Consequently the female relatives who managed and labored in the businesses in which special-immigrant men had invested were put under intense governmental pressure and scrutiny to make those businesses thrive through financial sacrifice and arduous labor.

Soon other bracero families who lacked special-immigrant status followed suit and tried to invest similarly in the town's economy to compete with special immigrants' families: their ability to thrive as members of the town's business community was also at stake. Working-class families were especially disadvantaged in this contest and especially hard-pressed to meet the financial goals required of them.

Among the most strikingly visible changes associated with special immigration was the conversion of town barbershops and *cantinas* into grocery stores and makeshift vending booths managed by women, usually between the ages of twenty to fifty-five years. Women also managed building material warehouses, bakeries, dress shops, and *cenadurías* on the town's outskirts or operated businesses from the comforts of their home. The women listed their special and other immigrant relatives as sources of financial business support and managed businesses associated traditionally with women's labor, such as baking, cooking, sewing, and retail. Records of their payment of annual business license fees reveal their careful management of remittances and labor in this town's business community.[21]

The assessment of special-immigrant moral eligibility by town officials intensified the alienation of special immigrants' families from other families in the town. Starting a business to raise one's standard of living had surfaced as a feasible alternative among bracero, special-immigrant, undocumented Mexican immigrant, and non-Mexican immigrant families alike, but it was rare overall for immigrant men to establish or expand businesses and trades under terms that legally formalized their female relatives' shared management of their investments. Nonetheless, this became common among special-immigrant families, since it was required by moral-eligibility standards. Certain that women were unqualified to assume legal responsibility for family business management, men who were not under special-immigrant requirements feared that the success of special immigrants' female relatives might motivate their own female relatives to pressure them into similar formal legalization of their labor and roles. This was a change they were unprepared to adapt to.

The success of special-immigrant female relatives was also contingent on their collaboration with supportive male relatives. To enter into prosperous and afford-able product agreements with surrounding town distributors, it was important that female business managers work with their male relatives. Traveling on their own and negotiating with surrounding town distributors without male relatives by their side and negotiating on their behalf were socially unacceptable for town women and cast doubt on their respectability and sexual virtue. Women risked ruining their reputations and marriages.[22]

Because women were restricted to laboring within the physical confines of their businesses, dealing with town distributors became a time-consuming, long-distance process for them. It exposed them to intense public scrutiny and placed them at a disadvantage compared to competing businesses because of product distribution delays. Nevertheless, special-immigrant female and male relatives continued work-ing under these conditions because they did not have any other choice. Their man-agement success was contingent on their flexibility and resourcefulness.

Working-class special-immigrant families invested their earnings and remittances in business fees, remodeling of homes into business spaces, and purchases of mer-chandise, often leaving them with very little left over to purchase and integrate new goods and services that were US manufactured or inspired. Instead, special-immigrant families used their talents and existing knowledge of working-class families' sensibilities to overcome discrimination, deal with town competition, and secure special-immigrant moral eligibility. They transformed their spacious kitchens into food stands and specialized in the preparation and sale of popular meat entrées and stews that they sold by the pot. Customers came prepared with pots in hand and purchased customized portions of either *birria* (spicy meat entrée) or *pozole* (hominy and pork stew). Allowing families to buy these in amounts that they estimated they could afford appealed to financially strapped families. Those who were too poor to purchase large portions of *birria* could buy cups of *caldo de birria* (*birria* stew) to pour over their home-cooked beans, adding flavor and sustenance to their meals. By allowing businesses to cater to struggling town families without drawing atten-tion to their financial need, this sales model won their loyalty and diminished town resentment against the special-immigrant families managing these businesses.[23]

Another business strategy of special-immigrant female business owners and managers concerned signage. Signs displayed outside their booths, stands, and storefronts advertised in plain view their price scales and policies as a way of avoiding on-the-spot negotiation and challenging customer miscommunication. Town discrimination already placed these women at a disadvantage. They could not afford losing customers to allegations of fraud or miscalculation of balances owed. Straightforward information allowed women to conduct business transactions without losing customers or friends. It was hard for these women to muster the nerve to charge friends for services rendered without having price charts in place.

Further, special-immigrant female business owners and managers aggressively built a clientele among women who worked similarly arduous schedules cleaning homes, harvesting crops, and vending outside their homes. They made prepackaged, handmade tortillas, loaves of bread, *chiles* (peppers), and other staple products available under production schedules that coincided with the women's commutes to and from work and times set aside for errands and meals, thereby nurturing strong female customer bases.[24] Maria Elena Medina explained that "you would not venture out unaccompanied at night or run your shop after eight o'clock in the evening. . . . Women did not run businesses or errands into evening hours."[25] Female entrepreneurs could not afford to work evenings because this would cast doubt on their honorability and sexual virtue, ruining their public reputation and diminishing their female clientele.

Special-immigrant female beauty salon and dress shop owners used personalized customer service and group rates to survive in an economy that made a fashionable wardrobe and haircut unaffordable luxuries. They traveled to Guadalajara, Jalisco, the closest large city, accompanied by their older male relatives, to purchase stylish apparel and beauty equipment, guides, and magazines. Displaying and using finished products to attract customers proved ineffective. Instead, dress shop owners sold *patrones* (handmade cardboard apparel patterns), thread, and cloth, or sewed customers' premeasured and cut apparel for a service charge. Beauty salon owners sold beauty products, offered family haircut packages, and gave discount prices on select days of the week.

Using business models that recognized the importance of town and family sensibilities was foundational to ensuring special-immigrant female business managers' success and male relatives' continued moral eligibility. This entailed abiding by strict gender norms and maximizing talents and resources to define services clearly and calculate reasonable service and product rates accurately. Every aspect of these women's business management required careful planning. The town's distrust and resentment did not leave them room for mistakes.

Despite their business earnings in Mexico, special immigrants and their families could not afford to forfeit their US earnings. San Martin de Hidalgo's farmers and

merchants had transformed special-immigrant status into a central organizing feature of town settlement. The insecurity of the town economy motivated this town's
business community to take advantage of special immigration in ways that continued to place excessive demands on unskilled, working-class women and men's
flexibility and labor. Extended contract labor translated into intense scrutiny, heavy
responsibility, and very little consideration for their parental and marriage concerns.
In their efforts to pay off loans, meet bills, and achieve some economic security,
special-immigrant men and their families postponed living together. A series of
unrealistic expectations plagued their immigration and settlement plans. Expected
to contribute to unfair solutions to international immigration issues, they found
themselves placed under intensive regulation and control whether they labored
under discriminatory and exploitative conditions in the United States or under
onerous governmental requirements in Mexico.

In August 1959, the US government finally terminated special immigration.[26] INS
and Bracero Program contractors agreed that undocumented immigration in general had become so prevalent and out of control that hiring special immigrants to
keep other Mexican immigrants from interacting with and being visible to the general US public was no longer an effective containment measure. But while the
program was in operation, the US government used it to reduce contact between
braceros and US residents, and both the US and the Mexican governments used it
to prevent bracero settlement in the United States and to take advantage of Mexican
immigrant families' sensibilities and needs.

Allowing the US and Mexican governments to manage their family life was not
an appealing prospect for Mexican children, women, and men eager to prosper as
families without having to separate for indefinite periods of time. Even those
families who were in desperate need of US wages did not idealize special-immigrant
status or shy away from acknowledging the extraordinary cost of maintaining this
status in Mexico and the United States. Throughout the Bracero Program, exposure
to the emotional, physical, and financial rigors of this contract labor category—and
of the program in general—motivated many women, men, and, increasingly, children to instead attempt to sidestep the program altogether. Unwilling to give up on
their dream of leading a personally meaningful life together and as a family, Mexican children, women, and men became emboldened to seek each other's assistance,
counsel, and support in order to lead a family life that met their expectations and
needs in Mexico and the United States. Nonetheless, this was not an easy task but
one that required much thought, effort, and experimentation.

CHAPTER FOUR

· Government Censorship of
Family Communication,
1942–1964

On November 3, 1943, one year after the initial implementation of the Bracero
Program, German Santander wrote his wife, Estefania Santander, his fifth letter
requesting that she pool his remittances, her earnings vending food items door to
door in Ameca, Mexico, and their savings so that she would have enough money to
finance her undocumented entry into the United States and reunite with him in
Fresno, California.[1] He had already proposed this in his previous four letters, starting in January of that year, and had become desperate at not having heard from her;
he worried either that something had happened to her on the journey or that she
had not received any of his letters. Distraught at the prospect that Estefania had
become demoralized at not having heard from him about his plans for their future,
German was among the countless braceros who feared that writing to suggest that
their wives cross the US-Mexico border without proper documentation had cost
them their marriages.

German had taken great comfort in having been responsible and cautious when
writing to Estefania. He had written his letters late in the evening so that fellow
braceros would not ask him about their contents or about why he wrote so often.
The bulk of his letters explained in detail the times that would be safest for her to
seek temporary shelter from any of the eight Mexican American families who had
agreed to house her should she dare to join him. He supplied her with his agricultural
labor camp address so that she could better identify him or confirm her identity and
relationship to him when seeking the assistance of these families. German had

developed a support network of settled Mexican American families willing to help them transition into working as an undocumented Mexican immigrant couple in the United States. These families responded to his pain at having to labor twelve- to thirteen-hour shifts harvesting crops or landscaping the exterior of their homes without a family with whom to share time. Feeling most fortunate to have developed friendships with these families, he did his best to write letters that would allow him and Estefania to share a future together in the United States.

German and Estefania did not reunite in the United States until December 1947. Estefania never received any of his letters. She did not dare to enter the United States as an undocumented immigrant until German had earned enough money so that he could skip out on his Bracero Program contract and labor as an undocumented Mexican immigrant at a restaurant and rent an apartment for them in Tulare, California. German did not know why his letters to his wife had not reached her, but he grew intensely distrustful of the Mexican and US governments. Eventually his suspicion that these governments were not handling braceros' correspondence responsibly drove him to abandon the program altogether.

German and Estefania's failure to correspond with each other successfully throughout their Bracero Program participation was most likely a result of a little-known fact: starting in November 1942, the US government censored letters written by braceros and other Mexican immigrants to their relatives and friends in Mexico and the United States. It called on its consular officials to block letters to loved ones that encouraged them to cross the border. Without publicizing or explaining its censorship or failure to deliver or return letters to these women and men, the US government depended on these officials to make full adherence to program rules the only gateway to living and laboring in the United States. Failure to publicize such censorship was justified as part of a broadly defined effort to control threats to US national security in a time of war, resulting in only select US government and consulate officials knowing about the interceptions. Women and men of Mexican descent and varying legal status who wrote to one another and to other entities participating in the program were never aware of the full extent of the censorship. The Mexican government knew of this policy but not the details behind its enforcement. Censoring letters was intended to prevent reunification in the United States with relatives and friends who did not have program contracts. It was also intended to demonstrate the wide and effective reach of the US government's border enforcement. Nonetheless, this policy often backfired. It was German's suspicion that his letters had been intercepted that finally compelled him to do everything within his power to reunite unlawfully with Estefania in the United States.

The consulate's censorship of correspondence between women and men of Mexican descent was intended to curb a spirit of rebellion against the conditions of the Bracero Program and of immigration generally. The demand for low-wage migrant labor in the United States emboldened migrants, and the US government knew it. Migrants could use their new connections in the States resourcefully and orchestrate transnational reunions through the mail. Further, their dissatisfaction with the Bracero Program could lead them to leave it and pursue aims of their own outside its legal structure. Laurence I. Hewes Jr., regional director of the US Postal Service in California, ordered consular officials throughout the Southwest to prevent letters from "going into Mexico distorting or exaggerating the experiences of the workers in this country for the purpose of causing disaffection between the countries."[2] He explained that "this material might simply appear as a letter of a disgruntled person" but that upon closer inspection it could reveal that bracero and other Mexican immigrants had "no intention of abiding by the contract" and instead planned to travel to Chicago and other cities throughout the United States to meet loved ones who had already ventured to these destinations.[3] Because Mexican workers had ideas, resources, and girlfriends and wives emotionally invested in reuniting with them, they sought to pursue personally meaningful goals in the United States with or without program contracts in place. Though recruitment aimed at men with families had attempted to play on their emotions to bind men to fulfilling their contracts, in many ways these emotional allegiances across borders led to the very behaviors that their recruitment had been designed to avoid.

Historians have been quite limited in conceptualizing the US government's implementation of the Bracero Program as involving only screening, managing, and routing Mexican immigrant men as bodies across the US-Mexico border.[4] Because braceros could help their undocumented Mexican immigrant and prospective bracero relatives in Mexico sidestep border enforcement, the US government placed a high premium as well on curbing the flow of ideas, feelings, and information. Its censorship policies had drastic effects on immigrants and their families in both Mexico and the United States.

Using the correspondence and files of consular officials stationed in Chihuahua, Mexico, oral life histories, and censored letters, this chapter demonstrates how the emboldening potential of transnational family communication provoked aggressive obstruction by US officials. The Mexican state of Chihuahua emerged as one of the main points of origin of braceros throughout the program's trajectory. Correspondence that had the potential to facilitate reunification in the United States was the most perused and censored. Officials categorically undermined familial communication without regard to the personal relationships that hung in the balance when they did not deliver or return letters.

DIVIDING COUPLES

The US government was concerned about correspondence between Mexican immigrants in the United States and their friends and families back in Mexico even before the Bracero Program was launched. On June 22, 1942, the secretary of state warned US Consulate officials that Mexican men were writing to their relatives and friends in the United States to seek their assistance in securing US employment unlawfully, and on July 24, 1942, he transmitted another warning, this time using the letter of S. Licano Anchondo, who was writing from Chihuahua, Mexico, to Francisca Vallejo in Trinidad, Colorado, to support their assessment of the situation and their proposed solution of censorship. Anchondo was reported as having dared to express "his desire to go and work in the United States, and asking Vallejo to interview ranchers and inform them of his desire to work. Anchondo asked Vallejo to "take immediate steps in making these arrangements" so that he might "proceed to the United States."[5] The US government claimed it was important to obstruct letters like these from reaching women and men in the United States to discourage Mexican women and men from believing that with each other's assistance they could successfully—even easily—sidestep the US government.

Beginning in November 12, 1942, and until the termination of the program in 1964, letters that had the potential to motivate reunions in the United States and therefore defy the conditions and terms of the program were systematically documented and never delivered to recipients in Mexico and the United States. Preventing these women and men from communicating as families was deemed a most effective approach to enforcing the US-Mexico border because it undermined their sense of readiness for border crossing.[6] Letters written by women came under special scrutiny, particularly those discussing or proposing plans to enter the United States unlawfully, providing instructions to enter the United States unlawfully, or expressing an interest in reuniting with a boyfriend or a husband in the United States unlawfully.

On December 10, 1942, a month into its postal censorship, the US Consulate identified and decided not to deliver letters written by Sonya M. Silverstone, a US citizen, to her undocumented Mexican immigrant boyfriend, Antonio Pineda.[7] Having met three months earlier, they bid each other farewell after the expiration of Pineda's three-month Bracero Program contract. Silverstone wrote and sent letters to his home address in Taxco, Guerrero, Mexico. The letters she wrote him provided Pineda with instructions about entering the United States, explaining what he should expect upon arriving and what to bring with him. She knew that it was possible to get a tourist visa to come to the United States for two months, and she believed that before his visa expired he could arrange to get temporary contract labor in the States that would extend his time there even further. So she wrote him, "Dear Toño, you can come here as a visitor and after you are here we can arrange to have you stay as an immigrant. It will be easier to arrange it from here, I am sure. So leave as a visitor, but bring your tools and all your things, and come right away, *querido* [beloved]. I wired you money, $40, yesterday. Love, Sonya."[8]

Silverstone's letter to Pineda did not explicitly advocate extending his stay in the United States under undocumented terms, but it nevertheless transformed their relationship into a perceived threat to US national security. US Consulate officials identified and documented her instructions to Pineda as evidence of her fearless intention to break the law. Advising and providing Pineda with funds to prepare him to continue their romantic relationship together in the United States defied the government's enforcement of the border as well as its vision concerning Mexican immigrant settlement in the United States. Even after Silverstone intuited that Pineda had not received her initial and subsequent letters, she demonstrated to US Consulate officials the intensity of her spirited investment in this relationship by continuing to write her boyfriend. The determination of many other women of Mexican descent to similarly embrace the pursuit of an unlawful romantic relationship and reunion in the United States fueled US Consulate officials' dedication to reading and assessing other letters of this kind and intercepting them as a border enforcement measure.

Because so many of these men were just completing their program when they met their US girlfriends—and because some were even skipping out on their bracero contracts and laboring as undocumented workers—consulate officials feared that the love that these women expressed would embolden the men to do much more than just write about unlawful reunion. They feared that these flourishing romantic relationships might prompt couples to marry and begin families. Censorship seemed an effective US border enforcement policy that would spare the US government publicity concerning the dangerous personal relationships born out of the Bracero Program. The lack of explanation might also estrange these women and men, causing them to abandon their romantic relationships and hopes for reunion in the United States. Finally, the measure would cast doubt on the effectiveness of readying undocumented Mexican immigrant men through instructions provided in letters—

and on their sense of the ease with which they could reunite in the United States unlawfully. The government was effectively disciplining the emboldening potential of emotions.

BLOCKING FAMILY SOURCES OF INFORMATION

Many concerned mothers and sisters wrote letters from Mexico to solicit the advice of their female relatives in the United States about the immigration options of family members, including illegal options. Officials documented and did not deliver letters that requested information on how undocumented Mexican immigrants could enter the United States unlawfully. The government would not stand for using the US Postal Service as an accessible and credible resource for breaking US immigration laws.

US consulate officials sought to discipline women on both sides of the border into realizing that indeed they were not accessible to each other and were not reliable sources of information for their undocumented loved ones in Mexico and the United States. Ideally, this would do more than discourage the women—it would decrease the government's workload. Yet Mexican women continued to query their female relatives in the United States concerning the challenges of crossing the border. For instance, on November 12, 1952, US Consulate officials deemed that Herlinda Zapien's letter from Churintzio, Michoacán, Mexico, to her Mexican American cousin Adela Vega, in Merced Falls, California, should not be delivered.[9] Zapien was asking Vega to honestly assess whether it would be more dangerous for their cousins Arnulfo and Enrique Rosales to cross the US-Mexico border as undocumented Mexican immigrants or to bribe their way into being selected as braceros. Even though it had become common for the US Consulate to prevent Mexican women from communicating with their female relatives across the US-Mexico border, Mexican women like Zapien were continuing to write letters requesting information that could help their undocumented Mexican immigrant relatives enter the United States.

Zapien explained that her cousins were "planning to leave any day with intention of trying to cross the border illegally [at a checkpoint]. If not successful they will try to be smuggled across." This substantiated US Consulate officials' assumption that the dangers associated with crossing the US-Mexico border outside the required checkpoints—most especially the hunger, thirst, desert heat, and theft that undocumented Mexican immigrants experienced along the way—had inspired women to persist in writing each other across the border to protect their undocumented

Mexican immigrant relatives from some, if not all, of these hardships. Zapien shared with Vega that although she had "tried to dissuade them, they insist on making the attempt."[10]

Other letters that the US Consulate obstructed were written by prospective undocumented Mexican immigrant men to female relatives in the United States. Belying widespread perceptions about the hesitation of Mexican men to seek the counsel of women on either side of the US-Mexico border, prospective undocumented Mexican immigrants often addressed their female relatives and friends in the United States as knowledgeable and reliable sources of information about the best ways to gain entry.

On May 18, 1954, on the heels of Operation Wetback, one of the largest US border-enforcement campaigns used to detect, apprehend, detain, interrogate, and deport undocumented Mexican immigrants in the US Southwest, the letter from Enrique Ayala in Michoacán to his cousin Maria Trinidad Aguilar in Los Angeles was among those that the consulate intercepted and withheld. Ayala wrote that he was "planning to go to the United States and may be followed by other family members if successful in entering." He explained that "the Mexican government has permitted no one to go to the United States since the war started unless it is possible to pass illegally."[11] He awaited word from friends being detained at the border and from those who had successfully crossed over.[12] Ayala's letter alerted US consulate officials that Maria's reply might educate Ayala and his relatives about how to enter the US illegally. Preventing Ayala's letter from reaching his cousin might cast doubt on his assessment of the ease with which he could deceive the US government.

In another case, a Guadalajaran man named Nieves wrote to his cousin Andrea, who worked packing fruits and vegetables in Oceanside, California, for frank advice as to whether he should pursue a Bracero Program contract or abandon the prospect of laboring in the United States altogether. Nieves began his letter by reminding Andrea that before the Program began he had been there for her and that he would continue to act in support of her and their family relationship, as well as take pride in their being there for each other. Insisting that he did not mean to pose a burden to her, Nieves emphasized that an honest response was all that he wanted and needed from her.[13] Her assessment would help him determine whether to risk his savings as well as his welfare for the sake of securing US employment. Many Mexican men wrote similar letters to their female relatives in the United States. The spirit of these letters raised the concern among program officials that Mexican women and men were stubbornly asserting transnational relationships on their own terms and independently seeking information on their immigration options rather than relying on government sources. Officials feared the consequences of migrants' feeling that a knowledgeable and supportive family relative was in the United States and within the writer's reach.

WITHHOLDING CRUCIAL OR TRAGIC NEWS

Beginning in 1945, US Consulate official Churchill Murray cautioned against obstructing letters that informed Mexican women and men in Mexico and the United States of time-sensitive and often tragic developments.[14] He criticized the US government's lack of accountability regarding some of the devastating consequences of censorship's use as a border enforcement measure. On that day, strict adherence to government criteria for censoring letters would have kept him from permitting either the delivery or the return of a letter in which a bracero laboring in Fresno, California, had written anonymously to Antonio Torres Vigil's family in Chihuahua, Mexico, to inform them of Vigil's death. Murray explained that the US government's insistence that consulate officials withhold letters from braceros that documented negative circumstances or outcomes they experienced in the Bracero Program was problematic in situations like this.[15] He claimed that it was far better to deliver letters informing families in Mexico and the United States of tragic events.

Even in the best of situations, the families of braceros often did not receive even vague details concerning their loved ones' deaths until well after a week of their passing. Despite Murray's warnings, the heavy workload of US Consulate officials, coupled with the inefficiency of US and Mexican postal delivery services, resulted in inhumane handling of such sensitive matters. In the case of Melecio G. Melchor, for example, US Consulate officials in Washington, D.C., recorded on July 18, 1945, that "on June 30, 1945 at 3:00 a.m. Melchor passed away in Casualty Hospital in Washington, D.C." and that "his death was not reported to labor camp supervisors administering the camp in which Melchor worked until 4:00 p.m. of the same day. He was buried at 1:00 p.m. on July 2, 1945, in the George Washington Memorial Cemetery." They passed along this information to Melchor's family in Guadalajara, Jalisco, Mexico, adding only that Melchor "was employed by the Pennsylvania Railroad. Father Ramirez [a priest who held religious services in the labor camp where Melchor lived as he completed his contract labor] reported that there was some uncertainty as to the cause of this man's death."[16] Up to that point the US Consulate official reporting the case had received no medical report establishing the cause of death.[17] There is no record of when Melchor's family received the tragic news and whether they sought additional information concerning access to his remains or the circumstances that led to his death. There is no documentation in the files about whether the US and Mexican governments did anything more than record and communicate the tragic news to his and other families facing similar tragedies in Mexico.

CENSORING CHILDREN

The censorship program of the US Consulate extended even to children. Throughout the Bracero Program, it became evident to officials that Mexican children were as persistent and resourceful as adults in attempting to reunite with their bracero and undocumented immigrant parents in the United States, and it concerned them that children wrote letters to their parents about this subject.

Consequently, US Consulate officials intercepted and withheld the content of the letters of Mexican children to their Mexican immigrant parents of varying legal status in the United States when they judged that these letters would embolden their bracero or undocumented Mexican immigrant parents to break US immigration laws in order to reunite with them as a family in the United States. An influx of undocumented Mexican immigrant children not only would draw unwanted public attention to the government's unsuccessful control of the US-Mexico border but also would make it unfeasible for their parents to labor in accordance with the expectations of the US government, especially in the Bracero Program. Harvesting crops with their children in tow would make it difficult for them to move from one state to another on a moment's notice to meet US labor demands, and child care responsibilities would make them determined to attain permanent settlement in the United States.

When Herminia Moreno from Ciudad Delicias, Chihuahua, wrote to her undocumented Mexican immigrant mother Maria Moreno Olivares in Proctor, Arkansas, "Mother, I wish you would make an effort to come even if you have to cross illegally," she revealed a child's confusion regarding what constituted undocumented immigration, as well as her yearning that her mother as her parent do everything possible to return to her.[18] But the fact that the child was requesting a reunion in Mexico rather than the United States was not reassuring to the US Consulate. Her letter was still an emotional and personal proposal that US Consulate officials deemed a threat to national security worthy of censorship. By withholding the letters of children to their Mexican immigrant parents in the United States, officials intended not only to keep families from reuniting in the United States but also to alert children in Mexico to the futility of trying to remain connected to their parents on their terms.

DOCUMENTING INDIVIDUALS LIKELY TO IMMIGRATE ILLEGALLY

US Consulate officials developed in-depth records of the personal information disclosed in intercepted letters from family (including children) and friends in Mexico to immigrant workers of Mexican descent in the United States. The information gleaned from the censored communication was used to compile a list of women and men who could be easily identified by the US government's immigration authorities if they sought to cross the border illegally or succeeded in doing so. They would be flagged for further interrogation about the lawfulness of their intentions and goals and then turned back or deported. Beginning in August 17, 1944, this was the rationale that informed US Consulate officials' creation of such a record for the sisters Juana G. Flores and Vicenta F. Garcia. Flores wrote from San Francisco del Oro, Chihuahua, to Garcia in Goldroad, Arizona, to express her "intention to see [her] even without a passport in hand" and her willingness "to be smuggled" with the assistance of Garcia, even if this meant "sharing time as sisters for only a short while."[19] Flores was apparently undeterred by the prospective dangers of the rough terrain she would have to cross or by the possibility that the family reunification might be cut short by her own deportation as an undocumented immigrant.

US Consulate officials intuited that Flores's personal investment in reunion reliably indicated that even their failure to deliver this letter to Garcia would most likely not deter Flores from reuniting with her sister in the United States. Concerned that the reunification of siblings under these terms could lead to more relatives feeling emboldened and ready to do the same, these officials not only withheld the letter but opened an in-depth record on the two women highlighting the risk to border security that they represented.

Many correspondents in Mexico, anguished after realizing that their letters might not have reached their relatives in the United States, were prompted to cross the US-Mexico border without those relatives' assistance. Their increased danger, and their increased difficulty in finding their loved ones, were not accounted for as consequences worthy of US and Mexican governmental consideration. Nor were the worries and the disruption of relationships that censored communication added to the already existing stresses of family separation and loneliness. Projecting a semblance of control over borders took priority over reducing the human toll of the Bracero Program and continued to make censorship most convenient for US Consulate officials. Only when undeniably tragic outcomes had occurred did the US Consulate collaborate with the Mexican government to share information with families, and then only superficially and belatedly.

THE TREASURE OF THE BRACERO

On September 1956, fourteen years after the US government's censorship went into effect, labor camp administrators developed and circulated leaflets among braceros that tried to address the consequences of censorship. These leaflets encouraged braceros to "write frequently to your loved ones and don't forget to pray that God protect them and help their loved ones."[20] This strategy made the braceros themselves responsible for somehow maintaining family ties despite disruption and enforced silences.

In Fresno County specifically, labor camp administrators alerted braceros that if they wished to communicate with their families and friends "in this community there are many people that write and speak Spanish that are willing to help you write personal letters without cost. When in need of such services, please contact Our Lady of Fatima Catholic Church."[21]

From August 1956 onward, the staff of this church (Nuestra Iglesia Catolica de la Señora de Fatima) had been among the few people to offer their services to braceros frustrated by their poor communication with their families in Mexico and the United States.[22] The emotional anguish and physical isolation of braceros motivated staff to volunteer to reconnect braceros with their relatives and friends in Fresno County by helping them locate and obtain each other's labor camp addresses so that they could at least write to each other when both were laboring in that county. Although the staff were sensitive to braceros' need to communicate as well with their families and friends in Mexico, they did not dare risk exposing braceros or themselves to the US or Mexican government scrutiny that such communication might entail.

Labor camp administrators also announced that "they were doing their best to provide the bracero with better service toward sending money to their families in Mexico through the American Express Company, the largest and safest money delivery service in the world. For thirty cents, you can send anywhere from $1 to $100. This represents great savings on such services for braceros."[23] But by speaking of communication with relatives in Mexico mainly in terms of wiring them money—as well as singling out and accounting for the lack of letters as an issue of bracero illiteracy—these administrators continued to avoid addressing why neither braceros nor their family and friends were receiving each other's letters.

In August 1961, the US government creatively expanded its use of censorship to manage bracero-family communication across the US-Mexico border. It encouraged the administrators of labor camps employing and housing braceros nationwide to instruct braceros to use an album entitled *El Tesoro del Bracero* (*The Treasure of the Bracero*) to communicate with their families in Mexico and the United States upon completing their program participation.[24] This album was produced by the Fisher Brothers Creative Printing and Stationary Company and was distributed among braceros so that they could write in it, filling in the blanks to share predetermined details of their Bracero Program participation with their families upon their return to Mexico. Encouraging braceros to settle for this form of communication provided them with a ready-made narrative that did not leave much room for criticizing the US government's administration of the program.

The Treasure of the Bracero was organized into sections that would allow workers to record the names, ages, and Mexican sending destinations of the people with whom they worked while participating in the Bracero Program. Spaces were provided to enter descriptions of the food they ate during lunch breaks, the crops they harvested and packaged, and the US destinations they lived and worked in. With this album, the government sought to provide braceros with a record that conveniently highlighted select details of their work using a narrative and a timing of communication that would not pose a threat to US national security or defy the US government's regulation of the border. *The Treasure of the Bracero* described itself as not your "typical album but a memory book of treasures." Portraying contract labor as a memorable experience worthy of being shared in a memory book promoted the program as a worthwhile, albeit temporary, venture. Captions explained to braceros and their families and friends that the US government had created and provided this album so that braceros "could preserve a portrait of what they held deep within themselves, so that they continued to possess such memories and their loved ones also experienced them, as well as the nostalgia of laboring in the United States."[25] None of the captions framing this album addressed braceros' memories of emotional or physical hardship.

Yet the book designed to promote the program unwittingly also revealed some of its harsher aspects. *The Treasure of the Bracero* made it obvious to the families and friends of braceros in Mexico that laboring under the program required a physical examination, living in labor camps, and at least eight to eleven hours of hard labor harvesting crops. Further, the controlled content, circulation, and design of this album showed it to be a form of attempted censorship in and of itself.

The combination of rarely receiving letters from their family and friends in Mexico, if at all, and being told by US labor camp administrators that they should restrict themselves to using *The Treasure of the Bracero* to communicate with their families in Mexico after their contract ended did not sit well with braceros or their loved ones in Mexico. Too few of these men benefited from volunteer services like those of Our Lady of Fatima Catholic Church, and many of their families and friends resisted the US government's approach to managing their communications and wrote to the US and Mexican governments respectfully seeking answers as to why they received no responses to their letters.

UNANSWERED QUESTIONS

In February 1945, US Consulate official Murray told US government representatives supervising the consulate's censorship of Mexican women's and men's letters to their relatives and friends in the United States that persistent Mexican women and men who had lost touch with their bracero relatives and friends were deluging him with questions and holding the US and Mexican governments accountable. At the same time, Murray wrote to one of those persistent questioners, Maria de Jesus Alvarez in Acambaro, Guanajuato, Mexico, that her son's failure to write back or return from his participation in the Bracero Program had been a product of his "no longer being employed by the US company who had hired him, that he could have deserted."[26] He urged Alvarez to consider that "plenty of braceros, attracted by wages in war industries or other temporary forms of employment have deserted and left without completing their contracts, this being the reason why companies do not know their whereabouts or the US Consulate of this respective region (Chihuahua, Mexico)." This ploy of proposing likely scenarios that held the bracero in question responsible for decisions that made his whereabouts untraceable was standard among US Consulate officials who wished to avoid accountability for the disruption of communication between braceros and their concerned relatives.

Another standard response used by the US Consulate, required of its officials by the US government, was to explain the failure to deliver or return letters as the result of random glitches in the system and to plead logistical difficulties in locating braceros. Beginning in March 1945, three years after having been instructed to censor the letters of women and men of Mexican descent writing to and from Mexico, US Consulate officials informed Mexican Consulate officials throughout the country that "owing to the changes that frequently occur with regards to the mailing addresses of braceros laboring in several US labor camps throughout one contract cycle, it is difficult to keep track of their whereabouts. Nonetheless, all the correspondence sent to them is mailed to the company that contracted them. This procedure has always been satisfactory to braceros and even the secretary in charge."[27] They did also explain and disclose selectively that censorship could be the cause of some delays in the delivery of letters written by and to braceros, but they did not tell the Mexican Consulate exactly what content in these letters was being censored or how the censorship of letters worked. Instead, they simply presented censorship as a wartime measure. When the Mexican Consulate tried to act as a liaison for the families and friends of braceros, the US Consulate afforded them the right to request the addresses of labor camps housing braceros during their contracts in the United States. This response was meant to reassure the Mexican Consulate that the US government was interested in improving the state of communication between braceros and their families in Mexico.

CARTAS A EUFEMIA (LETTERS TO EUFEMIA)

Josefina Rodriguez was among the countless women in Mexico worried by her husband's failure to respond to her letters. Between August 1947 and September 1964, she wrote numerous letters to her bracero husband, Jose Rodriguez, before giving up entirely. She wrote to obtain his counsel before making decisions concerning their household finances, asking him, for example, whether she should invest their savings in their family business or postpone the enrollment of their child in school until they had a better sense of whether they would be able to afford the supplies. Each time Josefina wrote and mailed out a letter to him, she felt "angry, anxious, ashamed, and desperate to hear from him."[28]

Like Josefina, many women and men gave up on letter writing, unaware that the censorship of their letters and not the indifference of their relatives and friends was in many cases to blame for their failure to receive each other's letters. Their emotional anguish led to the popularity in Mexico of films and songs that recommended that Mexican women be discreet and patient when relying on letters to sustain romantic relationships with bracero and undocumented Mexican immigrant men on the other side of the border.

The Mexican government did not publicize or investigate the censorship of letters to braceros. But in 1952 it used the feature-length film production *Cartas a Eufemia* (Letters to Eufemia) to address the love that made Mexican women eager to reunite with their bracero or undocumented Mexican immigrant boyfriends or husbands.[29]

This production focused on the emotional work of waiting for the return of one's boyfriend in the Mexican countryside. It cautioned women against acting recklessly out of their love for these men. Elite Mexican society embraced this film's spirited recommendation that Mexican women wait with the utmost patience for news in the form of letters and their eventual reunification with these men.

Because US Consulate officials' aggressive censorship of the correspondence of women and men of Mexican descent and varying legal status in the United States and Mexico was never made public, it is unclear when it ended or how effective it was in reducing undocumented immigration. Clearly many women and men were aware that their letters across the border would most likely not reach their family and friends. But their wish to confer with others to obtain approval or advice on serious matters, their feeling of moral obligation to write, and the sense of comfort and resolve that they derived from at least having written all motivated them to continue to write. They learned to understand and use letter writing as an unreliable yet necessary form of communication for making decisions for their family's sake in the United States and Mexico.

CHAPTER FIVE

In Painful Silence

The Untold Emotional Work of Long-Distance Romantic Relationships and Marriages, 1957–1964

In August 1957, Carmela Juarez went to purchase cornmeal and other food items. Immediately her daughter Hermelinda stopped her household chores and rushed to lock their family home's door.[1] Certain that it would take Carmela at least thirty minutes to walk to and from Doña Concepcion's dry goods and grocery store, nineteen-year-old Hermelinda used the time to retrieve her record of the song "Siempre hace frio" ("It Is Always Cold," 1956) from under the bed and play it at least a couple times on the family's record player as a way to indulge her longing for her twenty-two-year-old bracero boyfriend, Benjamin Guzman.[2] Carmela disapproved of Benjamin's courting Hermelinda, but the daughter maintained a secret, long-distance romantic relationship with him, and the spirit of this song helped her love in silence.

Nothing compared to the emotional comfort Hermelinda derived from listening and crying to "It Is Always Cold." She sought out these moments to "mourn the pain" of "acting out of love and being in love with a bracero." Her "deep love" for her mother and boyfriend had made the cold of the song feel like her own, since she was "longing for [her] mother's understanding and his return." Listening to "It Is Always Cold" kept her from "becoming emotionally undone." Throughout Benjamin's Bracero Program participation, she had pretended to her mother that she had given up on a romantic relationship with him. But she did not want to lose hope of sharing a future with him, even though she had not heard from him for five consecutive months. When she listened to sad songs she could relieve some of the tension and *desahogarse* (express and be true to her feelings).

Romantic ballads of longing and loss helped transnational couples cope with the emotional ruptures enacted by the Bracero Program. Throughout the Mexican countryside, the songs of José Alfredo Jiménez, one of the most celebrated and prolific Mexican composers and singers of Mexican *ranchera* music, were among the most requested by men who were about to leave the women they loved and their families and hometowns.

Mexican women and men who fell in love with each other and entered long-distance romantic relationships and marriages were expected to adhere to gender expectations. Women were supposed to continue writing and to remain devoted and faithful even if their boyfriends did not reply to their letters. They were also supposed to keep their anxiety, fears, and hopes for these long-distance romantic relationships to themselves if they were to be considered honorable, productive, responsible, and sexually virtuous—and thus eligible for marriage in the eyes of their families, prospective in-laws, and Mexican immigrant boyfriends. Married women did not fare any better. They too had to keep quiet about the suffering they experienced as a result of separation from their bracero or undocumented Mexican immigrant husbands.

Braceros and undocumented Mexican immigrant men were under similar pressures and public scrutiny regarding their feelings and their romantic relationships. Women's parents were often wary of their daughters entering romantic relationships with men participating in the Bracero Program or traveling to the United States as undocumented Mexican immigrants. Families did not necessarily approve of couples who had only the promise of their love for each other and their dedication to earning and saving wages sufficient to afford a future together under honorable terms. Irrespective of their initial promises of love, parents worried that these men would never prioritize their romantic relationship or pursue marriage to their daughters. Already familiar with braceros and other Mexican immigrants who had abandoned their girlfriends or wives shortly after joining the program, parents feared a similar fate for their daughters. Mexican immigrant men could not afford to be publicly perceived as emotionally vulnerable by their prospective in-laws, families, and peers. Their moral eligibility to enter long-distance romantic relationships and even marriage was often contingent on their enduring emotional pain as responsibly as possible. Wary of the consequences of using their own words to express and describe their anxiety, yearning, and love, they, like the women they loved, instead depended on the lyrics, spirit, and tone of popular songs of love to convey their feelings. The songs restored their spirit to persevere for the love of their girlfriends and wives.

CREATING RESTORATIVE MOMENTS

Creating and benefiting from an emotionally restorative moment of remembered love posed emotional risks for Hermelinda. In part, she understood and shared Carmela's fears regarding a long-distance romantic relationship with Benjamin. Having been left to raise Hermelinda on her own after her father Osvaldo Juarez had abandoned them shortly after joining the Bracero Program in 1943, Carmela worried that Benjamin, like her estranged husband, would "simply not return one day from laboring in the United States," abandoning her daughter. The emotional pain and public shame of having been abandoned six years into their marriage without any explanation or any money with which to raise Hermelinda had left Carmela to labor fourteen hours a day making curtains, tablecloths, and bed linens for sale from their home. Overwhelmed emotionally and financially, Carmela had not had time to mourn the dissolution of her family and marriage.

Thirteen years of parenting Hermelinda on her own, building a strong year-round clientele for her handmade home products, and mustering the emotional endurance to cope with having been abandoned by the man who had been the love of her life had left Carmela most unreceptive to Hermelinda and Benjamin's courtship. Nothing Benjamin had done to earn Carmela's approval had changed her mind. Beginning in February 1957 and leading up to his departure in July of that year to join the Bracero Program, neither his meeting with her to introduce himself and request her permission to court Hermelinda with his parents in tow nor his delivering crates of apples, pears, and mangos and canisters of sugar to her in person on a regular basis had earned him her consent to entering a long-distance romantic relationship with her daughter. She insisted that she loved her daughter too much to consent to her "being in what promised to be at best a tumultuous relationship." "Having already lost [Hermelinda's] father to the program, and as a mother and an abandoned wife," Carmela wanted to spare Hermelinda the emotional turmoil of losing love.

Neither Hermelinda nor Benjamin questioned or resented Carmela's reasoning behind her opposition to their courtship. Familiar with the unceasing intensity of Carmela's sadness and hard work, they understood that her abandonment by Hermelinda's father soon after he joined the Bracero Program fueled her unwillingness to give Benjamin a chance to prove the sincerity of his love for Hermelinda, even though he intended to complete only one program contract to save enough money to return to marry her. Hermelinda's respect for her mother's sacrifice moved her to counsel Benjamin to view her mother's refusal to support their long-distance romantic relationship as a temporary setback for them and to pursue asking for her mother's permission to court her upon his return from participating in the program.

Confident that when Benjamin, unlike her bracero father, returned he would finally persuade Carmela to approve of their love and relationship, Hermelinda and Benjamin settled for his courting her in secret.

By entering a long-distance romantic relationship with Benjamin without Carmela's permission, Hermelinda risked disappointing her mother and possibly even preventing her mother from ever approving of their relationship. But Benjamin, up to the time of his departure to join the Bracero Program, had proven most supportive of her without ever betraying her trust in him.

Five months into their secret long-distance romantic relationship, Hermelinda's love for Benjamin had not wavered but had become the source of emotional agony for her. Longing for Benjamin to return from the Bracero Program had inspired her to fear that, as the lyrics to "It Is Always Cold" described, he might have forgotten her, fallen in love with another woman, or, like her father, abandoned her. Not hearing from him or receiving news of his plans for return had transformed each day that they were separated from each other into an emotionally painful, cold time. Living and working with Carmela without her knowing of her persistent love for Benjamin made listening to this song's description of her longing for him painful, but also a means of holding onto her hopes for a better future.

On November 1958, Hermelinda and Benjamin finally reunited in their rural hometown of Ameca, Jalisco, near San Martin de Hidalgo. They married one month later with Carmela's consent. Upon his return, the change in Hermelinda's demeanor moved her mother to approve of their marriage. Although Hermelinda did not ever share with her mother that she had been in a long-distance romantic relationship with Benjamin, Carmela could not ignore that the happiness that Hermelinda radiated when he visited them to request her hand in marriage marked a dramatic change in her daughter. For months, Carmela had witnessed her daughter grow pale, despondent, and thin in silence. Out of love for her daughter, she became most supportive of her marrying Benjamin. She intuited that Hermelinda would most likely grow angry and bitter if denied an opportunity to forge a lasting emotional relationship with him.

Carmela's confidence in consenting to their marriage grew after she learned that Benjamin had invested his earnings from the Bracero Program in his family's roofing business. When making his marriage proposal, he shared with her and Hermelinda that his love for her had influenced his decision to marry her—and to steer clear of renewing his program contract. He doubted being able to endure another assignment without the love of his life by his side. Upon marrying on a cold, wintry evening in December 1958, Hermelinda waited until the end of their wedding reception to share a most longed-for moment of love with Benjamin. When retiring into their cozy apartment, as they did not have enough money to go on a honeymoon, she requested that they play "It Is Always Cold" on the record player she had asked him to buy as his wedding gift to her and to listen and dance to it together. His purchase of the record player and his promise not to renew his Bracero Program contract had been the only requests Hermelinda had made of him when they had discussed their marriage plans in secret. While they danced, Hermelinda shared with Benjamin that the song had helped her endure their separation across the US-Mexico border. His realization of the intensity of her longing for him inspired him to share as well that his longing for her had stirred much anxiety in his heart, and they both broke into tears. This time Hermelinda embraced her tears as expressions of joy. Sharing this moment with Benjamin reassured Hermelinda that he had kept and made personally meaningful promises to her out of his love for her, and that her mother had consented to their marriage first and foremost out of her love for her, making this "among the truest moments of love" she had "ever experienced."[3]

Like popular music, love letters, conversations, and strolls together became means of handling the emotional pain of transnational relationships. The future of long-distance romantic relationships, especially marriages between women and Mexican immigrant men, was often determined by their families' assessment of whether, on reuniting, the couple showed they had kept promises made to each other before the separation. Families decided whether to support a couple by focusing on whether the men who returned from laboring in the United States had saved enough money to make inroads toward marrying their daughters, and they gauged women's eligibility to continue a courtship or to marry by whether women had kept themselves honorable, sexually virtuous, and hardworking during their separation from their boyfriends or fiancés. Women married to braceros took promises seriously. Wives felt that men who made and kept promises about sending home remittances and returning to their partners in Mexico had earned the right to continue to pursue contract labor in the United States.

Maria Elena Lopez came to realize that her bracero husband Agustin Lopez inviting her for an evening walk was a sure sign of his intention to renew his participation in the Bracero Program.[4] At times between August 1947 and September 1956, they would take a stroll together in Ameca, Jalisco, so that they could privately discuss whether they were willing to part from each other. Their motivation was the opportunity to earn wages that could strengthen their ability to provide for their four-year-old daughter and two-year-old son, Maribel and Alejandro Lopez, in the long term. Making a promise to Maria Elena was easier for Agustin when they allocated time away from their children and busy caretaking and employment schedules to share an outing. His promise reflected his understanding of the emotional sacrifices they each would be shouldering to make program participation feasible and profitable, so their evening strolls became important moments in which Maria Elena and Agustin nurtured their love for each other and their marriage.

During each of these walks, Agustin promised to dedicate himself to earning and saving enough US wages to pay for Maribel and Alejandro's elementary and eventually middle school education, as well as items that he intuited would satisfy Maria Elena's desires and needs. These promises "made it emotionally easier for [her] to parent the children and labor twelve-hour shifts preparing and vending food throughout his absence." The wages from Agustin's labor in the United States allowed him to buy Maria Elena a new winter coat, pairs of shoes to comfortably complete day-to-day tasks and attend special family gatherings, a sewing machine to make her own dresses, warm and soft blankets to weather the winter months, and a record player for her to listen to her favorite musicians; to buy their children bedroom furniture that would make their home more comfortable for them year-round; and to build windows that would let the morning light into their home's living room. He made and kept his promises to earn enough to purchase items that would make the family's life easier out of his love for her as a person, the mother of their children, and his wife.

Throughout their Bracero Program participation, Carlos and Rosa Rodriguez used the memories of moments in which he made promises to her as a resource that helped them both to endure the anguish and longing that set in when they were separated by the US-Mexico border.[5] From July 1947 through October 1958, Rosa used remittances from Carlos to open a savings account in San Martin de Hidalgo's Banco Nacional under her name. Carlos pledged that upon his completion of his contract labor he would return to deposit into this account a minimum of $60 from wages that he earned while in the United States. Insisting that their separation, which included disruptions of their communication, was not worthwhile if it cast doubt on his laboring in this way out of his love for her and their marriage, he used the symbolism of this bank account to hold himself accountable to her and their feelings for each other.

LETTERS OF LOVE

Despite the unreliability of using letters to correspond with each other, Mexican women married or related to braceros did not abandon writing to their bracero relatives completely. Throughout their program participation, their emotional investment in their marriage or extended family moved them to write letters of love, or enlist others to help them write such letters, to their bracero husbands or other bracero relatives in which they expressed that they missed the braceros, prayed for their prompt return, valued them, and wished them well. Francisca Negrete Gonzalez was one of these women. Writing from Nuevo Leon, Guanajuato, in October 1943 to her husband, Juan Gonzalez Garcia, Francisca shared and requested information from him and reminded him that she was the "one who loves you truly, and wishes you the best, that you write me, your wife that loves you and never forgets you."[6] She began her letter by telling Juan to "receive greetings from my mama and my uncle and from me receive the finest memories." She reminded him that regardless of how much money he was able to earn and save from his contract labor in Bakersfield, California, he would not be forgotten; he and their memories together were very much in the hearts and minds of their family. Like many other young women in long-distance romantic relationships with braceros, she also asked him to send her a photograph of himself. Explaining to Juan that "I wish to see you instead of writing you," she urged him to "please have your picture taken if you have the way of doing so. I wish to see you again."

Mothers also wrote their bracero sons letters of love that reassured them of their emotional support. These women recognized that it was their obligation to try to use letters of love to help their sons endure the emotional isolation of being disconnected from their loved ones. Mothers' letters focused on appreciation for their sons' attempts to use any form of communication that would enable them to remain emotionally connected.

In October 1943, Fidencia Abila wrote her bracero son, Jesus Abila, from Mineral del Monte, Jalisco.[7] She confirmed having received the portrait of himself that he had sent from Indio, California. To her, it was an encouraging sign of his faring well in the United States. She expressed pleasant surprise that the portrait showed him to be "very plump." She opined that he had "become like a little policeman" and expressed her gratitude for the reassurance she derived from his efforts to remain connected to her through this portrait. She added that she thanked God "because I thought that you would have a bad life but I see that it is not so."

Enriching the emotional well-being of Jesus and their extended family relationship also motivated Fidencia to tell him in her letter that she was emotionally invested in strengthening her relationships with his prospective mother- and father-in-law. Stressing to him that neither she nor he could take their support of his long-distance romantic relationship to their daughter for granted, she frankly urged that he "commend them to God so that they don't take away the love of the girl" from him. Providing him with her honest assessment of the fragility of his long-distance romantic relationship was intended to caution her son against being reckless when courting the approval of his prospective in-laws and his girlfriend.

Out of consideration for their bracero brothers' longing to remain emotionally connected to their families, siblings also dedicated themselves to writing letters. Throughout the braceros' participation in the program their siblings did not allow concerns about the possible nondelivery of these letters to discourage them from writing. Letters could provide braceros with personally meaningful information and requests that would remind them of how much they were missed and loved. In October 1943, Jose Arciniega wrote to his brother Ricardo.[8] Beginning his letter by expressing their family's gratitude for remittances he had sent to their mother allowed Jose to advise Ricardo that he ought to send remittances to her through him and rely on his detailed accounting of her use of these funds to maximize his financial assistance. Jose feared that it had proven too risky for their mother to continue to pick up remittances herself, as she had been robbed when doing so as a result of people "fooling her because of her age." Jose also stressed his desire to remain connected to Ricardo. Writing to share with him that "there passed through here a boy who comes from over there where you are," and that he "told him that I have written about three letters while you write me only one, that it's been three months without word," was Jose's way of alerting Ricardo to his failed attempts at connecting with him to express his gratitude for the five hundred dollars he had sent their family. Expressing that gratitude again, he hoped that this letter and the previous ones he had written would reassure Ricardo of their family's appreciation for his labor and love. Ricardo's example of undertaking contract labor and sending remittances responsibly to their entire family had inspired Jose to "be more supportive of my son Juan learning mechanics, so that he too can follow your example of acting generously toward our family." This claim as well was Jose's way of making Ricardo feel loved.

Jose ended his letter by giving Ricardo information that captured the current state of their extended family. Anticipating that an honest account of their family situation ideally would encourage Ricardo to return to them, Jose recommended, "Gather as much as you can, and then we will work together." He highlighted where he and their mother could be found, as they had recently moved, and his inability to "tell you anything about Aurelia, because I do not want to write her." Although he did not elaborate on the reasons behind his not wanting to communicate with Ricardo's wife, he offered to "do whatever is necessary" to convey "whatever you order me to your children" and said he was willing to "take them to the station where you wish" upon Ricardo's return. Familiarizing Ricardo with the limitations of his support, as well as a sense of their family's goodwill and whereabouts, was meant to reassure him that Jose remained committed to him and to the family and eager and willing to help him. He concluded by urging Ricardo to "soon be with your own. Come, you are loved. "

Throughout the Bracero Program, the children of braceros were among the most emotionally invested in writing and having their letters serve as moments of bonding with their bracero fathers. On November 17, 1943, Teresa Garcia helped her ten-year-old daughter Rosa Lopez write to her bracero father, Jesus Lopez, from Distrito Federal.[9] Cautiously enclosing her daughter's letter in her own letter—perhaps to avoid attracting the unwanted attention of the US and Mexican governments—Teresa shared with him that she had carried out his request to provide fifty pesos of their family savings to his mother. Reassuring him that their hard-earned savings had also made it possible to provide comfortably for their children—"wanting in school nothing and already I had bought shoes for both of them"—was Teresa's way of demonstrating to Jesus that out of her love for him and their family and marriage she had honored his wishes and acted as responsibly as possible.

Teresa concluded her letter of love by encouraging Jesus to "receive many kisses from all your children," and "from me [to] receive the most sincere kisses, from your Teresa that loves you, and that prays to God that you will soon return." Her emphasis on return was meant to dovetail nicely with Rosa writing her father, "I hope that you are well," and asking him to "ask God that soon you will be with us to give you many little kisses and hugs as you give them when you are with us." By stressing that she and "my brothers say that you must not forget them," she tried to express the full extent of her affection for her father by echoing her mother's wish that he soon return to them. Writing to Jesus to make him feel their love, which was in no small part reciprocal for what *he* had done out of his love for *them*, was essential to Teresa and Rosa's pursuit of creating, providing, and sharing a moment of love with Jesus that did not discount the importance of their emotional needs.

MOMENTS OF LISTENING

Throughout the Bracero Program, Mexican men joining the program to finance marriages to the girlfriends they were leaving behind used recordings of love songs to express the emotional pain of the separation. The songs helped them persevere for the future of their long-distance romantic relationships or through the dissolution of these relationships. This was especially the case when men parted from women shortly after entering into relationships with them. Long-distance relationships that arose from the separations of the Bracero Program hinged on men and women's strict adherence to gender expectations that underestimated the emotional toll of parting from each other across the US-Mexico border.

Though entering and building on a long-distance romantic relationship were hard-earned privileges contingent on women and men's responsible enactment of their feelings for each other, over time the parents and relatives of braceros and other Mexican immigrants often became receptive to long-distance relationships because they considered them conducive to their sons' and daughters' enduring commitment to forging a future in rural towns throughout Mexico. They considered these couples' promises to endure temporary separation from each other as the strongest indicator that they were motivated to settle in close proximity to their extended families. Families' desire to remain connected to their sons as they matured into adulthood and marriage consequently led them to become more supportive of braceros' recourse to moments of listening, before their departure, to songs that had special meaning for them.

In 1956 and again in 1962, Alejandro Ortega was among the braceros whose family was receptive to letting him listen, in the privacy of their family home, to a song that expressed the pain that thwarted hopes in the Bracero Program had caused him. Every time he returned to Ameca, Jalisco, he would listen to the song "El hijo del pueblo" ("The Rural Town's Son") to face the fact that he still had insufficient money to buy land and build a home of his own or to pay for a wedding ceremony.[10] He had saved enough to purchase direly needed furniture for his family's home, pay his mother's medical bills as she recovered from a stroke, and construct additional rooms for his family's home, but lack of leftover funds discouraged him from courting women. Listening and reflecting upon this song was emotionally restorative for him and helped him endure the hardship of having to postpone a romantic relationship.

The emotional pain of having withstood the rigors of the Bracero Program in anticipation of proving themselves eligible to share a future with the women they loved made mourning a broken relationship a delicate undertaking for bracero and other Mexican immigrant men. Julio Valle would listen to the song "Sufriendo a solas" ("Suffering Alone," 1951) when the memories of the love of his life, Dolores Casillas, became too overwhelming for him to bear.[11] In 1952, he had separated from her temporarily to join the Bracero Program and earn enough money to purchase furniture for their family home. They had married each other only three months before he departed to the United States, and she had convinced him to participate in the program to finance expenditures that would afford them a comfortable home and, ideally, an automobile to share weekend outings throughout the state of Jalisco. Six months after his leavetaking he returned to reunite with her and learned that she had left him to begin anew with her former boyfriend in Guadalajara, Jalisco. The news that she had left him days after he had set out was devastating and a source of shame for him. Dolores's betrayal and memories of the moments they had shared together made it too painful to continue living in their home and rural town without her. Listening to "Suffering Alone" was his only solace.

Women in San Martin de Hidalgo, Jalisco, often used the song "La del rebozo blanco" ("The One with the White Shawl"), by Mexican singer-songwriter José Alfredo Jiménez, to create a restorative moment of listening, whether alone or with other women.[12] The song's title refers to a custom, among women in Mexican rural towns and villages, of wearing a white shawl to indicate that one was in a long-distance romantic relationship with a bracero or an undocumented Mexican immigrant working in the United States. Town residents were eager to know whether the indefinite absence of their boyfriends and fiancés had led these women to break their promise to wait patiently, flirt with other men out of disillusionment, or get sexually involved with someone else. Wearing a white shawl signaled to others not to ask a woman to account for the whereabouts of her boyfriend or fiancé, the state of her long-distance romantic relationship, or her own emotional welfare. The shawl, intricately woven using featherweight white yarn, sold in clothing and fine tailoring shops and stores for a modest sum of money, and worn by an honorable and sexually virtuous woman over her head and shoulders when she was making her way from her family homes to public functions and gatherings, made it possible to interact socially in public without being bombarded with emotionally stressful stares and questions. It also gave the family a way to declare and protect her honor and sexual virtue when she was out in public. The white shawl afforded her and her family respect. The emotional exhaustion of mourning honorably and optimistically heightened the personal meaning of the benefits to owning and wearing a white shawl. It gave women some privacy and served as a source of emotional comfort and empowering peace of mind. It was then easier to enjoy interacting socially with family and friends in public.

Throughout their separation from their bracero and other Mexican immigrant boyfriends and fiancés, women were made worthy of public confidence and trust precisely because they wore white shawls. Everyone realized that if a woman in this situation lacked a shawl it would be very difficult for her to be publicly perceived or treated as honorable and sexually virtuous. Wearing a shawl also meant it was particularly important to adhere to gender expectations regarding honorable and sexually virtuous behavior. This often meant limiting one's social interactions with men to the exchange of respectful greetings and brief formal conversations under the supervision of one's family and adopting a physical demeanor and presence that did not draw unwanted public attention to oneself or one's sexuality.

For some women, donning the shawl felt as though they were literally wearing and announcing their pain to everyone who cast eyes on them. Wearing these shawls rendered their predicament visible to anyone, making their heartache uncomfortably public. Nevertheless, some of these women learned to take comfort in wearing the white shawl because it allowed them to remain honorable and sexually virtuous in everyone's eyes, irrespective of the failure or success of their long-distance romantic relationships. They also might derive a glimmer of hope from the public's general assumption—which they were expected to embrace—that their boyfriends and fiancés could not have forgotten them and would return to begin a future with them.

The resonance of moments of love and moments of listening among and for women and men in romantic relationships that stretched across the US-Mexico border render especially meaningful and obvious the silences that these women and men had to maintain with regard to their doubts, fear, longing, and disappointment in the conditions and even outcomes of program arrangements or family adaptations to those arrangements. The rigor with which their relationships were obstructed by the US and Mexican governments and, in turn, scrutinized and monitored by their families illuminates the emotional lengths they went to and the risks they took to cope with being denied the freedom to express themselves or their feelings for each other in the comforts of their homes or in public. The emotional accountability that came with being in love across the US-Mexico border, as well as the resonance of moments of love and moments of listening, did not end with the termination of the Bracero Program. It is striking that many women and men did not allow themselves to admit and discuss the emotional toll of having been in love during the Bracero Program, when their emotional suffering had been too much to bear, until at least fifty years after the program ended. Other women and men in similar situations opted to express and convey their romantic feelings and commitment by daringly and cautiously documenting their love for each other through communications across the US-Mexico border. This undertaking posed its own set of emotional risks that over time became a bit easier to assume if they received the assistance of their families. Nonetheless, this was hard-earned support that continued to make their being in love under such constricting conditions tough emotional work for these women and men, and their families.

CHAPTER SIX · Hidden from History

Photo Stories of Love

On the afternoon of June 13, 1959, sixteen-year-old Esther Legaspi Delgadillo carefully packed into a satchel a dress she had purchased earlier that day along with a curling iron, stockings, and a pair of high-heeled shoes.[1] Ordinarily, she used this bag to carry food and other merchandise she purchased when shopping for her family at local stores in their Mexican rural hometown of Nochistlan, Zacatecas, but on this day she used it to hide and carry personal items that would help her create and share a photo story of love with her boyfriend, Antonio Sanchez, across the US-Mexico border. They had recently parted: he had migrated to the United States in search of employment as either a bracero or an undocumented Mexican immigrant. Esther didn't want her mother to know what she was about to do; although her mother had approved of their courtship, she was among the parents who expected daughters in long-distance romantic relationships to keep being in love to themselves.

Esther remained true to her distant love by using her errand time to take a portrait that would kindle her and Antonio's feelings for one another. Restrictive gender expectations and rumors of the US government's censorship of correspondence across the border had not discouraged her from doing so. Esther explained, "We loved each other, and were dedicated to our love for each other."

Love songs, love letters, and promises made to each other had not been enough for the couple to feel truly connected across the US-Mexico border. The story Esther sought to create and share with Antonio, then and at later points in their relationship, consisted of photographs of her and, eventually, them that captured the sincerity of their love and longing for each other. Esther provided Antonio with carefully crafted snapshots of her love for him that he could carry and contemplate so that he could experience moments of love wherever he found himself. Her courage to risk documenting her longing for him and their permanent reunification in this way was fueled by familial support as well as Antonio's love.

Her aunt had already obtained Esther's mother's permission to spend the afternoon with Esther. This would allow them enough time for her to chaperone Esther as she took a portrait that required her to change into a stylish dress and elegant hairstyle—all without raising her mother's concern. Their careful planning in support of Esther's photo story of love had been inspired by Antonio's own efforts to act out of love for her. He had already asked for Esther's parents' permission to court and write her before migrating to secure US employment. This gesture had revealed the honorability and sincerity of his love for her. Additionally, Antonio's request that, as soon as she could, Esther send him her portrait fueled her resolve to do so. Rather than keep her feelings to herself, Esther's love for Antonio emboldened her to provide him with a snapshot of her love. This first portrait captured the care with which Esther had styled her physical appearance to look beautiful for Antonio and reflected her emotional investment in their romantic relationship.

Before seeking the assistance of her aunt, Esther had sought out the counsel of her siblings. As she explained, "My brothers and sisters were very supportive of our love." They appreciated that she dedicated most of her day to helping care for them, cleaning their family home, excelling in school, and working in local shops, and they understood that whether or not Antonio had saved enough money for marriage, Esther desperately yearned to reunite with him. They did not judge Esther or Antonio for desiring and needing to see each other—even if only in the form of photographs—but they assumed that their sister would not dare to request a photo from him and they feared that it might be too reckless for her to send one of herself. Consequently they recommended that Esther be cautious in honoring Antonio's request so as to meet strict gender expectations.

Love for Esther moved her siblings to advise her to rely on their aunt to determine the most responsible way to take a suitable portrait. Her siblings intuited that Esther and Antonio fulfilling their emotional need for each other in this way—and with the Bracero Program very much part of the backdrop—would require mature supervision. After their mother, their aunt was the most generous and responsible adult they knew. Their aunt was entrusted to counsel and accompany Esther on whether she should take this photograph, who else should know about it, and what special precautions she should take when receiving this photograph and mailing it to Antonio. It was important to protect Esther and her family's public reputation, so Esther's attempt to remain emotionally connected to Antonio could not be misunderstood as a daringly reckless and sexually immoral expression of her desire.

Esther did not want to depend on her mother to oversee this venture. Already laboring tirelessly to provide for them, their mother would only be further overburdened by supervising Esther's correspondence with Antonio. Their aunt already spent considerable time with them, which made it easier for her to help Esther make a carefully crafted portrait (figure 10). Their aunt also seemed a most responsible adult to supervise such documentation of Esther's feelings, as she recognized that the correspondence between couples—although family approved and publicly accepted—could still be used to assess the honor and sexual virtue of the women in these relationships. It was in the best interest of young women to secure and benefit from the supervision of a close female family relative when using photographs or other documents to correspond with their Mexican immigrant boyfriends. This way, their correspondence would not be misinterpreted as immoral and reckless.

Throughout the Mexican countryside, young women taking and sending photographs to remain connected emotionally with their Mexican immigrant boyfriends were expected to have at least a chaperone by their side through each of the stages of taking these portraits. Their photographs and oral life histories reveal that a sense of public accountability inspired these women, as well as men, to take such emotional chances only with the utmost caution. Transmitting photographs during the Bracero Program was risky for couples, especially for young and single women like Esther. What makes these photographic stories of love so illuminating lies in how and why they could be both intimate and highly public documents, deeply meaningful to those involved but less transparent to their families, peers, and US and Mexican government officials. Using their portraits and other photographs to craft, express, and share their love for each other in ways that would not be too obvious or problematic for their families or the US and Mexican governments helped separated couples feel that they had successfully and responsibly taken an emotional risk for each other.

This is what makes understanding the spirit in which men and women embraced the taking, sharing, and preservation of photographs most historically generative. Women in long-distance romantic relationships with braceros or undocumented

FIGURE 10.
Studio portrait of Esther Legaspi Delgadillo Sanchez, 1959.

Mexican immigrant men could never afford to forget that the photographs they made and sent were not just intimate declarations of love but also public ones. It was their responsibility not to arouse the suspicion of US and Mexican government authorities, who intercepted letters and often deported braceros who corresponded with young women in ways that were incompatible with the program's aims. These young women could not afford for their photographs to be misinterpreted as an emotional appeal to reunite with their bracero or undocumented Mexican immigrant boyfriends in the United States. The US government did not welcome such a prospect and, rather than risk it, would often not deliver the photographs to these men and might even cancel their program contract and deport them. Further, if the photographs reached relatives or peers who perceived them or the couple's use of them as immoral or sexually aggressive, they would disapprove of and prohibit the courtship or disown or ostracize the women. Women's photographs, therefore, were potentially dangerous public documents. Esther would be among the women who did not take such consequences lightly.

Even when parents granted their daughters permission to enter long-distance romantic relationships, they tended not to support their writing letters or sending photographs. Parents doubted that men laboring in a different country and surrounded by women born and raised in the United States were worth the risk of public ostracism that their daughters would run as a result of trying to share love and longing for them. In parents' estimation, these women's portraits undeniably publicized that their daughters had acted out of love and in response to the advances of these men. The photographs were evidence of their vulnerability—their daughters were laying their feelings on the line, and they could very easily be made to look foolish upon the dissolution of their relationships with the braceros. Should their boyfriends not honor their long-distance romantic relationships, parents worried that their daughters' photographs and letters would make it difficult for them to deny that they had been poor judges of character—or even had acted too daringly, so much so that it had discouraged their boyfriends from remaining committed to their relationship. These women's parents worried that such suspicions would make it challenging for another man to court them honorably.

Sidestepping parents' responsibility for supervising women may have been permissible among relatives like Esther's aunt, but it also made these relatives feel extremely accountable for the risks young women under their supervision were taking in order to make these photographic stories. Like their parents, these relatives worried that the women in these long-distance romantic relationships had much more at stake than the men did. For example, if the men used the women's portraits and other photographs to share their intentions and feelings for these young women or to make evident how eagerly the women had expressed their affection and desire, then these young women's upbringing, honor, and sexual virtue would be publicly impugned. It would be difficult for other men participating in these conversations to avoid discrediting these young women's public reputation and dismissing the desirability of entering a romantic relationship with them. Men in these relationships were not as exposed. Their expression of longing for their girlfriends in the form of respectfully tasteful portraits was often accepted as part of their courtship. In sharp contrast, for women the recognition, expression, and documentation of their emotional desires and needs through photographs and at the request of their Mexican immigrant boyfriends was understood as unseemly. These documents and the conversations that they could potentially elicit among men would make it difficult for these women or their parents to defend their honor and sexual virtue against their public claims. Men's interpretation and use of these women's photographs were of great concern to relatives supervising the creation of the photographs. Thus Esther's aunt asked Esther whether she was confident that Antonio was in love with her. Her aunt wanted to avoid unnecessarily risking Esther's public reputation and the overall possibility of her obtaining a lasting and desirable relationship.

Historians of the mid-twentieth-century Mexican immigrant experience in the United States and Mexico have for the most part been hesitant to explore and assess the role of love, and especially its emboldening potential, in the experiences and aspirations of couples confronting their separation across the US-Mexico border.[2] The persistent refusal to engage with the entirety of these women and men's experiences has restricted our field's consideration of what it meant to confront, survive, and, in the best of cases, thrive in the face of the Bracero Program. At best, historians have investigated how couples of varying ethnic, legal, and racial status refused to adhere to conservative and often racist inter- and intraethnic and gender expectations.[3] The daring and resourcefulness exhibited by women and men separated by the US-Mexico border—all without jeopardizing their reputations, their relationships with their families, or their right to work in the United States as contract laborers and undocumented Mexican immigrants—remain underestimated and underinvestigated. But such an inquiry could be a pathway into understanding the emotional stakes of participation in the Bracero Program and the power of these couples' love for each other.

Photo stories of love from the time of the Bracero Program have often gone on to be the documents that families of Mexican descent throughout the United States and Mexico most value as they reflect on the Bracero Program's impact on their families. This chapter will demonstrate the extent of the emotional risks that women and men took for love, especially in hopes of benefiting from the morale-building potential of photographs during their separation. Resisting becoming emotionally disconnected from each other and stripped completely of their humanity by the US and Mexican governments' implementation of the program, these women and men dared to take themselves seriously as possessors of romantic feelings who were worthy of responsibly negotiating gender expectations and program conditions in Mexico and the United States. After all, it is the spirit with which they crafted and used these photo stories of love across the US-Mexico border that has endured in these families' sense of their history. Love inspired their grandparents, parents, sisters, brothers, aunts, and uncles to risk documenting what our long-standing conceptualization of the Bracero Program experience has rendered most undocumented. Their attempts at documentation have given us traces of what has historically been undocumented. They also show how important love was in determining where and whether migrants ultimately settled.

LOVING CAUTIOUSLY

Esther's confidence that her Mexican immigrant boyfriend Antonio longed for her as much as she did for him emboldened her to risk taking and sharing with him another portrait of love to enrich and continue their photo story of love. As she recalled, their love for each other "inspired an unwavering affection and goodwill." Throughout his years of laboring in the United States and their separation from each other, he carried his portrait of Esther with him at all times because it protected him against breaking down emotionally. Because he kept her portrait a secret, Esther was prompted to continue risking her public reputation and future prospects in order to fulfill his request to see more of her and her love for him.

Feeling obliged to adhere to gender expectations and the Bracero Program's conditions for the sake of their sharing a future together, Esther used a respectfully cautious approach when sharing additional portraits with Antonio. Heeding her siblings' advice, she used every element at her disposal to offset their anxiety concerning her portraits' being misunderstood as immoral, reckless, or sexually aggressive overtures. Her elegantly styled physical appearance in her portraits was meant to leave the lasting impression on him and anyone else who saw them that she was serious about acting out of her love for him with the utmost respect. She could not shake the feeling that her love for him was impeded by the program's pervasive presence in their relationship. Conveying her feelings for Antonio could not be a private matter, and it required emotional work to conform to the US and Mexican governments' expectations that she express herself without enticing Antonio to violate the conditions of the program. As Esther put it, "These photographs—our feelings—we could not take them lightly."

On July 22, 1963, four years after Esther took and sent her first portrait to Antonio, he had yet to return, but he did not betray her trust. His continuous employment

FIGURE 11.
Studio portrait of Esther Legaspi Delgadillo Sanchez, 1963.

in the United States had not yet made it possible for him to settle in Mexico to permanently reunite with Esther. Their continued separation and his responsible handling of her first portrait moved Esther to share photographs with Antonio that would make for moments of love that included the social world he had left behind and missed desperately.

Out of her deep concern for Antonio's emotional well-being and the future of their long-distance romantic relationship, Esther sent him a photograph taken of her on her eighteenth birthday. It showed Esther wearing one of her most cherished gold necklaces (figure 11). Through this photograph, Esther intended to transport Antonio back "to memories of her at her most beautiful." She would often wear this

FIGURE 12.
Middle school portrait of Esther Legaspi Delgadillo Sanchez and
Antonio Sanchez. Esther is second from the right in the second-
to-last row. Antonio Sanchez is first on the left in the last row.

necklace when going out with him on chaperoned dates. Esther's family had taken
this photograph of her to mark a special celebration of her coming of age. They did
not suspect that it would be duplicated and used to create a moment of love for
Antonio. Coupled with her original portrait, this photograph of Esther made for a
photo story of love that convinced Antonio of her unwavering love for him.

That Esther had given him a duplicate of a family photograph that at the time
was highly coveted made her emotional investment in his welfare and their relationship most obvious to him. Throughout the Mexican countryside, the production of
family portraits often cost at least one day's worth of an unskilled laborer's wages,
making such documents expensive and cherished family items.

Esther also sent Antonio their class portrait from middle school, the time when
they had begun dating (figure 12). She did so to transport him to moments and places
that they had shared. As Esther recounted, she hoped that Antonio would value her

sending him "a photograph of [their] love that would not inspire any suspicion" because it showed them only as part of a group of classmates. The photograph would not have revealed the affect behind sharing this "trace" of their courtship to those who did not know them or their relationship. For the sake of their love, she did not "shy away from parting from one of the only portraits [she] had of them together."

The middle school class portrait would be the last photograph Esther would send Antonio. When he had been gone for five years, laboring in the United States with other Mexican immigrants, Esther wanted only to reunite with him in person. Her patience with using this form of documentation to recognize, express, and share her desires and needs for and with Antonio had worn thin. Their long-distance romantic relationship had begun to take an emotional toll; when she was alone she cried more often out of her longing for him. It had become increasingly impossible for her to air her feelings, as she could recognize and discuss her emotional agony with her sisters only when not in the company of her mother. Weary of fueling others' concern, she often opted to keep her heartache over their separation to herself. She did not dare risk that the sight of her emotional pain might lead those most supportive of their relationship to disapprove of her love. Her resentment about the conditions of the Bracero Program had become emotionally devastating. Esther had become exhausted, and she longed for the story of love between her and Antonio to be constituted of much more than carefully crafted photographs.

In 1970, Antonio had saved enough money to marry Esther in an intimate ceremony in Nochistlan. Their marriage celebration confirmed to them and their families and peers that Antonio had honored his commitment to Esther. Overwhelmed with joy, Esther and Antonio embraced their wedding ceremony as a refreshingly public moment of love that they hoped would mark the beginning of sharing countless moments of love together, unseparated by the Bracero Program.

PHOTO STORIES OF LOVE
AS A RESOURCE

Alex and Mary Romero were among the couples who used their affectively charged photographs to create and share a photo story of love that strengthened their family ties and prospect of marriage.[4] In 1932, a few days after having met each other at the onset of the US and Mexican governments' repatriation of an estimated three hundred thousand people of Mexican descent, they exchanged portraits with each other in Los Angeles. Their fear of being separated from each other as a result of this governmental move to curb Mexican immigrant settlement in the United States inspired them to begin a photo story of love immediately after meeting and to marry only two weeks after declaring their love for each other in this fashion. Couples' fear that one of them might be repatriated on a moment's notice or without warning and separated from the other moved women and men in romantic relationships to exchange portraits. This way, they would remain connected emotionally to each other even if they ended up on opposite sides of the US-Mexico border. Their parents were also confident that their exchange of these portraits would create a positive, lasting impression on their partners and families and would facilitate their locating and reuniting with each other.

Mary's mother did not immediately approve of her romantic relationship with Alex. Since they had met in an LA train station, Alex and Mary's families were not familiar with either of them. They had expected them to enter romantic relationships with young people from their own neighborhood. Mary's mother did not welcome her romantic relationship with Alex because his laboring as a farmworker in Azusa, California, did not quite fulfill her plans for her daughter. Having done her best to raise Mary in Los Angeles as a single parent, her mother hoped that Mary would eventually marry a man who worked in a better-paid, skilled trade. Nonetheless, her mother's feelings toward their romantic relationship began to change when Mary shared Alex's portrait with her. He posed in a three-piece suit and dedicated the portrait to Mary. His clear expression of his *cariño* (affection) for Mary revealed the sincerity of his feelings and the polish of his personal sense of style when asserting himself (figure 13). Having exchanged his portrait with her daughter without hesitation also resonated as a quality that met Mary's mother's expectations. Similarly, Alex's parents enthusiastically approved of Mary and their courtship after they set eyes on her portrait (figure 14). His parents estimated that her wearing a refined suit stylishly was but a glimmer of the good character and beauty she possessed. Mary's beautiful portrait, along with Alex's enthusiastic account of her being a kind, responsible, and understanding young woman, earned them his parents' approval of their courtship.

Alex followed up their exchange of portraits by meeting with Mary's mother to ask for her permission to court Mary. This diplomacy moved her mother, as well as his parents, to approve of their marrying even though the couple had known each other for only a couple of weeks. (The parents were afraid that the couple would be unable to date much and would rush into marriage anyway without their approval.) In the winter of 1932, soon after their marriage, Alex and Mary settled in Los Angeles and were most grateful for how the portraits had allowed their love to flourish. In 1942, the inception of the Bracero Program encouraged them to

FIGURE 13.
Self-portrait of Alex Romero, 1932.

provide their own daughters with portraits. They hoped that photographs would enable their daughters and their suitors to similarly advance their romantic relationships. Parents often worked together to use their photo stories of love as examples to their daughters of long-distance romantic relationships across the US-Mexico border.

Parents also used photographs in an attempt to nurture an enduring support network for and among their daughters as they entered romantic relationships with their bracero or undocumented Mexican immigrant boyfriends. Worrying that their daughters would take for granted the affection and support of their siblings, especially their sisters, they requested that their daughters take some photographs posing with each other so that their photo story of love would include and celebrate the women who had been and should continue to be a source of unconditional love

FIGURE 14.
Self-portrait of Mary Romero, 1932.

for them. They hoped that upon contemplating and reflecting on photographs that celebrated their beauty, character, love, and solidarity as a group of sisters, their daughters would be reminded of the family ties and love that they shared and would be more supportive of each other.

Parents embraced the spirit of creating photo stories of love for their daughters as a way of tempering their emotional agony of being in love with men whose contract labor or undocumented Mexican immigrant status in the United States had the potential to make for challenging long-distance romantic relationships. In 1941, heading into the Bracero Program, and in the Mexican state of Jalisco, Katie and Sara Cobla were among the women raised to use their photo story of love to fuel their emotional investment in each other's welfare. These sisters' parents had pooled their earnings to finance their individual portraits and a photograph together (figure 15) so that Katie and Sara had photographs that would remind them of their individual self-worth and the loving bond they shared as sisters.[5]

AN EMOTIONAL YET SOUND PROPOSAL

In November 1964, Veneranda Torres and her eldest daughter Maria Francisca Torres packed their family portraits (figures 16 and 17).[6] These portraits were among their

FIGURE 15.
Family portrait of Sara and Katie Cobla, 1940s.

family's most cherished family photographs, as they had been taken before Jesus Torres, Veneranda's husband and the father of her children, left the family to complete his fourth Bracero Program contract. Having taken these and other portraits to remind each other and their children of the love that had moved them to marry and begin a family together, Jesus and Veneranda had used them to create a photo story of love for each other. Now that they were married, they were a bit more daring in using their

FIGURE 16.
Veneranda Torres, 1959.

personal style in photos to express and remind each other of their love. Veneranda described the portraits as "invaluable traces of him and of their love." They had made for countless restorative moments of love for her and the five children.

The emotional value of their photo story of love compelled Maria Francisca to help her mother wrap and store these portraits as carefully as possible, as she worried that if they were damaged in any way her mother and siblings would be emotionally devastated. The emotional turmoil of being separated from each other for extended periods of time had become too painful for everyone, and Maria Francisca did not dare take for granted the storage of portraits as they prepared to paint their family home before and for their father's return.

Throughout his Bracero Program participation, Jesus had been a responsible provider, husband, and parent as he labored in Delano, Victorville, and Wasco, California. Between 1958 and 1964, upon completing his program contracts, he would return to Veneranda and their children with savings to expand their quite profitable family-run business raising livestock and producing milk and cheese products, including ice cream, for a large distributor. Veneranda's enterprising management and investment of his savings and their business profits had made it

FIGURE 17.
Studio portrait of Veneranda Torres and her children, 1960s.

possible for her to finance raising their children, purchase furniture for their living room and the children's bedrooms, make home repairs, and paint the interior and exterior of their home in preparation for his return and permanent settlement in Acambaro, Guanajuato.

The photo story of love had prevented her from becoming emotionally undone by the overwhelming feeling that their children needed Jesus's constant guidance, as they "missed him terribly." But now Veneranda was determined to ask that Jesus consider leaving contract labor in the United States and settling permanently by their side. She recollected, "I was committed to our permanent family reunification, I dreamed of it." By adorning the very first room Jesus would enter upon his return from the Bracero Program with their photo story of love, Veneranda sought to create a moment of love that would give Jesus the courage to seriously consider her proposal.

Veneranda acknowledged the importance of Jesus's Bracero Program participation and the attendant sacrifices he had made in support of their family's well-being. She was well aware that without his US wages they would not have been able to marry or begin a family or launch a successful business of their own. Worried that Jesus would misinterpret her proposal and think she was underestimating the personal sacrifice he had made in laboring separate from them to earn money, she wanted to get across her own and her children's gratitude for all his emotional and financial investment in their welfare. But she also wanted to inspire him to embrace his family responsibilities in a new light. She was trying to remain true to her feelings and those that had moved her to take the pictures and support his program participation in the first place. Initially, she had agreed to take her portrait so that, irrespective of what happened to either of them when participating in the program, they would have a record of each other to remind them of their love. Now she hoped that the love with which the photos had been taken would prompt Jesus to realize that expecting Veneranda to continue to rely on these portraits to see and feel each other's love for most of the year was unfair to both of them. Reminding him of how much they had loved each other was integral to asserting how much she needed him to be by her side and making her proposal an act of love without questioning his sacrifice or his love for her and their children.

Veneranda was anxious and determined to use everything they had, including the family's photo story, to propose that Jesus settle permanently in Guanajuato. She intuited that as Maria Francisca and their oldest son neared adolescence she would need him physically present to help her parent them properly. She had already endured eight years of marriage that included giving birth and raising their children without him and maximizing their hard-earned savings and profits to build a successful home and business as he participated in the Bracero Program. Yet even as she took heart in having proven herself worthy of making such a serious proposal, she understood that by urging Jesus to prioritize meeting the family's emotional needs she was taking a great emotional risk. Wives of Mexican immigrant men were discouraged from asserting their own desires and needs without much careful forethought. Indeed, they were considered reckless just for being too emotionally invested or in need of their husbands.

Veneranda's particular approach to proposing that Jesus stop participating in the Bracero Program was partly inspired by gender expectations in the Mexican countryside. Veneranda knew that if Jesus decided to not renew his program contract, it had to resonate as a responsible decision before their extended family, customers, and neighbors. If these people doubted the soundness of his decision to stay or cast it as a reckless emotional whim, they could end their business dealings or friendship with the family out of fear that they too would become publicly perceived as reckless women and men. She described "decisions of this sort" as "very decisive and public." So even as Veneranda was firm in proposing that Jesus opt out of the program as an intimate family matter, she recognized that as business proprietors they could not afford for such change in their business management and family life to be publicly understood as strictly an emotional decision. Consequently the painting project and the photo display were aimed at convincing not only Jesus but also customers and neighbors that the healthy state of their children, home, and business no longer required him to participate in the program. Veneranda wanted Jesus to realize that his decision to stay would be publicly understood as a responsible approach to nurturing what they had been able to create as a result of their program participation. Wives' emotional desires and needs had to remain hidden from view or not publicly perceived as the sole reason for Mexican immigrant husbands to opt out of the program.

This was Veneranda's second attempt at using photographs to convince her husband to give up contract labor in the United States (the first was described in the Introduction). The freshly painted family home and the living room display of the photo story of love boosted the family's business sales and drew compliments from relatives, customers, and neighbors. But unfortunately, Veneranda's strategy did not have its main desired effect: that of immediately convincing Jesus to opt out of the Bracero Program to stay by her side. Though Jesus was most appreciative of Veneranda and their children's thoughtfulness, he did not think it prudent financially to forfeit renewing his program contract. Instead, he decided that it was in the family's best interest to persevere through their emotional longing for each other as he contracted for at least another season of harvesting crops in the United States. He thought it a worthwhile sacrifice because continuing in the program would enable them to purchase more equipment for their business. With the right refrigerators and mixers, they would be better equipped for him to stay by their side to run their business without having to overextend themselves physically when preparing their milk and cheese products for sale. The soundness of his decision was of some comfort to Veneranda. It demonstrated his willingness to continue to make the personal sacrifice of separating from them for an indefinite period of time out of his emotional investment in making their day-to-day life easier in the long term. Nonetheless, this did not protect Veneranda or their children from feeling bruised emotionally. Even as they embraced the spirit of the photo story of love that adorned their living room, they could not help grieving and expressing their longing for Jesus by praying for the permanent reunification of their family as soon as possible. Veneranda learned to take "heart in the separation of their family being born out of his love for them."

Jesus did not meet Veneranda's and their children's emotional need to live as a family together until after the termination of the Bracero Program. In 1966, they reunited permanently in Wasco, California. The success of their family business had not persuaded Jesus to settle for living together in Mexico. Instead, he found it most strategic for them to pursue a prosperous future in the United States together. He had been able to save enough money for their family to finance initial entry as undocumented Mexican immigrants harvesting crops together and then to finance the legalization of their immigration status with the help of their US employer.

After six consecutive years of family separation across the US-Mexico border, permanent reunification of their family had become very much a priority for everyone. Despite public criticism against their reuniting as undocumented Mexican immigrants in the United States and accepting life under the constant fear of deportation, their love for each other moved them to take great emotional risk once more. Neither Veneranda nor Jesus could contemplate enduring the pain of being separated from each other much longer. Their yearning for each other and their longing to raise their children together could no longer be quelled by contemplating, crying, and praying before their photo story and forging moments of love when separated.

The emotional turmoil of a long-distance marriage inspired women married to braceros to cautiously assert their longing to reunite with their husbands. Their being married did not make it any easier for these women to express their longing to know more about the whereabouts and plans of their husbands, or to reunite with them permanently. The gender expectation that they hide the emotional work of repeatedly separating from and reuniting with each other left these women depending on photo stories to inspire moments of love during the extended periods of time in which they had to live and raise families on their own, as well as to persuade their husbands to recognize the hardship when considering the renewal of their program contracts.

Married women had to be most resourceful when striving to convince their husbands to opt out of the program and reunite with them. It fell on them to remain true to their feelings without making an already emotionally stressful situation worse. They were expected to endure the pain of separation in silence, and their attitude and conduct throughout their long-distance marriages, unlike their husbands', were used to judge their moral character and sexual virtue. These women could not afford for their emotional desires and needs to cast doubt on their public reputation. Staying behind to capitalize on a bracero husband's savings from the program and to raise the children born out of the marriage was expected of them. The soundness of their judgment was under much public scrutiny and could potentially make fulfilling their obligations more challenging. As Veneranda noted, "waiting in love" was "hard yet underestimated work."

A RESTORATIVE PHOTO STORY OF LOVE

On May 22, 1959, Artemio Guerra de Leon and Maria Graciela Garcia Guerra's respective parents crafted a transnational photo story of love for them in the form of photographs they could display in the comfort of their respective family homes. Like Esther and Antonio and Alex and Mary, these parents created a photo story of love that provided Artemio and Maria with moments of love "that would help them meet their emotional needs."[7] In 1959, Artemio's parents enlisted the services of a professional photographer to begin their photo story of love for him. They convinced Artemio to pose for a portrait of himself wearing his perfectly ironed and washed standard button-up work shirts and dark pants before setting off to clean barns, harvest crops, raise cattle, and stock dry goods merchandise throughout Doctor Coss, Nuevo Leon (figure 18). Deeming it important to document the optimism and work ethic that characterized his day-to-day work life before migrating to the United States in pursuit of a Bracero Program contract or entering into marriage, they wanted to celebrate and remind him of the qualities that had made him an upstanding, hardworking member of their family and Mexican society. For the same reason they also paid for another portrait after he had successfully completed his Mexican government–mandated three-month military service requirement.

Artemio's parents were confident that these photographs would make evident to him the strength of his character, work ethic, and promise when he was undergoing

FIGURE 18.
Self-portrait of Artemio Guerra
de Leon, Mexico, 1950s.

the emotional hardships of his likely migration to the United States and his long-distance courtship of Maria. His parents not only provided him with a photo story that would fuel his emotional endurance but also framed and displayed these portraits in their household's living room. Artemio's easy access to seeing and reflecting on his portraits was intended to make for moments of love that would inspire him to persevere in pursuit of his goals in Mexico or the United States. As Artemio recounted, "My parents' love for me and my future was of great help to me and my love for my then girlfriend and now wife, Maria." In 1960, when Artemio began to court Maria as he began his Bracero Program participation, his parents wanted Maria's parents to learn as much as possible about Artemio by conversing with them and by seeing the photos so that her parents would be reassured that Artemio's contract labor in the United States and temporary separation from Maria were an extension of and consistent with his trajectory of hard work.

In 1961, after completing his first six-month Bracero Program contract, Artemio had not earned or saved enough to marry Maria. But the pain of this realization was made bearable by his seeing and reflecting on his portraits. These portraits provided him with snapshots of his successful completion of responsibilities and tasks that had made it possible for him to contribute financially to their family's welfare, as well as honor his family's commitment to him. He remembers that "they made it less easy for me to forget my potential—what I wanted for myself and Maria." They also moved him to recognize the spirit in which he had worn and worked in the clothes and military uniform used in each of his portraits, and to remember, in restorative moments of love, day-to-day interactions such as working alongside his childhood friends and attending chaperoned social functions with Maria. They gave him much-needed emotional comfort by reconnecting him with the optimism with which he had labored to help his family, shared time with Maria, and established productive friendships before joining the program and separating from Maria and his family.

Protecting Artemio against underestimating or forgetting his experience in Mexico as he confronted his failure to optimize his first Bracero Program contract emerged as a very personal priority for his parents. Fearing that pointing to the program's exploitative conditions as the main reason for his unreadiness to finance his marriage to Maria or to make progress toward other personal goals would be too emotionally painful for everyone, his parents depended instead on their photo story of love of him to let him know that he was not a failure and that his first program contract was not a complete loss. They anticipated that the portraits would move him to have faith in himself and to recognize that participation in the program did not automatically translate into immediate success. Reflection on their photo story of love of him was intended to encourage him to place his failed first contract in perspective with other formative experiences that had required him to remain steadfast in his resolve despite the initial disappointing outcome.

Maria's parents also used portraits of her to craft a photo story of love that would embolden her to remain true to her feelings and potential.[8] They determined that the emotional turmoil of the Bracero Program had made it imperative for their daughter to have a photo story of love in place, a narrative that she could use to experience moments of love that would protect her from becoming emotionally devastated. Providing her with a photo story of love that did not center entirely on her long-distance romantic relationship with Artemio or the outcome of her likely migration to the United States, they sought to meet her emotional needs of having an accessible record of her beauty, strong moral character, and work ethic (figure 19).

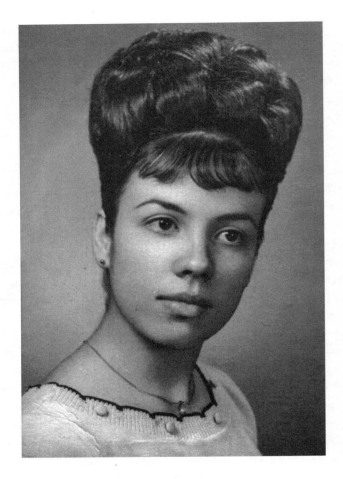

FIGURE 19.
Self-portrait of Maria Graciela Garcia Guerra in Doctor Coss,
Nuevo Leon, Mexico, 1960s.

Maria wanted to migrate to the United States and work there, using her savings to finance her marriage and begin a family of her own with Artemio, as well as to purchase home appliances that would make their day-to-day lives more comfortable. Even as Maria's parents did not oppose this plan, they worried about the longing that would set in as soon as she separated from Artemio.

Like Artemio's parents, Maria's parents used their photo story of love to protect their daughter from becoming overwhelmed emotionally by her feelings of love.

Throughout the Mexican countryside, women who migrated to labor in the United States on their own were often deemed reckless and sexually immoral. It was believed that they would be exposed to obstacles and relationships that would trap them into becoming aggressively assertive and sexually promiscuous. Worried that such attitudes concerning female immigrants would harm Maria's own perception of herself, Maria's parents pooled their earnings to finance portraits that would remind her of the dedicated, self-sacrificing, and optimistic spirit in which she was pursuing her goals. Maria described her parents as "most committed to loving me generously for my sake."

Beginning in 1960, portraits of Maria in beautiful and fashionable hairstyles and dresses and assuming graceful poses among family were at the center of her parents' photo story of love for her. Through these photographs her parents tried to celebrate and remind Maria of how, in the days before her migration to the United States, she had bestowed great care on her appearance, even after a hard day's work. By documenting her beauty and her emotional investment in herself, the photos were intended to encourage Maria to resist becoming indifferent or emotionally devastated by the outcome of her migration or the status of her long-distance romantic relationship.

Because of the risks associated with women's being photographed, some women avoided having their picture taken even when in the company of their friends. This outlook is revealed in the photograph featuring Maria enjoying a social function with Artemio (figure 20). The other young woman featured in this photograph is expressing her refusal to be photographed alongside them by covering her face from the camera. Maria had to be most receptive to her parents' plan of protecting and helping her emotionally by taking and using these photographs.

In 1965, after the Bracero Program ended, Maria began to appreciate the photo story that her parents had made for her. It gave her the courage to separate from Artemio and her family in pursuit of earning and saving US wages as an undocumented immigrant in the United States. Maria explained, "My parents understood and respected my acting out of love and counted on me doing so responsibly." Seven years after completing his first program contract, Artemio was able to secure his US employer's sponsorship and legalization of his US immigration status. This allowed him to labor in the United States for an indefinite period of time, but it did not make it any easier for him to earn and save enough money to marry and begin a family with Maria. His earning sixty cents an hour harvesting crops often barely afforded him enough money to pay for his daily expenses in the United States. Although Maria did not doubt his intention to marry her, she anticipated that if she worked

FIGURE 20.
Maria and Artemio Guerra de Leon sharing a good time
after a date at the movies in Doctor Coss, Nuevo Leon,
Mexico, in the 1960s.

in the United States, even if not alongside Artemio, and they pooled their savings they could most likely afford to reunite and marry earlier in Nuevo Leon with the support of their parents. Seeing and reflecting on her parents' photo story of love for her further fueled her self-confidence to act out of her love for Artemio and her desire to finally share a future with him.

That year, when Maria was working twelve-hour days harvesting crops in Delano and Wasco, California, the emboldening potential of her parents' photo story of love resonated most powerfully with her. After laboring under the scorching sun, wearing clothing that covered every inch of her body except for her face and often only her eyes, Maria searched the recesses of her mind to return to and ultimately see and lose herself in those photos. The portraits of her wearing her favorite dresses and having a good time with family, friends, and Artemio in Mexico evoked distant yet vivid memories and allowed her to contextualize her arduous labor in the United States as just one—not the only—experience defining her life. This realization protected her from becoming overwhelmed emotionally.

Between 1965 and 1967, as Maria labored in Wasco and Delano, California, harvesting grapes and other crops, she was inspired to pose for photographs of herself laboring with her coworkers (figure 21). Documenting experiences that were

FIGURE 21.
Maria Graciela Garcia Guerra, at right, picking fruit in
Delano, California, in May 1966.

difficult to describe and explain but that in her estimation "should never be forgotten" became her way of developing a well-rounded transnational account of her
resilient spirit. She intended for these photographs to make it clear to herself that
she had done everything within her reach to remain true to her feelings so
that whatever the outcome of her migration or her relationship she would not
become too critical of herself. In this use of photographs, she was following her
parents' lead.

For two consecutive years, Maria drew the emotional endurance to labor in the
United States "from every photograph she took and carried with her." These photographs, coupled with the recollections they induced, made her optimistic about
her pursuit of her emotional desires, regardless of the outcome of her migration,
and encouraged her not to underestimate her potential. Laboring in the United States
had required her to stay emotionally whole despite her longing for Artemio and her
family.

In 1967, when Maria returned from laboring in the United States and reunited
with her family, it was difficult for her to share with her parents photographs that

showed her harvesting crops. She chose instead to give them pictures where she was surrounded by coworkers who had become her close friends and where she was facing the camera and smiling. That way, her parents would not dwell on her plain clothes, her labor on bended knee for hours at a time, and the heavy loads of crops that she carried. She feared that these images, which differed so much from the portraits taken before she left to the United States, and the accompanying stories about the conditions of labor she had endured would break her parents' hearts. She also intuited that they might make her parents angry about all she had sacrificed for her relationship with Artemio. It took Maria several months to get up the courage to share with her parents any photographs that showed the physical rigors of her labor, but these were integral to the transnational photo story of love her parents had worked so hard to begin and provide for her.

On March 12, 1967, Artemio and Maria reunited and married in Doctor Coss. They took a wedding portrait together to record this hard-earned moment as part of their shared and individual photo stories of love (figure 22). This portrait became the first professionally taken photograph of them together. It adorned the living rooms of their own and their families' homes. It would prove seminal to their continued documentation of their love when they were separated from their parents. Throughout their marriage, Artemio and Maria's emotional investment in continuing and using their photo story of love was also steeped in their need to remind each other that they valued each other and their shared life together. Like their parents, they embraced the documentation of their time together, so that the photo story of their life together would not consist solely of their laboring to make ends meet. They took photographs to continue to capture traces of their beauty, promise, and resilience and to remain true to their parents' advice: that they not forget but rather document and carry in their hearts and minds that an emotionally fulfilling life was composed of moments that marked accomplishments, character, and the enjoyment of time with loved ones. This made photographs a priority and an essential component in the story of love that Artemio and Maria wrote together.

Artemio and Maria's dedication to maintaining a thoughtful and transnational photo story of love was among the many qualities that made them most generous in conveying to me the range of emotions shaping the mid-twentieth-century Mexican immigrant experience in Mexico and the United States. When sharing their oral life history, they insisted that I learn more about and from their photographs and said I would not otherwise be able to understand their story. Together their photographs told a transnational photo story of love all its own—

FIGURE 22.
Maria Graciela Garcia Guerra and Artemio Guerra de Leon on
their wedding day, March 12, 1967.

a story that reveals that, had they not embraced the spirit behind their parents'
beginning the tradition of sharing these photo stories of love with and for them, it
would have been far more challenging for them to have remained emotionally
invested in their long-distance romantic relationship in Mexico and the United
States.

SUPERVISING THE CREATION OF
PHOTO STORIES OF LOVE

By 1960, throughout the Mexican countryside Mexican mothers started to become
more receptive to paying for at least one portrait of their daughters to nurture a
healthy sense of their self-worth and confidence. This was especially the case among

Mexican mothers left to raise their daughters on their own as their bracero or undocumented Mexican immigrant husbands labored in the United States. Raising their daughters on a tight budget, these women could not afford to craft photo stories of love comprising several photographs and had to derive emotional comfort from single pictures. Being held solely responsible for supervising their daughters' love lives throughout their immigrant father's absence motivated these women to allow their daughters to pose for and use photographs under their close supervision rather than forbid that they use this form of documentation altogether. Pretending that these relationships or photographs did not exist struck them as a far more reckless course of action.

By becoming involved in taking and sharing their daughters' portraits, mothers influenced the style their daughters used to craft their physical appearance, as well as the content of the letters or messages they used to send these photographs to their Mexican immigrant boyfriends. These mothers anticipated that their counsel on these matters would make for prosperous long-distance romantic relationships between their daughters and their Mexican immigrant boyfriends and saw the portraits as integral to such relationships. These women tried to ensure that their daughters' portraits would reflect their beauty, moral character, and work ethic. Protecting their daughters from taking portraits that would expose them to negative public criticism or, in the worst case, public ostracism as a result of too daring a pose, too revealing a dress, or too explicit a message, they wholeheartedly encouraged their daughters to use these portraits to create photo stories of love that were beautiful yet discreet, and to share them with their boyfriends if they had proven sincere in their courtship. With much sacrifice, mothers sought to provide their daughters with portraits that would fuel their self-confidence, allow them to remain emotionally connected to their Mexican-immigrant boyfriends, and protect them from being publicly perceived as recklessly aggressive women.

In 1962, twenty years into the Bracero Program, Esperanza Rodriguez was among the mothers who became involved in this way. Her daughter Ramona wanted to give a portrait to her boyfriend, Salvador Frias, and Salvador's plans to go to the United States to labor as an undocumented immigrant had finally led Esperanza to yield to her daughter's wish. Her concern that Ramona might take too daring a portrait or that it might end up in the wrong hands motivated her to take an active part in the proceedings.[9] After having saved what amounted to two weeks' worth of her earnings harvesting crops, Esperanza agreed to pay for the portrait. She approved of the couple's courtship and had consented to their writing each other

FIGURE 23.
Self-portrait of Ramona Frias, 1960s.

during their separation but did not want Ramona mailing her portrait to Salvador because she feared the photograph might be intercepted and used by the Mexican and US governments to detect or deport him, a turn of events that would upset her absent bracero husband upon his return. Consequently Esperanza made certain that Ramona and Salvador exchanged their portraits with each other before his departure to the United States (figures 23 and 24). She also insisted that Ramona pose for her portrait wearing her favorite dress and a serious expression to instill a shared sense of responsibility with regard to the discretion and respect each deserved. Esperanza sought to supervise as many aspects of Ramona's photographs as possible.

Esperanza knew that her close supervision of Ramona and Salvador's photo story of love did not mean that she had nothing more to worry about. She feared that

FIGURE 24.
Self-portrait of Salvador Frias, 1960s.

despite the couple's love for each other any misstep by either would ruin Ramona's public reputation and her own reputation as a parent, as well as the couple's future prospects of a romantic relationship. Ramona shared that her "mother's love moved [her] to be most vigilant when following her instructions without question."

For Mexican couples to have photo stories of love that they created for each other or that, increasingly over time, their parents created for them to a certain degree spared them from breaking down under the emotional exhaustion of the Bracero Program. These photo stories revealed to them dimensions of their love and their long-distance romantic relationships that only they knew. Once we begin to consider those dimensions in relationship to their own and their families' oral life histories, we start to see the documentation of love as generative emotional work that transcended the US-Mexico border. It suggests the value of considering as well other risks, strategies, and relationships these children, women, and men used to deal with the emotional consequences of the Bracero Program and its legacies in Mexico and the United States while remaining first and foremost true to their feelings.

PART THREE   ·   DECISIVE MEASURES

CHAPTER SEVEN

Awake Houses and *Mujeres Intermediarias* (Intermediary Women), 1958–1964

The Bracero Program was targeted at men with families. Its administrators believed that affective ties across borders would guarantee that contract laborers would return home on the expiration of their contracts. The program ripped families apart but promised them eventual reunification. It promoted the feelings of longing and loss that permeated popular songs, love letters, and staged family photographs. In order to contain the effects of the emotions it provoked—to prevent women from crossing the border and to preclude workers from returning home prematurely—the program policed Mexican families. Postal officials read letters between loved ones, refusing to deliver missives that might promote what they judged to be premature reunification. On the US side of the border, local officials virtually quarantined contract laborers in their migrant camps, limiting the mobility that might provoke desires to establish new families in a new country. In Mexican towns, relatives of contract laborers were socially stigmatized and found their economic strategies frustrated by newly exploitive labor conditions.

Yet Mexican workers and their families were not passive victims. As this chapter demonstrates, the state's manipulative exploitation of family ties generated unexpected outcomes. As women and children in Mexico found themselves forced to inhabit new roles, they developed active strategies that fundamentally changed the form of the families they sought to preserve. Women not only filled new jobs outside the home but became managers of family finances and initiators of family businesses. They left their homes to pursue educational opportunities to equip themselves with the skills needed to cope with the economic obstacles their families faced. Perhaps most important, they formed "awake houses" (*casas despiertas*), consciousness-raising collectives in which the problems facing individual women could be addressed as stemming from shared gender and class vulnerabilities. The language of love, loss, and longing that the Bracero Program's disruptions of family life provoked sounds traditional in every respect. Yet under conditions of dynamic transformation and change, preservation of putatively traditional gender and family roles required their radical transformation.

On October 26, 1958, Ignacia Zarate Mandujano Rios came together with other Mexican women eager to transition out of their emotional exhaustion. Her strong reputation for acting in support of heart-weary women had earned an invitation to Rosa Ramirez's family home.[1] Several married women between the ages of twenty and sixty-six in San Martin de Hidalgo, Jalisco, Mexico, had requested that Ignacia join them to share her advice on how to overcome their fatigue with being married to a bracero or undocumented Mexican immigrant man as part of an awake house. In striving to remain true to the spirit of an awake house, a house in which women tried to act in support of each other out of their solidarity for each other, Ignacia took this invitation seriously.

Ignacia was one of many Mexican women who emerged as *intermediarias*, or intermediary women, although they did not formally identify themselves as such. These were women of extraordinary courage, endurance, and vision who, upon frankly assessing the consequences of the Bracero Program, tried to respond to these consequences. Acting as go-betweens for receptive children, women, and men, they initiated and facilitated women's difficult conversations with each other and with other family members, including their bracero relatives, with the aim of finding remedies for the emotional exhaustion that the burdens and separations of the program had caused.

Five years after Mexican women's suffrage, and sixteen years into the Bracero Program, these women did not appeal to the US or Mexican governments for support or hold them explicitly accountable for their exhaustion. Instead, they acted on their own to bring women together in the comfort of their family homes to listen and talk to each other and to collaborate with one another to improve their emotional welfare. Their concern moved them to dare to initiate spaces, conversations, collaborations, educational programming, and training for skilled employment conducive to bringing children and women together to derive much-needed emotional strength from each other. This emotional work paved the way for their creation and maintenance of awake houses and other productive spaces throughout the Mexican countryside.

Intermediarias encouraged women to be candid with each other about their fatigue caused by the fragile state of their marriages and the stresses of their other family obligations. Ignacia believed firmly that one voice could help transform a family home or any other space into an awake house, and therefore she treated earnestly each invitation. She "did not dare take women—their time, trust, pain, and work—for granted, knowing it all too well." Women like her described these spaces as awake houses, but this was not a formally recognized title or designation. Rather, *casa despierta* became a term widely used among women when describing these spaces. This term was most appropriate for capturing that these spaces were meant to inspire reflection on how being married to a bracero or undocumented Mexican immigrant and heading a household with hardly any emotional support was exhausting emotional work for children and women. Ignacia did not discount that marriage had always been challenging for women and men, but she recognized that when this personal relationship stretched across the US-Mexico border as a result of the two governments' implementation of a binational contract labor program, marriage became "a far more fragile emotional connection to sustain." Her own marriage to a bracero, Ramon Rea Rios, and her estimation of other women's emotional suffering and the instability of their marriages as a result of the Bracero Program influenced Ignacia to become part of an awake house as an *intermediaria* who was emboldened to listen to women's feelings honestly and responsibly.

Beginning in 1958, sixteen years into the US and Mexican governments' implementation of the Bracero Program, the emotional strain of the constant separation of their families across the US-Mexico border similarly emboldened women from the Mexican rural towns of San Martin de Hidalgo and Ameca, in Jalisco, and Acambaro, in Guanajuato (two Mexican states aggressively targeted for program participation), to confront the program as *intermediarias*. These courageous women forged restorative sites to initiate, share, and benefit from refreshingly frank conversations. Drawing on the oral life histories, writing, and careers of *intermediarias* who acted on behalf of and in support of families across the Mexican countryside, this chapter analyzes the emotional exhaustion, courage, and influence of *intermediarias* and their establishment and participation in awake houses, and explores Rosa de Castaño's creation of the play *Braceros: Mojados* as a similarly intermediary act.

The mostly young women who became *intermediarias* decided to take their potential seriously by seeking better-paid skilled employment in accounting, banking, custom tailoring, nursing, teaching, or other areas of interest. Confronting their family's situation honestly, they had the spirit to acknowledge that they had a future to protect. They dared not explicitly justify their actions as an outcome of anger, anxiety, desperation, frustration, or emotional exhaustion resulting from the Bracero Program or the decisions of their Mexican-immigrant relatives and families because they needed their families' permission and support to attend a trade or vocational school program, gain skilled employment, and open the family home to other women in the form of an awake house. These women excelled at being daring yet generously responsible daughters, sisters, and wives. Ignacia explained, "We cared about and prioritized being there for each other responsibly."

IGNACIA ZARATE MANDUJANO RIOS: A DARINGLY RESPONSIBLE *INTERMEDIARIA*

On August 26, 1958, at thirty-four years of age, Ignacia Zarate Mandujano Rios suggested to Rosa and the other twenty women in attendance at their meeting in San Martin de Hidalgo that they keep meticulous records of their expenditures, write regularly to their bracero or undocumented Mexican immigrant husbands to receive helpful information on their progress and plans, and share candid conversations about feeling emotionally exhausted with their parents or other relatives who had already proven supportive of them. Realizing that deciding on actions that would help them face their emotional exhaustion was in itself emotionally arduous work, she did not impose her expectations or views on women who had braved forming part of an awake house. She understood the courage it took for women to allocate time from their already hectic schedules to admit that they deserved and needed each other's support when facing an emotional exhaustion that usually went unacknowledged. She recollected, "Accepting hard and painful truths even among women in similar family situations was extremely difficult emotional work." Conceptualizing women's awakening to their need for each other's emotional support as a gradual process, Ignacia deemed it most productive to share strategies with these women to help them immediately cope with their problems. She was confident that the peace of mind that ensued would stir an emotionally restorative awakening among these women.

When striving at these meetings to assert her role as an *intermediaria* in support of women, Ignacia prioritized recognizing and responding to the stress of assuming the head-of-household role. These women had made household decisions without the support of their absent partners, and they faced the consequences of the decisions that their husbands, as household heads, had made, often without consulting them. To Ignacia, this was an urgent matter. Unwilling to risk criticizing their husbands, or to question women about the decisions that were most challenging for them to make, carry out, or deal with on their own, she advised the women to maintain meticulous records of both the expenditures that informed their decisions and the outcomes of their decisions. Maintaining transparent records of their finances would make it easier for them to consider this information when making decisions, as well as when sharing this information with their husbands.

In response to the emotional devastation of being in marriages and raising children without much emotional support from their partners, Ignacia recommended that women make and implement decisions that adhered to gender expectations without becoming emotionally drained. She specifically recommended that they consider their children's feelings when making decisions or facing the outcome of their husbands' decisions, as well as when delegating to their eldest children, in moderation, certain household chores, tasks associated with the operation of their businesses, and care of younger children. Urging women to help preserve children's affection for their absent fathers and to help children understand that their fathers' absences made for a stressful family situation that required more of them, she emphasized that it was up to them to "truly protect our children by loving them unconditionally." *Intermediarias* made women aware of the importance of sharing and discussing their feelings with their children, who needed to be alerted to the emotional rigors and gender expectations of accommodating to a most unfair family separation. This way, their children would not grow resentful of them or their fathers.

During these meetings, Ignacia dedicated much of her time to encouraging emotionally exhausted women to consider initiating honest conversations with their bracero and undocumented Mexican immigrant husbands. For instance, she urged women not to allow their anxiety over making their husbands uncomfortable to discourage them from writing them letters to pose important questions about their plans for return. She encouraged them to consider that it was in their family's best interest and "their obligation to themselves and their marriage" that they attempt to establish communication, even if letters hardly ever reached their destinations. Letter writing in pursuit of relevant information would give them some much-needed peace of mind.

Ignacia concluded her facilitation of what, even in the company of receptive women, were difficult meetings by urging the women to confide in their parents, or in other relatives who had already proven supportive of them, that their marriages had drained them emotionally. Seeking out emotional support from their family was crucial if they were to successfully pursue an education and transition into employment opportunities that would prevent them from becoming completely demoralized by the instability of their marriages and the obligations of heading their households, and family cooperation might be helpful in many practical arrangements to make these changes easier. Ignacia recommended that women share with their family whatever proposals they thought would make it less emotionally exhausting for them to undertake their head-of-household obligations. Convincing their loved ones not only of the depth of their emotional pain but also of the seriousness of their commitment to improve everyone's well-being struck her as the most productive approach to these conversations.

Ignacia recognized that it was hard for women to admit that they needed emotional support and to seek it from family members, since women were expected to stoically confront difficult situations for the sake of their families. If they were married to braceros, they were supposed to accept that their husbands would eventually earn enough money to settle permanently by their side and that their decision to constantly migrate to and from the United States was well intentioned, a desperate response to the lack of well-paying employment opportunities in Mexico. Meanwhile, wives were expected to endure anger, fatigue, loneliness, and sadness honorably and in silence. Ignacia had found, however, that breaking this silence and initiating honest conversations could be a most productive outcome. Before bidding each woman goodbye, and in anticipation of their next meeting, she emphasized that it would be most emotionally restorative for them to pursue meeting with supportive relatives, as they had with other women in this awake house, to express that they needed their support to transition into a less stressful situation.

EMBOLDENING MOMENTS

Ignacia's impetus to act as an *intermediaria* between emotionally exhausted women had been years in the making. Her personal investment in encouraging women to confront their emotional pain was fueled by her recollections of the importance of having shared frank conversations about her feelings with her own parents, Jose and Guadalupe Zarate Mandujano. Had she not had the courage to share with them that excelling as an overburdened head of household to accommodate the constant migration of her bracero husband, Ramon, was crippling her emotionally, they would not have been motivated to support her successful transition into skilled employment in teaching at their local elementary school, La Escuela Rural Niños Héroes of San Martin de Hidalgo.

The first time Ignacia had dared to share her feelings with her parents was in December 1944. She had invited her parents to enjoy an early dinner that took her hours to prepare. In the midst of cooking this meal, she had broken down in tears at least three times. But she had finally mobilized her courage and shared with her parents that her marriage to Ramon had become too exhausting for her and that neither her wages from unskilled labor nor Ramon's savings had enabled her to comfortably care for her children. Two years into the marriage, she felt disconnected from Ramon, anxious because of her inability to meet the basic needs of her family on her own with very limited emotional or financial support from him, and frustrated at the thought of her marriage becoming a permanent long-distance relationship as a result of Ramon's repeated renewals of his Bracero Program contract. It had all made for a burden that she could no longer carry in silence. Learning that she was pregnant for the second time, and recognizing that Ramon's savings after having labored in the United States had not improved their finances, Ignacia felt angry, sad, and tired. Her breakdown in the presence of her parents finally revealed to her that it was far more likely that she would derive emotional comfort and eventual financial relief from better-paid, skilled employment in elementary school teaching than from her meager unskilled worker's wages. Years later, when readying herself to meet with women as part of an awake house, she remembered the restorative qualities of discussing her harsh reality with her parents. It had been her and her parents' honest assessment of her emotional welfare that had inspired her to undertake meaningful work for wages that would make it financially feasible to care for her children and manage her household without becoming devastated by the burden of her family's program participation. Improving her earning potential was an important step toward eventually having some peace of mind.

Ignacia and her parents had determined that she could greatly improve her wages as an elementary school teacher, as she stood to earn 350 pesos a month, compared with the 100 pesos she earned helping them prepare food items for sale and washing and ironing other people's clothes. Once Ignacia decided on this step, she felt less overwhelmed by the financial burden of Ramon deciding to renew his program contract. She felt that without the love of her parents she would have been "unable to face such a difficult family situation."

One reason that Jose and Guadalupe were so unconditionally supportive of Ignacia was their own familiarity with the tumultuousness of her marriage. It was hard for them to overlook that in 1943, two weeks into their marriage, Ramon had decided to separate from Ignacia to join the Bracero Program. Upon learning of the program, he convinced her that his working in the United States temporarily and earning US wages would bolster his earning potential and facilitate his transition into marriage; while well intentioned, this had broken their daughter's heart. As Jose and Guadalupe saw it, Ramon's separation from Ignacia so early into their marriage, and her learning of her being pregnant with their first child shortly after his departure, had paved the way to her emotional exhaustion.

Jose and Guadalupe's resolve to act in support of Ignacia was also fueled by their assessment of Ramon's unwillingness to risk settling permanently in San Martin de Hidalgo. They feared that he would continue to pursue Bracero Program participation, as he had done with one contract after another. Between 1943 and 1946, Ramon had labored for eleven months in the United States, returning periodically but never staying. He insisted that raising their children required contract renewal, urging Ignacia to understand that they could not afford to forgo US wages. His failure to consider Ignacia's emotional exhaustion when renewing his contract after spending barely a month with her and their children heightened Jose and Guadalupe's interest in helping their daughter face what they feared would be the long-term separation of her family. Jose and Guadalupe intuited that they could not rely on Ramon's eventual return to permanent settlement. They decided to be as considerate of Ignacia's emotional pain as possible.

UNCONDITIONAL SUPPORT

In September 1945, Jesus and Guadalupe were among many parents who were emotionally supportive of their daughters' completing vocational education. After having discussed with Ignacia the fragile state of her emotional well-being, they did not waver in their support of her becoming eligible for a well-paid teaching position at their local elementary school. Their enthusiasm for the idea motivated her to apply for admission to the Instituto Vocacional San Angel, located in Sayula, Jalisco. Upon applying, she joined single, middle-class women between the ages of seventeen and twenty-nine who also prioritized pursuing academic degrees and vocational credentials. Since the inception of the program, the enrollment of women from San Martin de Hidalgo in surrounding towns' vocational institutes throughout the Mexican state of Jalisco had increased from 30 to 120. Most of these women wrote in their applications that they had applied because they were committed to accommodating the absence of immigrant men responsibly, asserting that they were among the most qualified to pursue teaching and other service credentials because of their educational and family backgrounds. Unlike Ignacia, these women were earning vocational credentials as a preemptive measure, not a matter of necessity. Additionally, their middle-class parents were better prepared to pay for them to live near these vocational institutes under the supervision of relatives and friends. This way, women avoided the exhaustion of long commutes to school, as well as public suspicions of their possible interactions with men during their commute.

With a child in tow and another on the way, Ignacia wrote a different kind of vocational institute admission application, asserting that she needed to complete an education and achieve skilled employment to pay for her dependent children's care. Applications helped admission committees determine a student's overall purpose and support networks. It was Ignacia's obligation to prove that her children would be cared for adequately and would not distract her from her studies. Vocational institutes were strict about whom they trained, as they did not want their reputation to deteriorate. Hence, before applying, Ignacia and her parents carefully structured her transition into schooling and skilled employment, setting up child care arrangements and an employment schedule in advance so that she could describe these to the vocational institute and confirm that she had the support network in place to excel as a student, parent, and wife.

In January 1946, Ignacia's application was approved. The vocational institute was located a couple of hours away by car from San Martin de Hidalgo, so she would need to relocate temporarily to this town with her mother and children by her side. Moved by her application, and especially by her sketch of the sacrifices she and her parents had made for her education, the vocational institute's clergy agreed to house her under the auspices of their town church.

Although Ignacia helped Guadalupe clean, cook, and care for her children, her mother undertook most of this work so that Ignacia could attend courses and complete demanding course work and related activities successfully. Jose provided financial support toward payment of her tuition fees and visited occasionally to deliver Ramon's remittances personally. Ignacia's household management and pursuit of an education were contingent on their all acting in support of each other. Out of consideration for everyone's welfare, Ignacia attended her classes, prepared and vended food items after school hours, helped her mother care for her children, and completed homework assignments efficiently.

Once Ignacia had earned her teaching credential in September 1949, her commitment to acting as an *intermediaria* grew. After her mother's death, her father remained committed to his daughter's success. Even as he recovered from poor health, he cared for Ignacia's children so she could teach early mornings and afternoons. Jose remained steadfast in his support of her thriving as a parent, wife, and teacher. His unwavering optimism and the emotional comfort she derived from earning higher wages made it possible for her to adapt to Ramon's constant migration with less emotional and financial stress. Ramon temporarily returned several times from laboring in the Bracero Program, and he paid for a few months' expenses and regularly sent remittances, but he refused to settle down, always confident that another stint in the United States would bolster his potential for long-term settlement. His absence and their growing emotional disconnection from each other were still painful for Ignacia, especially coupled with the pain of her mother's passing and her recognition of her father's fragile health. But she persevered in refusing to become emotionally overwhelmed. Her improved financial situation had inspired her to consider continuing her education. After months of teaching, she learned that her teaching credential restricted her to elementary school teaching; applying for better-paid, middle school teaching positions that would allow her to work longer hours required another year of course work. Having already successfully collaborated with her parents emboldened Ignacia to go further in enhancing her earning potential while also acting as an *intermediaria* for other women.

In October 1950, Ignacia began her advanced educational training in collaboration with other women who were doing the same thing. Ignacia proved to be a most helpful *intermediaria* among these women. It was important for others in their lives to understand that these women's pursuit of an education was a responsible measure and not a distraction from their head-of-household obligations to their children or marriage. With so much at stake and despite his poor health, Jose continued to play a formative role in Ignacia's, and now these women's, further accreditation. He would drive them to and from their assigned vocational institute to prevent public misunderstandings that might arise if they commuted alone. Under his supervision, their commutes were accepted as solely intended to advance their education, earning potential, and management of their household obligations. Additionally, Jose purchased a *sevillana* (shawl worn over women's head and shoulders) for Ignacia to wear when traveling to and from the vocational institute because wearing a *sevillana* commanded respect. Jose advised Ignacia that "even though she was accompanied she bore much responsibility." Out of respect for her father's counsel, she counseled her colleagues to do the same. The need to protect each other from unwanted forms of public scrutiny inspired her to be as honest in her advice as possible. Striving to be a supportive *intermediaria* for these women meant helping them adhere to gender expectations while achieving goals that could improve their emotional welfare.

In May 1953, with each other's and Jose's unconditional support, Ignacia and her colleagues secured accreditation. Now they could work mornings and afternoons in San Martin de Hidalgo's schools, teaching various academic subjects. This combination of teaching positions made it feasible for them to earn enough to cover the basic needs of their families, household expenses, operating costs for the preparation and vending of food items from their homes, and any outstanding loan agreements incurred to help finance the migration of their bracero or undocumented Mexican immigrant husbands. Ignacia's awareness that she would not have secured such well-paid employment without the unconditional support of her father and colleagues made her even more determined to act as an *intermediaria* in support of more women and to take her potential as an *intermediaria* seriously.

AN AWAKE CLASSROOM

In 1955, with Jose's continued aid, Ignacia began to expand her support of emotionally exhausted women. She used her second-grade classroom to host and lead after-school meetings with the children of emotionally exhausted women so that they had a time to themselves to discuss how they were feeling and what was proving most difficult when supporting their mothers during the absence of their bracero or undocumented Mexican immigrant fathers. Respectful of the intimate bond between these children and their parents, she did not encourage these students to criticize their parents but rather reassured them that if they were a bit more understanding and tried to help their parents, their parents would gradually regain their optimism and energy. The mothers or other relatives entrusted to care for these students had to consent to their participation in these after-school meetings, and they were informed of the goals behind gatherings and provided with progress reports upon their request. Teaching, reaching out, and refusing to underestimate the emotional toll of the Bracero Program on children and women became an integral dimension to her acting as an *intermediaria* between her students and their emotionally exhausted mothers.

In 1957, Ignacia expanded these efforts even further. With the support of fellow teachers, she coordinated and participated in neighborhood cleanup campaigns, school cleanup drives, and student recognition events to boost the morale of her students and their mothers or other caretakers entrusted to look after them. She and her fellow teachers anticipated that collaborating to clean classrooms, front porches, and stoops of family homes would make it easier for everyone to enjoy healthy spaces without becoming emotionally or physically overwhelmed and would remind everyone of the benefits of focusing on what they could do together as a way to cope with their emotional pain. It also strengthened Ignacia's resolve to uphold these hard-earned lessons when parenting her own children and to participate in meetings in which emotionally exhausted women sought her counsel.

Although Ignacia remained committed to her marriage and her children, Ramon's decision to prolong laboring in the United States made these meetings personally meaningful for her as well as for the women she counseled. In 1963, her father's passing made an awake house in which women frankly shared their feelings with each other an emotionally restorative space for her. Ramon's constant migration to and from the United States under the promise of eventual settlement and their failure to use contraceptives had also resulted in unplanned pregnancies. She kept writing letters to him to learn more about his whereabouts and plans so that they did not become completely estranged from each other, but meeting with women in the awake house reminded her of her ability to raise their seven children without becoming overwhelmed.

Accepting women's invitations to share her experience and advice with them as they struggled to transition out of their emotional exhaustion was most helpful to Ignacia. Ramon was consistent and responsible about sending remittances to contribute to the family's welfare, and she derived some emotional comfort from this, but the fact that the two of them had to lead separate lives for over fifty years, as they did not permanently reunite until 1995, was made bearable primarily by her meeting with other women to act as an *intermediaria*. Everyone recognized that it was crucial to not dwell on what they did not have or what they had lost as a result of the Bracero Program's separation of their families. Coming together to discuss this source of enduring emotional pain more productively and to inspire even married women with children to work toward meaningful goals that could improve their day-to-day lives prevented them from becoming paralyzed by resentment, sadness, and loss. Throughout the years, the honesty with which Ignacia strove to act as an *intermediaria* made forging and sharing an awake house with these women emotionally restorative for her.

AZUCENA LOPEZ: EMOTIONAL COURAGE AND THE FORGING OF AN AWAKE HOUSE

On the evening of May 30, 1959, after having met with women like Ignacia as part of an awake house in Ameca, Jalisco, nineteen-year-old Azucena Lopez embraced the goal of confronting the emotional exhaustion of the Bracero Program for her and her family's sake.[2] She had been inspired by these women's advice to use the intensity of her family's emotional pain as a personal incentive toward initiating a conversation on the subject with her bracero father, Domingo Lopez. She explained, "I learned that I could not afford to shy away from tough emotional work. That was a much too dangerous course to take." She hoped that if she frankly admitted to her father that she was exhausted by the family's participation in the program and feared he was too, the conversation could help to overcome their estrangement.

As she recollected, "I owed it to our family and myself." The prospect of improving their father-daughter relationship and, in turn, the emotional welfare of their family influenced Azucena to act as an *intermediaria* between herself and her father and siblings.

Domingo had not abandoned or neglected Azucena or her three younger siblings, Paul, Miguel, and Ricardo. From 1944 to 1957, when undertaking his contract labor in the United States, he would either send them remittances or return with savings to finance a few months' worth of their household expenses. Throughout the separation of their family, Domingo had tried his best to lend them financial support, but with each of his successive contracts, connecting with them emotionally had become harder for him to do. In 1956, the passing of their mother, Laura Lopez, had further diminished the family's ability to confide their feelings in each other. Wary of overburdening each other, they repeatedly separated and reunited without admitting that the passing of their mother, the absence of their father, and Azucena's being left to act as a head of household at such a young age had created a painful silence among them. Nonetheless, the emotional exhaustion had become too unbearable for Azucena; she finally risked bringing their family together to reconnect with each other as a decisive step toward their recovery from the emotional turmoil of the Bracero Program.

Azucena shared with Domingo that his having "returned an emotionally bruised man from his last Bracero Program contract had made for an emotionally devastating family situation." He hardly ever talked to her or her siblings about his feelings, family finances, or plans for their continued collaboration, thereby making evident his growing indifference to the emotional welfare of their family. Having acted as the head of household throughout her father's absence, Azucena was particularly troubled that he did not discuss with her the family's financing of day-to-day expenses. Domingo preferred to keep his feelings and plans to himself, which made Azucena anxious, sad, and tired. As his daughter, she was also burdened by gender expectations that discouraged daughters from questioning the decisions of their fathers or initiating conversations on family finances with them. Hence, Azucena was most cautious when sharing her feelings with her father. Despite the emotionally restorative potential of establishing an awake house, she knew it would be tough emotional work for their family.

Azucena decided to recommend that her father consider allocating some of their energy, money, and time to her completion of an education that would make her eligible for skilled employment in accounting in Ameca, Jalisco. She felt that a skilled and well-paid job would help her to remain an optimistic and productive member of their family. She also anticipated that her success in achieving this goal would motivate her siblings to do the same and would make it possible for their family to avoid further separations across the border. Her careful consideration of the family's emotional state had made evident that their constant separation from each other was at the heart of their disconnection and her father's indifference toward the future of their family.

Azucena had found that listening to each other generously was integral to the work of the women she had met with to forge and benefit from an awake house three nights earlier. Therefore, she did not want to startle her father into this conversation, which was to be especially delicate because his own exhaustion had intensified her emotional suffering. Instead, she prepared a cup of coffee and his favorite pastry, *empanadas azucaradas,* to entice him to listen to her feelings and to share the source of his anxiety and sadness with her. Confronting such a sensitive family situation together would require Domingo to be receptive and forthcoming. Azucena also wanted to share the importance of their family becoming personally invested in her transition into adulthood. The despair that had accentuated the seemingly permanent dark circles under her father's eyes and the wrinkles framing his forehead and jawline influenced her to share her proposal in a way that would help him see that their emotional suffering had become too much for both of them to bear in silence. Azucena intuited that beyond his parental concern for her emotional well-being, the dramatic deterioration in Domingo's own demeanor and mood after his completion of thirteen consecutive Bracero Program contracts without significantly improving the family's financial welfare would motivate her father to listen and respond to her generously.

After Azucena and her father had admitted their exhaustion to each other, Azucena learned that Domingo had already taken steps of his own toward addressing the issue. He admitted to her that his own exhaustion had moved him to leave the Bracero Program for good so that he could *reposar* (rest) and finally focus on being a good father to her and her siblings by their side. Although she was immediately struck by and grateful for his having taken such a critical first step toward their family's emotional recovery on his own, Azucena came to value most the fact that he shared his frank assessment of the program with her. His candid discussion of how the program's conditions had harmed his ability to be an emotionally supportive father resonated as an invaluable, productive step toward their improving their family's welfare in the short and long term. Domingo embraced his need to remove himself from the program so that he could eventually transition into emotionally reconnecting with her and her siblings. He agreed with her that he needed to do more for their family now that they were finally in one place together, thereby laying the foundations for mutual emotional support through a most difficult transition out of the program. Domingo recognized his recruitment into the Bracero Program as a source of enduring emotional pain for him and his family. He explained that the exhaustion of laboring in the fields of Fresno, California, was not as devastating as the emotional shocks that the program had inflicted on him.

Although Azucena did not call herself an *intermediaria*, it was not lost on Domingo that his daughter was striving to be receptive and forthcoming in listening to him, and he considered her initiation of a conversation that her younger siblings were too young to share a responsible intermediary act on behalf of the family. His immediate appreciation for his daughter's emotional maturity influenced him to tell her that the Bracero Program's selection and renewal procedures, conducted with the utmost disregard for his humanity, were a most lingering emotional wound for him. He told Azucena that he could not forget the shame of being required to answer personal questions; sign forms he did not have a chance to read or did not understand; strip to varying degrees of nudity to undergo humiliating photographs, physical examinations, and delousing procedures; and be corralled into large, open-air waiting areas as part of an assembly line of Mexican men managed by women and men of Mexican descent in Empalme, Sonora, Mexico.

The feeling that he had grown to identify Mexican women as a source of danger, especially women employed to enforce these processing procedures as administrative assistants, nurses, and secretaries, haunted him most. Not being able to trust that Mexican women administering the program would have some respect for Mexican men's humanity, he feared that Azucena might follow in these women's footsteps out of her desperate need for well-paid, skilled work. The zeal with which these women had asked him intrusive questions concerning his sexuality and assisted doctors in their physical examination of his body had been publicly humiliating and shocking. Each time he underwent such mistreatment at the hands of Mexican women he was emotionally devastated by his and their compliance with a degrading program. Azucena explained, "My father was tormented by his recollections of such procedures." That emotional pain that had made it difficult for him to approach his life and family relationship with optimism.

Domingo explained to Azucena that the similar contracting procedures that he subsequently went through in the United States had intensified his emotional suffering. His experiences at US contracting centers revealed to him that the Mexican American women and men who administered the procedures valued not his humanity but his silence. During the contracting process in El Centro, California, Domingo, like his fellow prospective braceros, was never allowed to speak unless he was answering a question posed by the Mexican American women and men implementing contracting procedures. These individuals watched over the prospective braceros as they waited to be escorted into large rooms so that US employer representatives could inspect them and determine their physical eligibility for work. Hours of being under these women and men's humiliating supervision and custody without ever being treated as a human being had made him feel deep shame and sadness for accepting such mistreatment out of his financial desperation. Unable to resist or avoid such employment practices, he found it difficult to shift into a healthy state of mind during and after a program contract. His disappointment with himself and with the reluctance of both governments and the Mexican and Mexican American women and men who worked for those governments to improve the program's conditions had depleted Domingo's spirits to the point that he had become emotionally distant from his family. He admitted to Azucena that it was difficult for him to transition out of the mood occasioned by his mistreatment when he reunited with her and her siblings. It was actually difficult for him just to cope.

Domingo concluded his discussion of his feelings by admitting to Azucena that her and her siblings' labor exploitation at the hands of local families in their Mexican hometown of Ameca had been an enduring source of emotional pain for him. That pain led him to invest willingly in her plan to obtain a trade school education in accounting. His continuing failure to save enough money from the Bracero Program to remove his children from unskilled labor for the families who had lent him money for Bracero Program expenses had filled him with much heartbreak and shame. Those families often employed his children to clean their homes, harvest their crops, and deliver heavy items door to door for at least six consecutive hours a day without affording them even five-minute breaks. His inability to protect them from that mistreatment had infuriated him. But now, he said, the fact that Azucena had persevered in pursuing an education for herself and her siblings and had come to him to collaborate with him in improving the emotional welfare of their family was a source of emotional comfort that made her most worthy of his unconditional support. His interest in honoring her generous care of their family moved him to finally express his deep appreciation for her courage in initiating a most emotionally restorative conversation with him.

Facing the reality that hardly anyone had thought of them as worthy of humane treatment on either side of the US-Mexico border made it feasible for Azucena and Domingo to experience and share an awakening to each other's emotional exhaustion. Azucena admitted to him that indeed it had been emotionally exhausting to accept being exploited by hometown families for the sake of repaying Domingo's debt in his absence and in silence. The conversation energized Azucena and Domingo to prioritize collaborating in support of her transition into skilled employment in accounting so that she could move out of the poorly paid, unskilled employment opportunities otherwise awaiting her on either side of the US-Mexico border.

The comfort that Azucena and Domingo derived from having confronted the sources behind their emotional exhaustion inspired them to pursue maintaining an awake house. They agreed that taking a break from their hectic schedules to share conversations would prevent them from taking each other's efforts for granted and would be foundational to a healthy family life. Unfortunately, Domingo could not afford for Azucena or her siblings to dedicate themselves exclusively to their education because he had no one else to depend on when operating their store, but he continued to help finance their basic needs and tuition fees. And his continued reliance on Azucena to act as an *intermediaria* between him, her, and her siblings made their collaboration to promote the welfare of their family less stressful for everyone. They shared frank conversations about each other's feelings as they completed demanding schedules, and Azucena helped Domingo understand that her siblings felt overwhelmed by her dedicating so much of her time to her trade school education. She felt that they were "finally feeling and talking like a true family." Maintaining and benefiting from the honest spirit of an awake house made for a most heartening approach to their family's difficulties.

In 1960, after Azucena had earned her certification to work as an accountant in their hometown, she and her father continued to be grateful to each other for their unwavering commitment to maintaining an awake house. Their dedicating time to listen and talk to each other about their feelings as they worked long hours in the family business and cared for younger siblings during Azucena's trade school course work had improved the morale of their family and dramatically diminished their emotional exhaustion and disconnection from each other. It had also been restorative for her siblings. Finally feeling emotionally connected to Domingo had made them increasingly optimistic about the promise of their elementary and middle school education. Azucena's successful pursuit of a trade school education and her personal investment in conveying their feelings to their father—combined with Domingo's receptivity to their feelings and decision to settle permanently by their side—had made it feasible for them not to labor for town families and had encouraged them to aspire to better employment opportunities themselves. The possibility that the family might reach a point where none of its members would need to migrate for work in the United States nurtured Azucena's, Domingo's, and the younger siblings' spirit to remain invested in maintaining an awake house with each other and for each other's sake.

VENERANDA TORRES:
A MOST HUMANE *INTERMEDIARIA*

In June 1957, Veneranda Torres earned her nursing certificate from El Program Federal Rural de Enfermería, sponsored by a modest trade school in her rural Mexican hometown of Acambaro, Guanajuato.[3] Two years' training had made for long days of studying and caring for child patients and had prepared her to set and meet her own goals as she transitioned into adulthood in the midst of the Bracero Program. With her nursing certificate in hand, Veneranda finally felt ready to adopt a humane approach to women's emotional exhaustion from accommodating the constant separation of families across the US-Mexico border. In the spirit of Ignacia and Azucena, she embraced acting as an *intermediaria,* taking it upon herself to craft and transform her family home into an awake house for emotionally exhausted women, all with the support of her mother.

Throughout her upbringing and education, Veneranda had grown in her commitment to excelling as an *intermediaria* on behalf of and in support of emotionally exhausted women. Exhausted herself, she recognized that women needed to do more for each other so that they would benefit from each other's trust in the form of an awake house or a safe space that brought women together to act in support of each other. Like Ignacia Zarate Mandujano Rios and Azucena Lopez, she embraced using her transition into adulthood, and specifically her attainment of a nursing certificate, as an opportunity to act as an *intermediaria* who dared to confront women's exhaustion responsibly. To do this, Veneranda enlisted the support of her mother in making the family home a safe space where women could take a moment out of their busy schedules to lend each other comforting advice and assistance on a moment's notice. She explained, "Deep in my heart, I intuited that this was a major first step in the right direction for me and for other women."

Earning the trust of these women was integral to Veneranda's transition into acting as an *intermediaria* on their behalf. Her education and skilled employment in nursing enhanced her credibility as someone who would not separate from her family to labor in the United States as an undocumented Mexican immigrant woman, but she also had to project an enduring personal investment in supporting her family unconditionally. If these women misunderstood her intentions, they would not come. She had to be especially careful to adhere to gender expectations when pursuing her education and skilled employment in nursing so that she kept a good reputation and these women would not fear attracting unwanted public attention by visiting her home.

Further, she had to ensure that her confrontation of the emotional toll of her father's decisions, especially his laboring in surrounding towns away from her family, would not be misinterpreted as her disapproval of his or her mother's parenting and choices. And without a healthy relationship between her and at least her mother in place, her family's home would not have the public credibility that would persuade emotionally exhausted women to consider her family's home as an awake house.

Adherence to gender expectations that required her to care and labor for her family unconditionally was not new for Veneranda. It had been at the heart of her relationship with her mother and father. As one of the oldest children in her family, she had been raised to be as helpful to her parents as possible. Working by their side as they harvested crops, raised livestock for sale, prepared family meals, cared for her siblings, or completed household chores framed her deep respect for following their instructions and living up to their expectations. Beginning in 1950, her father separated from their family for months at a time to labor throughout the Mexican countryside, returned for a couple of months at a time to reunite with them and pay for a few months' worth of their family's basic needs, and then left them again in search of profitable domestic employment opportunities without considering the full extent of his decision's implications. Veneranda and her mother were left to work increasingly longer days making and selling cheese and other milk products from their home to make up for his absence. The emotional toll of accommodating her father's decisions had been exhausting. Though Veneranda recollected, "I always felt loved," she also stated, "My childhood was not the easiest."

As a fifteen-year-old girl, Veneranda did not have much time to socialize with girls or boys her age or to do much more than care for her siblings and labor by her mother's side. Asking questions concerning the whereabouts and plans of her father was also not an option. This made for an emotionally painful family situation that over time brought her and her mother together. Their mutual personal investment in not allowing the separation of their family across the border to drive them apart would later set the stage for her mother's receptivity to supporting Veneranda's pursuit of an education and skilled employment in nursing as well as her plan to act as an *intermediaria* for other women.

Over the years, Veneranda's mother had seen that Veneranda often took the time to ask her about her health and her doubts and fears regarding her father's decisions and the separation of their family, and that she took care of her siblings to afford her mother time and space to herself. Veneranda's mother thus decided to collaborate with her in using the family home as an awake house or restorative space for women who in her estimation were too emotionally overwhelmed to act in support of each other in this way.

DESPIERTA Y DEDICADA (AWAKE AND DEDICATED)

Having her mother's approval and unconditional support bolstered Veneranda's self-confidence in undertaking this project. Her mother's backing also made her careful about adhering to gender expectations. Out of her love and respect for her mother and her respect for her mother and father's marriage, Veneranda did not judge the personal relationships of the women who embraced their family home as an awake house. As she had done when conversing with and helping her mother, she limited herself to affording these women a space, listening to them, and answering their questions if she knew her mother would not object to her doing so. She carefully considered the relationships at stake and the age differences between her and the women who sought emotional comfort from restorative moments in her home (most of them were older than her, their ages ranging from twenty-three to sixty). Her mother advised Veneranda to steer clear of asking women questions about the healthfulness of their marriages to braceros or undocumented immigrant men and lending her opinion on the status of their marriages. Understanding that her age, gender, marital status, and role within her family did not entitle her to initiate such conversations with her mother or with other married and often older women was integral to Veneranda's achievement of her goals. Veneranda explained, "My mother did not allow me to forget that I had to be most respectfully cautious when interacting with women much older and experienced than myself." According to her mother, marriage and women's personal relationships with men were intimate matters that, at best, married women should discuss with each other out of their own volition. Adhering to the soundness of her mother's gender expectations compelled Veneranda to capitalize on their relationship and her education, employment in nursing, and deep-seated concern for women's well-being to forge a space that was of emotional comfort to everyone.

Veneranda did not object to her mother's gender expectations because she did not forget that her attitude and actions were a reflection of her and her parents' moral character. Her good relationship with her mother and their mutual investment in unconditionally supporting each other and their family, including her father, were critical if she was to establish the public credibility necessary to successfully transform her family's home into an awake house. Women did not interact socially or visit each other's homes if this could potentially tarnish their public images. They could not risk making their already difficult situation worse.

It became equally important for Veneranda not to criticize the US and Mexican governments' implementation of the Bracero Program or its impact on the welfare of her family and that of other similarly exhausted families. Both her mother and father had discouraged her from ever expressing her criticism of either government's involvement in framing the Bracero Program. They were fully aware of the personal hardships that had generated her resentment of both governments, and they shared her disappointment and frustration at how the lack of well-paying employment opportunities in Acambaro had compelled her father to traverse the Mexican countryside in pursuit of labor that indefinitely separated him from their family. But they still insisted that as the daughter of a Mexican immigrant man and as a young woman coming of age she could not afford to share with others her negative assessment of the US and Mexican governments' treatment of Mexican families. Her expression of such views could draw unwanted public attention to her, her father, and her family and thus would make others see her as recklessly opinionated and outspoken. Unwilling to risk her public credibility before she even began her acting as an *intermediaria* and careful not to defy her parents and gender expectations, Veneranda accepted that when confronting her and other women's exhaustion she could not hold the US or Mexican governments accountable in this way.

AN *INTERMEDIARIA*'S EDUCATION

Between 1955 and 1957, Veneranda continued to depend on the strength of her relationship with her mother and their shared awake house. Recognizing that their restorative conversations had emboldened them to confront the difficulties of long-term separation of family members, both of them tried to keep honestly sharing their feelings with each other. Conversations in which Veneranda shared with her mother that she felt anxious about taking challenging courses in nursing made it possible for her to complete her course work and household chores and help produce cheese and other milk products for sale that paid for the family's basic needs. Further, both mother and daughter did everything they could to diminish each other's exhaustion. Benefiting from each other's trust nurtured their willingness to provide each other with the space and time to take short breaks when the stress of responsibility for the welfare of their household became too unbearable. Dedication to nurturing a relationship and family home life that was based on mutual consideration not only rendered Veneranda's mother-daughter relationship with her mother a source of emotional energy but also allowed her mother and other women to understand her pursuit of an education as an expression of her commitment to supporting her family.

In June 1957, Veneranda earned her certificate in nursing. It was a restorative moment that symbolized for her the successful culmination of her and her mother's labor spending entire weekends together preparing and selling baked goods from their family home's kitchen to finance her tuition and other expenses associated with her pursuit of the nursing certificate. This had been the only way they had been able to pay for what amounted to an annual expense of an estimated 420 pesos (300 pesos for tuition fees, 50 pesos for supplies, and 70 pesos for her uniform) given their already tight family budget. Laboring tirelessly together every day of the week for two consecutive years had also provided many opportunities for conversations that helped them remain optimistic about their potential to support their family and her education with each other's support.

Veneranda realized that earning her certificate and sharing this goal with her mother had boosted her mother's morale. The possibility that she could obtain well-paid and personally rewarding employment was most comforting to her mother. It reassured her that her energy and time was advancing her daughter's transition into a meaningful adulthood that, unlike her marriage, would not depend on the instability of migration. Her newfound optimism and belief motivated her to adorn their house with the portrait of her daughter's nursing school graduating class.

With each conversation she shared with her mother, Veneranda noticed that their courage grew as a result. As she recounted, "We became closer and learned to care for each other unconditionally." Together they acknowledged and discussed their aspirations, doubts, and fears regarding the absence of her father, increases in the price of food and other basic necessities, the risks of diversifying their food sales to include more items, and other matters of concern, and they provided each other with the time to pause and consider their options carefully before making difficult decisions concerning their family relationship, finances, and time management on a moment's notice. The ease and trust that fueled such humane consideration of each other's emotional exhaustion struck her as qualities that had transformed their home into a most heartening awake house.

THE EXPANSION OF AN AWAKE HOUSE

In the winter of 1957, three weeks into Veneranda's new job as a nurse at Acambaro's local clinic, Veneranda, with her mother's assistance, rearranged their living room so that women who came to the family home could embrace it as a comfortable space in which to process their feelings with them and with each other. The initial expansion of their awake house required Veneranda to depend on her mother to invite women into their home. Her mother had to be the one to convince these women to confide in their family out of trust in her honorable reputation and genuine concern. Married with children, owner of the family home and business, head of household during her husband's absence, and closer in age to most of the exhausted women they were striving to support, Veneranda's mother was most qualified to encourage women— who had already come into the family home to purchase their cheese and other dairy products—to venture into their living room, take a break from their hectic schedule, sit down and catch their breath, drink a cup of coffee or a glass of lemonade or water, listen to a song of their choice as it played on their family's record player, and join conversations in which they could share their feelings with her and other women who had opted to accept her invitation as an extension of their workday.

Veneranda, meanwhile, adhered to gender expectations that restricted her initial involvement in the expansion of their awake house to choosing, creating, and maintaining the interior design of their living room, preparing the cold and hot drinks and snacks offered to the exhausted women who came to rely on this space and its social interactions, and sustaining her own public reputation as a caring, discreet, and supportive daughter and nurse to help her mother make their family home a comfortable space for these women to express their feelings with each other. Every day before going off to work, Veneranda would clean their family's living room, refill water pitchers, and prepare sufficient coffee and lemonade for her mother to offer these women, and she would frequently talk with her mother to ensure that the expansion of their awake house was feasible for her. She did not take for granted her mother having to add at least two hours to her workday to be able to host these women as she operated their family business, managed their household, and cared for their family.

Veneranda's limitations to acting as an *intermediaria* inspired her to focus on her attitude and actions as her most important contribution to her family's successful expansion of their awake house. She believed that if she had not persevered in conversations with her mother about sharing their family home as an awake house, her mother would not have had the courage to collaborate with her on this project. Veneranda undertook the work of listening to these women, cleaning the family home, and preparing beverages and food for these women to enjoy. That way everyone could relax without having to maintain this space or prepare the food and drinks. In her mother's estimation, Veneranda's work of maintaining her family home as a comfortable, reputable, and humane space for these women to share with ease was a most productive way of acting as an *intermediaria* between these women.

Over time, as Veneranda got a reputation for looking after child and elderly patients with the utmost care, the women of these patients' families came to the awake house as well. There they could take much-needed breaks from looking after their children or elderly relatives. Veneranda's nursing care of child patients had exposed her to the desperation of these children's mothers. They did not have anyone with whom to share their feelings of sadness, worry, or longing for the medical recovery of their children. Veneranda described them as "facing a most desperate situation without much in the form of information or services."

The women who shared conversations and moments of solace at Veneranda and her mother's awake house were under great stress, as temporary heads of households, from their constant and unconditional accommodation to their bracero or undocumented immigrant husbands. This difficult situation had caused them chronic back pain, headaches, and sleepless nights. Sharing their concerns energized them to embrace the emotional and physical work they had to do, thereby reassuring their families that sharing time with other women as part of their workday was indeed a worthwhile priority. Wary of betraying anyone's confidence, they did not tell others about what exactly they had shared with other women when in this space. Instead, they depended on their increased productivity when operating their family businesses, producing and selling clothing, food, and other items, and caring for their families to make the positive influence of spending time in the company of women most obvious to their families. They did everything within their reach to preserve their easy access to a space with other women who recognized the emotional, physical, and financial stresses of their work and did not judge them. As temporary heads of household, they made difficult decisions about their financing of their families' basic needs, parenting, the use of their energy and time, and records of their expenditures—but always under the expectation that upon their husbands' return they would relinquish such roles and responsibilities automatically. Conversing about this was restorative for these women.

Upon their return, husbands often did not discuss their thoughts on what should change or stay the same in their management of their families, businesses, energy, resources, and time. This lack of communication emotionally devastated their wives. Their husbands' indifference to discussing the important work they had undertaken as heads of households made these women feel taken for granted. Their disappointment in their husbands' underestimation of them as heads of household gave them the need to vent. Conversations at the awake house made it safe for them to admit to themselves and each other that raising their families while separated from their husbands had caused them anger, fatigue, and frustration. particularly when their husbands repeatedly decided on a moment's notice to separate from them without consulting them. All this made it even more important to share their feelings with women who were also treated as temporary heads of household at the convenience of their husbands.

At any given time, an estimated eight to ten women might gather in Veneranda and her mother's living room to talk to each other and listen to music together. They were not expected to disclose information that would make them uncomfortable or to do much more than listen to each other. At no other time during their day were they afforded such humane understanding of their exhaustion. Unwilling to add to the burden of completing a multitude of tasks in the best of spirits, women merely tried to treat themselves to an evening cup of tea and to prepare certain soups and stews to nourish their immune system. All the while, they reminded themselves that just being by their children's side to care for them was a luxury that many men and women were increasingly unable to enjoy. As Veneranda explained, "Families were committed to being practical and loving in their care for their children. They tried and for the most part did their very best for them."

Combining their honest assessment of the emotional toll of accommodating the constant migration of their husbands with humorous personal anecdotes helped to make being there for each other restorative for everyone. The fusion of laughter and tears comforted women into feeling less anxious about the pressure to produce more clothing or food items for sale, caring for their children while doing so, and hoping that they would actually sell everything they produced to at least make ends meet. Their husbands often left them with very little or no money to meet existing and new expenses associated with their operation of their family businesses and management of their households, which required them to work longer hours. This state of affairs only heightened the importance of sharing their feelings about this situation with women weathering similar hardships. The "added pressure to make this work look easy, so that their children and other relatives did not become demoralized," moved women to seek each other's company at least three to four times a week during the middle of the day and early evening hours.

A year into maintaining the awake house, Veneranda was finally welcomed to share helpful information with these women. Her diligent care for patients made the women receptive to her joining them. Having earned their confidence, Veneranda could lend them emotional support and, on their request, give them helpful information from her training and practice as a nurse: telling them which local medical doctors would be friendliest and most generous in caring for their children and elderly relatives, giving them helpful tips for completing medical forms required by their local clinic, and sharing strategies for successfully pursuing trade school education.

Veneranda's and her mother's humane approach to sharing their awake house, and its influence on their attitude and actions when they got together with women who shared their emotional exhaustion, outlived the Bracero Program. To this day, women heading households with hardly any emotional support from their Mexican immigrant husbands in Mexico or the United States continue to benefit from Veneranda's personal investment in sharing time, conversations, and information that can restore their spirit to care for their families and manage their households optimistically and resourcefully. Seeing firsthand the newfound energy women had and continued to derive from sharing and discussing their feelings with each other moved her to remain true to acting with concern and discretion on behalf of women who were trying to responsibly deal with the emotional consequences of the Mexican and US governments' enforcement of the US-Mexico border, especially the predicament of having to excel as heads of households without emotional support from their bracero or undocumented immigrant husbands.

ROSA DE CASTAÑO AS *INTERMEDIARIA*

In 1953, Rosa de Castaño published *Braceros: Mojados,* a play that warned and held women and men in the United States and Mexico accountable for the emotional exhaustion of braceros and undocumented immigrants in Mexico and the United States—an achievement that made her a uniquely revealing *intermediaria* for migrant workers.[4] Although Castaño did not describe herself as fulfilling this role, she cautioned everyone who read her play that their failure to recognize and respond to the exhaustion of these women and men would intensify the longevity and pervasiveness of this form of alienation in Mexico and the United States. At the time, it was a daring assertion to make. Writing what could have been seen solely as a source of entertainment, she called for a broader sense of cultural responsibility. By holding men publicly accountable for their and women's emotional exhaustion, she emerged in some ways as even more of a risk taker than the women who ran awake houses. Throughout her play she dared to explicitly and publicly identify the attitudes and actions of people of Mexican descent and of varying legal statuses as a source of emotional pain for each other in Mexico and the United States. In the spirit of later *intermediarias* like Ignacia Zarate Mandujano Rios and Veneranda Torres, she portrayed their mutual indifference to or abuse of emotionally exhausted women and men's emotional vulnerability as in part to blame for the propensity and prevalence of emotional suffering among bracero and undocumented Mexican immigrant women and men. In the midst of the Bracero Program, she used her position as a playwright—who had spent a considerable amount of time in both countries—to publicly declare the lack of solidarity between and among people of Mexican descent as an underestimated source of emotional exhaustion for both women and men. Castaño joined *intermediarias* in courageously acknowledging that women were among the hardest hit by the emotional repercussions of the Bracero Program's separation of Mexican families.

Little is known about Castaño. She was born in 1910 as Rosa Garcia Peña in Camargo, Tamaulipas, Mexico. Her education began in El Colegio del Verbo Encarnado in San Antonio, Texas, and culminated in Monterrey, Mexico, where she is believed to have completed college. In 1934, after having married Luis Castaño, she changed her name to Rosa de Castaño. By 1941, she had made her way to New Orleans, Louisiana. During this time, she published a series of novels and plays, among them *El Coyote* (The Coyote), which in 1941 earned her national acclaim in Mexico. *Braceros: Mojados* revolves around the emotional exhaustion of braceros and undocumented Mexican immigrant women and men in the United States and Mexico. The play illuminates the dangers of not looking inward. Castaño crafted it so that women and men are understood in relationship to each other, sharing an inability to admit and cope with disappointment in the form of failed migrations to and from the United States. Her play makes evident that immigrants' reluctance to help each other cope with having returned from laboring in the United States without any savings, or with having been physically attacked and robbed of their money on their journey to and from the United States, paved the way for a most painful cultural silence.

The title of Castaño's play, *Braceros: Mojados*, in itself illustrates an intermediary spirit in that it suggests the equality and shared experiences of those with legal status and those without, prompting braceros and undocumented Mexican immigrants to consider each other in relationship to each other rather than as competitors. Much of the play highlights the emotional pain that immigrants of varying statuses experienced. It tries to break the silence about intraethnic violence, harassment, and labor competition. The exploitative conditions that Mexican immigrants have shared become obscured when people believe themselves either superior or inferior to each other and thrive on each other's emotional vulnerability and suffering.

In a spirit much like that of the *intermediarias* who opened up their family homes to let groups of women gather there, Castaño uses her play to manifest the importance of coming together. Throughout *Braceros: Mojados*, she asserts that underestimated and unresolved forms of tension and competition between immigrants of Mexican descent inspired cruelty and criminal acts that compounded the damage wrought by externally imposed immigration conditions. By encouraging women and men to understand that being of Mexican descent did not automatically make immigrants treat each other humanely or fairly, she prompts her audience to reconsider and change their own attitudes and actions when dealing with intraethnic tensions.

Throughout her play, Castaño raises awareness regarding women's distinctly gendered emotional pain. Immigrant women struggled not only with financial needs but with families who pressured them to consider entering romantic relationships with settled Mexican immigrant men in the United States. Castaño uses these typical situations to indicate that women's adherence to gender expectations that they heed the advice of their families could have dangerous consequences. Women are warned that they should not automatically trust or favor settled Mexican immigrants who are thriving in the United States, since these men could potentially compound their pain through sexual coercion or exploitative employment conditions. Prefiguring the bold spirit of *intermediarias* in the Mexican countryside, Castaño alerts women and men to the reality that undocumented Mexican immigrant women were most vulnerable to being coerced into traumatic relationships and situations by women and men of Mexican descent, including their relatives and Mexican hometown friends. As she presents it, coming together to establish and maintain a common ground is crucial for discouraging women and men from ignoring or taking advantage of each other's vulnerabilities in Mexico and the United States.

By portraying ways that Mexican immigrants treated each other inhumanely and showing the full ramifications of these acts, Castaño held the women and men in her play publicly accountable and implicitly prompted her audience to consider their own role in an emotionally devastating situation. She also publicly recognized the poor choices and difficult decisions of male and female relatives as a source of emotional exhaustion for women. In doing so, she expressed and shared what women steered clear of explicitly recognizing or discussing when they got together in "awake houses": that Mexican men of insecure legal status needed to be held accountable for the emotional suffering that they inflicted on each other and on women and children. Her play—its scope, cast, and spirit—created a moment in which emotionally exhausted women and men felt heard, as she dared to write what few women and men felt emboldened to say about each other or their relationships. Capturing the feelings of so many women and men distinguished her writing as a risky intermediary act.

Although Castaño's play did not hold the US and Mexican governments' implementation of the Bracero Program or deportation of undocumented Mexican immigrants responsible for the exhaustion of women and men of Mexican descent, just her recognition of the socially inflicted suffering that these women and men endured was a most illuminating intermediary act on their behalf. It showed the high stakes, for women and men in both countries, of ignoring this immigrant population's emotional anguish, doubt, estrangement, and fear. Encouraging these women and men to value caring for and understanding each other was an intermediary act on their behalf among audiences who were rarely brought to acknowledge Mexican immigrant women and men's exhaustion as a traumatic outcome of the Bracero Program. By using her writing to expose women and men to the consequences of their indifference to or abuse of each other's emotional suffering and to encourage the cultivation of humane relationships, Castaño's work was part of a larger move to restore or protect the community's emotional welfare and is consistent with the spirit of the awake houses. In writing, publishing, and circulating her thoughts on the situation at hand, she did not allow her being a Mexican married woman and a Mexican female writer to stop her. Her public warning that if women and men did not dare to do more in support of each other their emotional exhaustion would continue to devastate them and would drive them apart expressed the emboldened spirit of the *intermediarias* of the Mexican countryside.

Unfolding in 1953 in the Mexican rural town of Arandas, Jalisco, *Braceros: Mojados* begins with a group of five men who leave the Mexican rural town of Arandas, Jalisco, and travel toward the border in hopes of crossing illegally and then gaining bracero contracts once they are in the United States. Journeying through rough terrain without much information, support, or other protection, these men do not have a clear sense of where they are or what to expect, and in this vulnerable condition they are attacked and robbed by Manuel, a childhood friend of theirs who has become "El Matabraceros" ("The Bracero Killer"). As Castaño makes evident, pursuing contract or undocumented labor in the United States was not only dangerous but traumatizing in that assaults like this left immigrants unable to trust anyone, especially men familiar with their doubts and fears. The incident prompts audiences to consider that it is emotionally devastating for Mexican immigrant men of insecure legal status to experience violence at the hands of other Mexican men who, instead of being sympathetic, are eager to benefit from their vulnerability. Throughout her play, Manuel beats, cheats, robs, smuggles, emotionally abuses, and kills Mexican immigrant women and men as they migrate to and from the United States. His own Mexican descent and his familiarity with immigrants' already desperate emotional and financial situations do not prevent him from preying on them. Instead, his ambition for financial gain prevails. Castaño makes obvious that Manuel's abuse, betrayal, and, in the worst case, murder are motivated by his desire for other immigrants' hard-earned US wages and savings.

Castaño devotes the remainder of the first act of her play to depicting the traumatic aftermath of Manuel's attack. Once his former childhood friends have regained their consciousness, they realize that one member of their party, Victoriano, a close friend, is nowhere to be found. Nonetheless, they do not stop to look for him or to learn of his fate. Their friendship and concern for him are outweighed by their fear of being blamed for his disappearance and possible murder. Left with nothing but the clothes on their backs, they ignore their guilty feelings over not searching for Victoriano or returning to Arandas to inform his family that he has probably been kidnapped or killed. Going on instead is painful for them to consider: "What are we going to tell his wife and children when we come back from the United States overflowing with dollars and good things?" (4). Ultimately, however, they decide not to deal with his disappearance until their return. When they stumble on his religious token in the form of a stamp of El Señor del Buen Camino (patron saint of Mexican immigrants journeying to the United States), they are inspired to take comfort in praying for his safety by asking for the pardon and protection of this patron spirit before they resume their journey. Castaño uses Manuel's physical attack on this group of men, and these men's failure to search or to alert Victoriano's family of his disappearance, to expose audiences to the reality that not even close childhood friends could be trusted to act in support of Mexican immigrant men.

Castaño emphasizes that men like Manuel used their own sense of superiority to justify their abuse and murder of their compatriots, reasoning that nobody cared about these women and men. Thus members of the play's audience could see that their own indifference to the suffering of Mexican immigrants emboldened men like Manuel to exploit or even murder them for financial gain.

Castaño also uses Victoriano's friends' rationales for their decision to abandon him to illustrate these men's distrust of Mexican government authorities. Fearful that Mexican police officers will not believe their account or care much about the disappearance of their friend, they opt to believe that El Señor del Buen Camino will lead Victoriano safely to the United States. By dramatizing the dangerous potential of Mexican immigrant men's indifference to the welfare of Mexican immigrant women and men, Castaño encourages them to hold themselves accountable to act in their fellow immigrants' support. She captures the intensity of immigrants' anxiety and fear to show that the audience's personal investment in these women and men's emotional welfare is a promising source of solidarity for everyone in the United States and Mexico.

Castaño holds the audience of *Braceros: Mojados* accountable for diminishing the pain and exhaustion of Mexican immigrants. One incident in particular convey the severity of the consequences of simply abandoning these women and men to their fate. Shortly after his friends have resumed their journey, Victoriano reappears, but now he is insane. It was too much for him to accept that Mexican men posed a danger to each other. After being attacked, robbed, and left behind by men he thought would not make an already challenging journey dangerous, "Victoriano Reyes, the bracero from Jalisco who separated from his friends with crazed eyes, was left to the mercy of his patron saint" (6). Abandonment by his friends has pushed Victoriano to "become lost and mad from hunger and thirst" (7).

Castaño uses Victoriano's mental breakdown to suggest that for Mexican immigrants the realization that even their fellow immigrants did not hold themselves accountable to act humanely toward them was highly traumatic. Not shying away from an almost taboo subject, Castaño acts as an *intermediaria* who acknowledges these men's disappointment in each other as a source of intense emotional suffering. This was a perspective that very few Mexican women dared to assert and promote in Mexico or the United States.

Castaño uses the character of Manuel to underscore how Mexican immigrant women and men of varying legal status migrating to and from the United States were preyed upon by their own countrymen. Manuel smuggles immigrants into the United States and guides them back to Mexico in order to earn enough of their trust so that he can then physically attack and rob them of their earnings and savings when their crossing of the border becomes too risky or when physical altercations between them become too violent. As Castaño points out, Mexican immigrants were most vulnerable to these men when they were coming back to Mexico with their earnings: "The real danger lay in their return" (13).

Castaño presents Manuel as posing a danger to Mexican immigrant women and men even after having smuggled them into the United States. Many of these women and men then have to rely on him to secure a Bracero Program contract or employment in farms and packinghouses stretching across the United States. After securing them employment, Manuel is left to determine whether they keep their jobs with their US employers. This creates a stressful relationship of dependence between him and these women and men when they are laboring as either braceros or undocumented Mexican immigrants under his supervision. Manuel demands a percentage of their earnings in exchange for submitting positive assessments of their work performance to their employers. Such employment conditions intensify what Castaño shows as these women's and men's already traumatic situation: they are ridiculed in public as a result of their recently arrived Mexican immigrant status. Settled Mexican immigrants and Mexican Americans join Manuel in publicly humiliating them as "'wetbacks' who had become lighter in their physical complexion as a result of their being prohibited from leaving or venturing outside their place of employment, and whose clothes had finally dried up completely when they took it upon themselves to sneak out of these farms and packinghouses to interact socially with fellow workers" (23). Castaño keeps a relentless focus on the vulnerability of these immigrants, who were often locked up day and night inside their place of employment and were often scorned and exploited by other Mexicans. Providing a glimpse of their lives in the United States was the act of an *intermediaria* that urged a wider recognition of the negative impacts of exploitation and public humiliation in deepening the emotional exhaustion of Mexican immigrant women and men in Mexico and the United States.

By showing the crimes that Manuel commits with the assistance of his Mexican immigrant sidekick, Picacho, Castaño conveys the dangerously wide reach of US and Mexican society's indifference to the travails of Mexican immigrant women and men. In the second act of *Braceros: Mojados,* Manuel employs his Mexican hometown friend Picacho to help carry out his emotional, physical, and financial abuse of Mexican immigrants. Manuel depends on Picacho to intimidate these women and men into submitting to his demands. Because the immigrants fear that Manuel and Picacho will cost them their Bracero Program contracts or other US employment, get them deported, or retaliate against their families in Mexico, these women and men endure the abuse in silence. Seeking Manuel's services to enter the United States or to secure employment there is at least emotionally taxing and can be a fatal misstep. Picacho's indifference to the women's and men's humanity makes him a truly dangerous person. Throughout the play, Castaño holds Mexican immigrant men accountable for initiating and maintaining personal relationships that diminish each other's suffering instead of augmenting it, but this stance is most striking in her consideration of Picacho's failure to resist following in Manuel's footsteps.

Throughout the third act of *Braceros: Mojados,* Castaño focuses on the consequences of the emotional exhaustion of undocumented Mexican immigrant women and men in the United States to emphasize that as a result of such trauma it was challenging for them to befriend anyone. She describes how their exploitation and public humiliation by people like Manuel and others of Mexican descent intensified their isolation. A fear that, like Manuel and Picacho, settled Mexican immigrants, Mexican Americans, and undocumented Mexican immigrants would abuse new migrants' trust or treat them as people unworthy of humane social interactions made it most difficult to confide in often similarly exhausted women and men. Castaño uses the courtship of Miguel, an undocumented Mexican immigrant man, and an undocumented Mexican immigrant woman, Rosaura, who like himself has relied on Manuel to enter into and labor in the United States, to demonstrate that it was difficult for undocumented Mexican immigrants to move past the anxiety born out of their interactions with inhumane acquaintances in their past.

Upon meeting Miguel, Rosaura resists the prospect of beginning a romantic relationship with him because she believes that "if she had already met her great love, she would not have left her country to look for one," implying that it is difficult to meet men worthy of her love in either country (12). The exhaustion of having endured inhumane treatment from Manuel and other women and men whom she assumed were in some way like her, or who shared a desperate need for US wages and personal connection to Mexico that should have made for friendly interactions between them, inspires Rosaura to doubt that their ethnicity or familiarity with hardships is in and of itself an adequate basis for a humane romantic relationship between them in the United States or Mexico. Castaño presents the emotional anxiety of Mexican immigrant women and men who struggle to trust each other as a result of their exposure to indifference—and this work makes her an *intermediaria*.

Castaño's most daring intermediary act on behalf of and in support of women is to dedicate the fourth and final act of *Braceros: Mojados* to exploring the emotional exhaustion of an undocumented Mexican immigrant woman through her treatment of Rosaura's experience. Rosaura is introduced as a beautiful young woman from Arandas who—accompanied and pressured by her much older aunt, Cuca—enlists the services of Manuel to enter and labor in the United States as an undocumented Mexican immigrant. Her emotional turmoil begins shortly after she meets Manuel. After helping her enter the United States, he becomes aggressive in expressing his affection for her, even saying he wants to marry her upon their return to Mexico. His feelings for her take a violent turn when he realizes that she wants to begin a romantic relationship with Miguel, who despite her initial refusal of his affection is most friendly and supportive of her. Manuel's anxiety over the unlikelihood of having a romantic relationship with Rosaura compels him to use his influence over her continued employment to pressure her into at least going out on one date with him.

Castaño uses Rosaura's doubts and fears about socially interacting with Manuel and Miguel to echo something Miguel tells Rosaura: that they need each other to cope with the emotional toll of "having been blindly enthralled with the United States! So many stories are told about the United States, that it is beautiful, that there are so many things that are affordable and so much money" (11). Miguel's warning captures Rosaura's emotionally brutal reality. She has not found or benefited from abundance and opportunity in the United States. Instead, her options have been restricted: she fears that acting on her affection for Miguel or refusing to go on at least one date with Manuel will cost her her work assignment or hours or, worse, result in her deportation to Mexico. Castaño uses Rosaura's exhaustion and especially Manuel's manipulation of her to show how vulnerable undocumented Mexican immigrant women were to unfair and stressful personal relationships. Her humane presentation of the undocumented experience urges audiences to act far more humanely toward these women. Given that hardly anyone in Mexico or the United States dared to write about or discuss these women's experience with concern or humanity, Castaño's writing, publication, and circulation of this play constituted a truly intermediary act.

To immerse women and men reading *Braceros: Mojados* in the gendered intensity of the ethnic tension fueling the emotional pain of undocumented Mexican immigrant women in the United States, Castaño presents a heated exchange between Rosaura and a settled Mexican immigrant woman who throughout this scene remains nameless and is merely described as a *pizcadora* or agricultural field worker. The argument takes place at a local bar where Rosaura is out on her date with Manuel. Seeing this young woman dance with Miguel shocks Rosaura and prompts her to tell Manuel that she wants to leave. She pleads with him, "Why did you bring me here—look how many drunks and gamblers, dirty women too. I am decent. I am not like them" (22). The date with Manuel has been disturbing in itself, and realizing that Miguel is socializing with another woman makes Rosaura feel even worse. Shortly after having overheard Rosaura's dismissal of this venue and its patrons, the woman dancing with Miguel confronts her. This woman's immigration status and her employment harvesting crops instead of packing them hidden from view embolden her to assert an air of superiority over Rosaura. Resentful of Rosaura's negative reaction to her dancing with Miguel, she confronts Rosaura about her noticeable disapproval of both her and her dancing with Miguel.

Beginning her public confrontation of Rosaura by referring to her as a *mojada* ("wetback") whose illegal status forces her to labor hidden inside a packing plant, the woman provokes Rosaura to dismiss her as an "ordinary and dirty agricultural worker" (22). Even though their exchange does not escalate into a physical fight, Castaño uses their public humiliation of each other's employment, as well as their differing immigration statuses, to illustrate the ease with which everyday differences could create traumatic situations for undocumented Mexican immigrant women and settled Mexican immigrant women who were indifferent to each other's emotional pain. Castaño makes clear that being publicly humiliated as a "wetback" emotionally devastates Rosaura. It confirms for her, and for the play's audience, the depth of her plight. Such altercations are an ever-present yet underestimated source of emotional pain for Rosaura and, in Castaño's estimation, for everyone to consider when determining whether to act in support of these women's humanity.

Castaño's *Braceros: Mojados* is also intermediary in its account of the inhumane terms that settled Mexican immigrant women and undocumented Mexican immigrant women new to the United States used to distance themselves from each other. Throughout the play, whether Rosaura is laboring in agricultural fields or hidden from view in cramped and poorly lit and ventilated packing plants, it is difficult for her to befriend other women. A realization that shared exploitation does not discourage women from drawing unwanted public attention to each other's US immigration status when striving to disparage each other shocks Rosaura into resisting conversations or altercations with fellow women of Mexican descent and distancing herself from everyone. When she is publicly humiliated about her undocumented status by a similarly exploited but settled Mexican immigrant woman, she takes the drastic measure of refusing to socially interact with settled Mexican immigrant women, refusing to date Manuel irrespective of the consequences, and refusing to trust anyone. This decision, which is likely to intensify her emotional exhaustion, shows how difficult it could be for undocumented Mexican immigrant women to lead lives that were true to their feelings. Castaño's nurturing of an understanding attitude among women and men who might otherwise be indifferent or reluctant to acknowledge these women or their emotional exhaustion is consistent with the spirit that energized women who came together in awake houses to admit and discuss their anxiety concerning the undocumented immigration of their female relatives in the United States.

Braceros: Mojados alerts women and men to the family expectations that added stress to the lives of undocumented Mexican immigrant women. The final act of the play presents Rosaura's tension with her aunt Cuca as a source of emotional pain. Castaño focuses on their relationship to show how difficult it could be for undocumented Mexican immigrant women to sustain supportive relationships with female relatives that had begun in Mexico. Rosaura's aunt Cuca finds laboring twelve-hour days in a cramped packing plant to be physically unbearable, and this motivates her to pressure Rosaura to begin a romantic relationship with Manuel so that he will support them financially and Rosaura "would not need to migrate, labor, or suffer in the United States to begin a promising future" (11). Rosaura, however, does not have romantic feelings for Manuel but fears him. Her aunt's failure to respect that, and her tendency to corner Rosaura and question her about getting to know Manuel, make her very anxious. It becomes emotionally draining for Rosaura to worry that her aunt's interactions with Manuel will overexpose her to his advances, anger, or resentment. For Castaño to use her play to hold Mexican women accountable for the emotional welfare of their undocumented Mexican immigrant female relatives and to support women facing such emotional pressure was a most fearless act. Holding female relatives responsible for affording each other some much-needed peace of mind was not an easy argument to make to women who thought that they knew what was best for the daughters, nieces, and other female relatives under their supervision in the United States.

Castaño culminates her account of the exhaustion of Mexican immigrant women and men with the death of Manuel. Manuel is guiding a group of undocumented Mexican immigrants that include Rosaura, her aunt Cuca, and Miguel back to Mexico after their labor in the United States when his loathing and jealousy toward Miguel, who has successfully entered a romantic relationship with Rosaura, inspire him to rob and beat Miguel and to plan to kill him and the others as he leads them across the US-Mexico border. His plan, however, is derailed when his father learns that he is the widely feared Bracero Killer. Devastated by this news, his father takes matters into his own hands.

At the end of *Bracero: Mojados*, the confrontation between Manuel and his father escalates, culminating in Manuel's murder by US and Mexican government authorities. This is not the father's intention—originally he sets out to express to Manuel his disgust and shame at Manuel's criminal behavior before he turns his son over to US and Mexican government authorities. Nonetheless, he is unable to convince Manuel to turn himself in peacefully, and their exchange ends in violence. In the confusion, Rosaura is able to escape to ask for help for Miguel, her aunt, and other women and men in their group. Caught in the crossfire of the US and Mexican government authorities who are attempting to arrest Manuel, Rosaura's cry, "Oh God! Oh God! Protect us and protect all of the braceros! Protect all of the braceros! Protect them! Protect them! Oh God!" stops the authorities from shooting them (31). Agents did not risk shooting braceros, which would draw unwanted public attention to their enforcement of the US-Mexico border. Such a turn of events urges audiences to consider that it was up to those closest to Manuel to put an end to his criminally inhumane behavior and to come to the defense of each other and braceros. By having Manuel die after being shot by the US and Mexican government authorities that his father summons, as well as showing a father with the emotional courage to hold his son accountable in this way, Castaño imposes a severe penalty for betraying

Mexican immigrant women and men and the values instilled by one's family. This was an intermediary act that made it possible for women and men to consider the emotionally painful consequences of Mexican immigrants' indifference to and exploitation of the emotional, physical, and financial vulnerability of their fellows.

We know little about the reception of *Braceros: Mojados*. It is unknown whether Castaño's play was performed for US or Mexican theater audiences. Even so, her writing, publication, and circulation of this play was a daring intermediary act in support of Mexican immigrants of varying legal status in Mexico and the United States that held everyone who saw or read her play responsible for finding common ground with these women and men that would prevent them. from becoming indifferent to their emotional suffering. This was especially important because the women and men involved in this chapter of North American history rarely had the energy, networks, resources, time, or training to undertake or use written arts to express themselves.

The courage and achievements of *intermediarias* throughout the Mexican countryside capture the expansiveness of their assessment of the Bracero Program's reach and consequences. Their work makes obvious that these women were far more responsible and inclusive than either the US or Mexican government. At each other's urging, *intermediarias* confronted the emotional, physical, and financial consequences in real time. They did not wait for their emotional exhaustion to completely devastate them or their families—or for the US and Mexican governments to instruct them—but instead took matters into their own hands as responsibly as possible. Sometimes this meant taking on more emotional work to hold themselves and each other accountable for a family situation that they did not create on their own and that stretched across the US-Mexico border. Hence, unlike these governments or even women and men of our current generation, they recognized that children, women, and men's emotional well-being and humanity were at stake and deserved their full attention.

CELEBRATING ALL OF THE
INTERMEDIARIAS

To this day, *intermediarias'* daring and responsible spirit is unparalleled. It is striking that a plaza in San Martin de Hidalgo, Jalisco, has two statues honoring the townswomen's spirit. One depicts a mother holding her child. Without a plaque or any reference as to what exactly the statue honors, the monument is meant to do much symbolic work without reference to any specific woman, much less to *intermediarias* like Ignacia or other women who courageously confronted the emotional exhaustion of the separation of their families across the US-Mexico border alongside and in support of similarly exhausted women.

Initially, and for years, this statue alone adorned this town's plaza, but in 2011 San Martin de Hidalgo's municipal government decided to honor with a statue one of the few townswomen who had become a local and nationally elected government official: Maria Guadalupe Urzua Flores. The statue includes a plaque describing her accomplishments in support of town families, and it was moved to the plaza to stand in close proximity to the other statue. Maria Guadalupe is beloved by this town because throughout the 1940s and 1950s she helped build a medical dispensary for leprosy, opened a night school for adults, organized for the rights of farmworkers, was elected four times to serve as federal deputy for the Mexican state of Jalisco (1955–79), served as the state's vice president of the Chamber of Deputies (1957), and acted as the town's president (1999–2000). Although she actively initiated and furthered causes that benefited the women who throughout this town's history excelled as *intermediarias* for and in support of their families, she is most publicly acknowledged and celebrated for having served as an intermediary between the residents and the Mexican government at the local and national levels. She successfully forged a working relationship with local and national Mexican government officials that made possible a series of much-needed community development projects. These earned her the commemorative statue and many other accolades, including and during this town's annual Day of the Dead festivities.

Maria Guadalupe has earned this public recognition. But so have *intermediarias* like Ignacia, Azucena, Veneranda, and all the other women who forged and sustained awake houses, as well as Rosa de Castaño, whose writings held people of Mexican descent accountable for aiding and supporting one another during the continuing immigration crisis. This chapter is an attempt to bring their essential work to light so that one day they too are celebrated in such spirited and public fashion in Mexico and the United States.

CHAPTER EIGHT

· *Ejemplar y sín Igual*
(Exemplary and
without Equal)

The Loss of Childhood, 1942–1964

The activity of Mexican women as *intermediarias* establishing awake houses reveals how attempts to preserve the family led to its dramatic transformation. Yet some disruptions in family life were not as easily addressed. An entire generation of children experienced uniquely difficult childhoods because of the Bracero Program. This chapter focuses on the ways in which the advantages the program secured for nation-states and corporate farmers came at the expense of the life courses of children in Mexico.

Andres Ramirez was born in Ameca, Jalisco, Mexico, on February 8, 1950.[1] In 1951, his father Paul Ramirez joined the Bracero Program, leaving his mother on her own to care for him and his three siblings. Two years after his father's departure, his mother died, leaving Andres an orphaned young boy under the care of his extended family. He sang in local bars throughout the Mexican rural towns of Ameca, El Crucero, San Martin de Hidalgo, El Tepehuaje, and Villa Corona, Jalisco, to help provide for his siblings. He would sing *ranchera* ballads and *corridos* late into the night every day of the week for departing and returning braceros. Desperate to earn a healthy sum in tips and eager to learn more about *El Norte* (the United States) and his father's whereabouts, he was never too tired to sing of longing and loss.

In 1962, at the age of twelve, he joined his uncle Tomas Ramirez and journeyed to the United States via the Bracero Program in search of his father. He traveled across the states of Arizona (1962), California (1963, 1968–72), and Texas (1964–67), harvesting crops alongside other Mexican immigrant children similarly seeking to reunite with their bracero or undocumented Mexican immigrant parents. Still singing in local bars and bracero labor camps in the evenings, he became very popular and highly sought after for his soulful interpretation of José Alfredo Jiménez's "El Jinete" ("The Horseman"), a *ranchera* ballad that captures the pain of lost love.[2] For ten consecutive years, he migrated and sang songs of yearning for country, lovers, and opportunity before reuniting with his father in Los Angeles in 1972 at the age of twenty-two.

Andres's journey in search of his father had been difficult. As an elderly man, he shared that it had transformed him into *un niño ejemplar y sin igual* (an exemplary child without equal). Exemplary children were Mexican children who labored as if they were adults, in the place of or alongside adults. They were entrusted to undertake any task with the utmost attention to completing it perfectly. Andres could not afford to make his relatives, employers, coworkers, or friends "uncomfortable or inconvenienced by his laboring with them or for them." He embraced the spirit of thriving as an exemplary child without equal. He shared, "I had to or else I would be fired, penniless, and homeless." His attitude and actions would be seen as a reflection of his family upbringing and would be used to judge his and his entire family's moral character. His desire to locate and reunite with his family moved him to live up to these expectations. These "children without equal" had to prove themselves in silence, paving the way for an alienation that they rarely dared to discuss with anyone.

Historians of the mid-twentieth-century Mexican immigrant experience have for the most part neglected the migration and labor of children who journeyed in search of their bracero or undocumented Mexican immigrant fathers. Some traveled to labor alongside them to earn and save enough money to allow them to finally live together as a family in the United States.[3] These children's feelings of accountability were part of the human toll of the Bracero program. They had very little opportunity to experience life as children. They were lauded for caring for themselves without becoming burdensome nuisances to adults as they harvested crops, shined shoes, cleaned labor camp barracks, delivered heavy items door to door, maintained labor camps, and packed fruit.

This chapter demonstrates that the Bracero Program placed insurmountable pressures on children. Laboring in the place of their Mexican immigrant parents or by their side under exploitative conditions to complement their parents' wages, they relied on each other for emotional support as they tried to evade unwanted forms of public attention that would make them vulnerable because of their status. Andres recollected, "We only had our talents and other children on the same journey to confront a most brutal reality of being invisible for everyone's convenience." Listening to the stories these now-adults but once-children tell, we see the sting of rejection they experienced. In their recollections, these women and men recall the pain of being dismissed as undesirable Mexicans.

EXEMPLARY CHILDREN WITHOUT EQUAL

The songs that Andres and countless boys in similar family situations performed after endless hours of hard labor were carefully crafted performances. Stirring workingmen to listen to him meant selecting songs that addressed their "yearning for the sense of belonging they had lost." Andres performed songs that captured these men's longing for their loved ones and their friendships in Mexico. When being transported from their US labor camps to their places of employment, braceros would board and ride in old model trucks, crammed together alongside some forty boys and men. Without seat belts or enough room to stretch or see past the people standing directly in front of them, children like Andres often sang a selection of songs that connected these men to their Mexican rural towns and villages. Being allowed to travel and work alongside the men as part of the work crew was often based on whether their singing distracted the other workers from the indignities of their employment. Songs sung by these children helped remind workers of who they were, what they needed, what they deserved, and what and whom they valued most in life in the face of intense forms of dehumanization.

Singing to acknowledge, echo, or offset widely felt yet intimate fears without risking becoming overwhelmed emotionally themselves required a certain degree of trust and shared accountability among these children and men. Singing or listening together to songs of this sort, with an emphasis on the quality of the musical performance, encouraged these children and men to feel comfortable enough with each other to sing about the intimately painful transnational reality of being in long-distance romantic relationships, being away from family and friends as they struggled with physical illness and poverty, and fearing for the safety of family and friends attempting to join them by crossing the US-Mexico border. Songs of farewell and good wishes were among the most solicited and sung by exemplary children. Andres recalls that he was constantly urged to sing "El Bracero Mexicano" (1944), by the musical group Los Braceros, when beginning his thirty-minute musical performance for men after a hard day's work.[4] This song was a tribute to the Virgin Mary's protection of braceros as they journeyed and labored throughout Mexico and the United States.

In 1963, at the age of fifteen, Maria Francisca Torres would bury herself under layers of clothing that revealed only her eyes, nose, and hands to protect herself from the scorching sun as she harvested crops and to disguise her gender.[5] Young girls were not automatically welcomed as laborers in the fields, in competition with fellow Mexican immigrant male laborers, and Torres, having migrated to join her father as an undocumented Mexican immigrant child, could not afford to get deported or to get her family deported. Torres adopted the posture, work ethic, and know-how of an adult when working alongside her relatives as part of their crew. It was integral to her being accepted as exemplary and without equal. Afraid of drawing unwanted attention to herself and family because of her age, her gender, and the nature of her work, she could not afford to slow her family down when laboring, or to make fellow workers uncomfortable. Francisca shared, "Out of my love for my family and our future, I was determined to prove an exemplary laborer and member of our family. I could not—our family could not—afford for me to be detected as a young girl laboring in the fields." Being tall, she hoped her height and work performance would make her seem like a young adult and not the child she was as she worked energetically under the supervision and protection of her grandfather and father. Maria Francisca's "love for her family inspired her deep investment" in becoming exemplary and without equal as she labored among and in competition with men.

This also meant that Maria Francisca's social interactions with Mexican immigrant men who were not her relatives were extremely limited. Like the young boys who excelled as exemplary children without equal through song, proving herself to be a competent worker was critical to her remaining safe in the company of mostly Mexican immigrant male workers. She recalled, "I did not dare risk socializing with them or sharing with them that I found the labor emotionally and physically exhausting."

Not all children laboring as exemplary children without equal fared well. On August 10, 1948, the US Department of Labor's Child Bureau began to receive reports of abuses against children.[6] In San Antonio, Texas, it was reported that at the Barn Hill Ranch Mexican immigrant boys were being locked inside the labor camp barracks and pistol-whipped when they attempted to escape from the employment site. These children between the ages of nine and fifteen were instructed to work long hours. They were rarely allowed to socialize with adults. Although official investigations of the mistreatment of Mexican immigrant children did not endorse this child abuse, they generally simply itemized the children's injuries.

There were also reports produced by US charities like the Bayside Social Center of California that revealed that undocumented Mexican immigrant children as young as twelve years old were found crying on the steps of churches throughout San Diego, California.[7] Some of these children out of their hunger and fear had boarded northward freight trains in search of their Mexican immigrant relatives in the United States.

The Bayside Social Center staff described these children as quite remarkable, praising them for handling adult tasks. Casting them as young women and men in desperate need of work so that they could send remittances to their families in the Mexican countryside, the center's staff did not advocate reuniting them with their families. Instead, the organization argued that much more should be done to place these children in agricultural labor camps because they had demonstrated a remarkable ability to exceed employer expectations without making any demands.

Beginning in May 14, 1949, and continuing until the termination of the Bracero Program, the Works Progress Administration adopted a different course of action.[8] Instead of recommending that the children work longer hours, the WPA developed a toy loan program. Using an honor code and a merit system designed to promote the appreciation and care of private property, WPA administrators allowed each eligible child to select a toy that she or he could take home for a period of two weeks. When the toy was returned, it could be exchanged for some other toy. The child was expected to take reasonable care of the toys, but there was no penalty when a toy was accidentally broken. Children who took good care of these toys would become "Honor Borrowers" and were permitted to choose the most desirable toys. Scooters, skates, wagons, tricycles, and bicycles were among the toys in greatest demand. The privilege of borrowing such toys was used as an incentive to teach children to be careful when handling the property of their employers.

This toy loan program was made accessible to undocumented Mexican immigrant children throughout Southern California at the request of their US employers. The employers administering this program often took advantage of these children's desire to in some way enjoy their childhood: they often required the youths to excel as workers who harvested and packed fruits and vegetables with the utmost care and precision before they could be lent a toy.

Beginning in August 8, 1949, and until the end of the Bracero Program, under the supervision of Tom Clark, the US Immigration and Naturalization Service also took notice of exemplary children without equal. But rather than valuing the lengths to which they were willing to go for the sake of reuniting with their parents in the United States, the agency imprisoned them in block-shaped barbed-wire stockades in El Centro, California.[9] The government was frustrated by children who insisted that they were eighteen years old when it was obvious that they ranged between twelve and fifteen. The children's refusal to provide information on their family background or present family contact information out of their loyalty for their families moved Clark to instruct INS officials to threaten them (especially young girls between the ages of thirteen and fourteen) with head shaving unless they admitted their illegal entry.

On October 26, 1950, third and fourth graders from the Aguas School in Beverly Hills, California, were not as inhumane in their reaction to children who had been stripped of their childhood. They donated the money inside their piggy banks to provide children laboring in the fields with some school supplies.[10] They were appalled at news stories featuring children who labored fourteen-hour shifts working in the fields, cleaning the exterior of labor camp barracks before the crack of dawn, and polishing the kitchen and recreational areas till midnight. The Beverly Hills students evidently recognized that these eleven-year-old children were not being treated like children. Hence, they dipped into their piggy banks and gave all the proceeds toward purchasing books, a chalkboard, chalk, pens, paper, pencils, crayons, and toys for migrant children.

In 1963, twenty-one years after the Bracero Program's inception and on the cusp of its termination, the *Los Angeles Times* drew attention to these children. The newspaper featured a story that centered on the experience of fourteen-year-old Pepita Jones. It reported that she passed herself off as "a sixteen-year-old Mexican American young woman, so that she could live and labor on the fringe of the law so long that [*sic*] it is easy for her to do so." Her need to be accepted on the job was portrayed as an act of opportunistic deception.[11] The newspaper reported that Pepita had been born in the United States. While searching for her parents she had been adopted by a Mexican American migrant family, only after she had contributed to their light purse. The story did not present Pepita's own understanding of her family situation. Nor did it report the difficulty of working as an adult when actually a child. Even as it reported that 5,477 undocumented Mexican immigrant children under sixteen years of age were working on similar terms as those framing Pepita's employment and that 3,946 of these children laboring in this way were at most fourteen years of age, Pepita was simply cast as "cheerful and illegal." The story questioned her claim of having been born in the United States to Mexican immigrant parents. It stated that Pepita's school enrollment had lasted only three months and that her parents' abandonment of her had led to her dropping out of school. Her teachers noticed that when in school she couldn't read or write—"Since she was a large girl who would move on to another job shortly, they let her sit at the back of the class, or do odd jobs scrubbing floors and washing windows." Her anxiety over being without her parents and limited to exploitative employment was not discussed. Instead, Pepita was portrayed as a most happy woman, not a child, who, when interviewed for this news story, shared a "cheerful smile, flashing dark eyes, and willingness to help."

LOCAL PROGRAMS FOR BRACERO
CHILDREN IN MEXICO

In December 1942, five months into the Bracero Program, middle-class families throughout San Martin de Hidalgo, Jalisco, and other Mexican rural towns and villages began programs to educate and give employment to children left behind by braceros and undocumented Mexican immigrant male relatives Their rationales for doing this, which emphasized transforming backward, illiterate, and malnourished children into disciplined, literate, and productive citizens and employees, were much like President Manuel Avila Camacho's rationale for working-class people's participation in the Bracero Program in that they depicted working-class people negatively and emphasized plans for their improvement. Illiteracy, disease, poverty, and unskilled labor were represented as factors that made working-class women and men unfit parents. According to middle-class families, working-class parents had not been exposed sufficiently to culture and were not adequately positioned to raise responsible and productive citizens. Although middle-class families wanted to teach working-class children to read and write, they still wanted to consign them to unskilled labor, claiming that this was what they were best suited for.[12]

Middle-class families employed the children of Mexican immigrant families (families with either bracero and/or undocumented Mexican immigrant male relatives laboring in the United States) to undertake the work that had been previously performed by their own bracero and undocumented Mexican immigrant male relatives. The children were expected to meet and exceed the middle-class families' expectations without complaint. Middle-class families were also struggling to cope with the Bracero Program's impact on their earning potential, as they were mostly young wives left behind and single adults who prided themselves on being successful entrepreneurs, professionals, well-educated teachers, or large landowners. Their employment of working-class children was a part of their own family plans for economic progress. These families were committed to preserving their middle-class status throughout the duration of their own bracero relatives' contract labor, and they hoped to transition into revitalized businesses and even more comfortable homes upon their bracero relatives' return.

Middle-class men did not teach academic subjects to these children. Women were encouraged to take a public role in the town as teachers, even if this meant working longer shifts. The daughters of middle-class families became those most responsible for the employment of children who had recently separated from their immigrant fathers and other immigrant relatives across the US-Mexico border. They targeted and employed immigrant families' children by appealing to overworked grandparents and parents, saying that demands on their labor and time, as well as their own backwardness and poor education, were preventing them from raising children adequately and responsibly and that their children were entitled to learn how to read and write and to develop a strong moral character and work ethic.[13] Often these children were not attending public schools because they could not afford to pay for school uniforms or supplies. Middle-class families who offered to be the educators and employers of poor immigrant families' children highlighted their arrangements as superior to what public schools could offer. They promised to reinforce the parenting of working-class families during their immigrant male relatives' absence and to supervise children carefully during their employment.

Anxious and overworked working-class grandparents and parents embraced the idea of their grandchildren and children obtaining employment and some sort of education. Already familiar with youngsters excelling as exemplary children without equal in the United States, they did not object to their children laboring and being educated in the Mexican countryside. In any case, refusing or publicly questioning the terms of middle-class families' offer was not an option. The families of these migrating laborers had often entered Bracero Program loan agreements with the middle-class families who made the offer. Working longer shifts for lower wages had "made it difficult to pay off their loans immediately, so they were economically beholden to these families."[14] Confident that their children's employment would appease these lenders, making it feasible for their families to transition out of debt and eventually out of contract labor, they allowed their children to be employed by these families without question. Immigrant families were committed to staying on good terms with their lenders; middle-class families were aware of this and took advantage of their vulnerability.

In December 1942, an estimated forty children in San Martin de Hidalgo began working for these middle-class families.[15] Elementary and middle school–age children were divided into groups of four and taught reading comprehension, writing, and basic math for two-hour intervals five days a week, by middle-class families. But under the guise of being educated, children were being exploited for their labor. They had to work twenty hours a week to obtain such reading instruction. Like their Mexican immigrant male relatives, children felt bound to these requirements. Their failure to comply would jeopardize their parents' loan agreement with these families.

Mexican national public school standards required a minimum of seven hours of school each day to be dedicated to the study of letters, arts, and sciences. These middle-class families clearly violated these standards. Children were required to spend half of their school days working. Each child was required to work four-hour shifts five days a week for successful entrepreneurs and large landowners throughout town. Children between the ages of seven and ten were assigned to work in groups because that way they were expected to get more done efficiently. Those between the ages of eleven and fourteen were assigned individual tasks. The employer families claimed that the work would help children develop marketable skills. However, children were confined to exploitative unskilled labor: they cleaned, cooked, delivered products, harvested crops, organized goods and wares, tended to livestock, and washed and ironed clothing for middle-class families. The logic was consistent with Camacho's justifying working-class men's bracero contracts: by exposing children to unfamiliar customs, the work would raise their earning potential and improve their work habits. In fact, it served only middle-class interests. Children's labor was largely responsible for an increase in productivity among middle-class entrepreneurs. Not surprisingly, the quality of customer service at these businesses had improved dramatically.

The middle-class families kept detailed attendance records. They met with students' grandparents and parents to discuss children's progress and their work ethic. Although such employment improved children's literacy, working-class bracero families still resented the exploitation and imperious management of their children.

In January 1943, middle-class families overstepped boundaries by recommending that parents and grandparents discuss with their children the importance of education, family sacrifice, and the nurturing of strong lines of communication with Mexican immigrant relatives. They advised grandparents and parents to prompt their children to write and pray for their bracero and undocumented Mexican immigrant male relatives' safe return. Such activities were meant "to facilitate children's transition into their employment, and to remind them that they were members of two-parent families and a town in great need of their labor."[16] The middle-class families reasoned that it was in the town's best interest to inspire children's commitment to their education through those they trusted most: their caretakers. They considered these activities expressions of genuine support and understanding toward children's emotional well-being.

Bracero grandparents and parents, however, considered their suggestions to be profoundly manipulative. Being advised to discuss family sacrifice with their children and to encourage their children to write to and pray for their immigrant relatives was humiliating in that it implied that their bracero relatives had neglected or abandoned them and that the children had forgotten their bracero relatives or did not honor and respect them. It cast doubt on these families' commitment to one another and invaded their sense of privacy. The intrusiveness of middle-class families discussing sensitive aspects of their lives under such terms, coupled with exploitative management and supervision of children, heightened tensions between middle-class and working-class immigrant families and inspired concerned bracero grandparents and parents to nurture children's self-esteem and belonging in the intimacy of their own homes and neighborhoods.

Rosa Rodriguez relied on her children and similarly struggling neighbors to overcome the hardships of negotiating middle-class families' expectations and her husband's absence.[17] The entire family would arrive home at seven in the evening and cook and help each other clean and prepare for the next day. They looked forward to dinner, as this was the only time they had to themselves. Most of their day was spent working. Weekends were when neighborhood block parties took place. Neighbor families compared plans, pooled their resources, and invited each other to community-wide group birthday parties, dinners, and curbside chats. Individual birthdays or other milestones were rarely celebrated. Working-class Mexican immigrant families collaborated closely to cultivate a healthy sense of self-esteem capable of offsetting middle-class families' emotionally and physically draining management.[18]

Nonetheless, some parents found it difficult to express their affection. Single-handedly raising their children was challenging. Women left behind had to take on the roles of both parents in their children's lives. This implied disciplining them while still trying to instill healthy self-esteem and convey affection. In an effort to negotiate such family obligations, Ignacia Zarate Mandujano Rios expressed her affection discreetly, hugging her children and kissing their foreheads only after they had fallen asleep. She explained, "It was difficult to express my affection. I feared my children would detect my vulnerability. It was difficult to maintain their affection and trust and simultaneously to teach them discipline with so much work and responsibility to take care of. I couldn't afford to openly express my affection."[19]

Overwhelmed by middle-class families' expectations, the mothers of these children sought support from their relatives working as braceros. They urged bracero relatives to send remittances to pay off their program loan agreements immediately and make their children's transition out of employment possible. They explained that accommodating their husbands' contract labor had forced their children into exploitative arrangements.

The grandparents, mothers, and other caretakers of these children were pained by their inability to support their children. Working thirteen-hour shifts as agricultural day laborers, cooks, customer service representatives, housekeepers, vendors, and waitresses, they earned an average eighteen pesos a week, roughly the equivalent of the wages that a bracero or undocumented Mexican immigrant laborer would get in a day.[20] Their earnings were not enough to raise their children; families implored bracero relatives "not to forget about those they had left behind."[21]

These letters were difficult to write. Grandparents and parents in the working class feared that if they conveyed the full extent of their exploitation, their immigrant male relatives would become disillusioned and estranged. Their contract labor had been motivated by an already desperate situation that their letters confirmed was worsening. Families speculated that Mexican immigrant male relatives were not earning enough to make their loan payments and that news of their children's exploitation and town employment conditions would discourage them from returning. Nonetheless, families had no other choice but to confide in their relatives and request their help.

Working-class immigrant men responded by emulating the approach of repatriates. They claimed that they would eventually return from US employment with enough savings to improve the family's socioeconomic status and make their permanent settlement possible. Meanwhile, they saw family members back in Mexico as laborers confronting exploitation and racism under conditions similar to their own. They advised their families to administer enclosed remittances carefully and to keep children laboring and to a certain extent learning under the supervision of these middle-class families.[22] By taking advantage of middle-class families' employment opportunities and by temporarily obtaining US wages, their families would eventually transcend the circumstances that restricted them to poorly paid unskilled labor on both sides of the US-Mexico border. Their vision of a better life for the family thus required long-term family sacrifice.

The immigration histories of mid-twentieth-century working-class Mexican immigrant men reveal that US wages and discretionary return became the touchstones of their vision for family reunification. They envisioned that uninterrupted Bracero Program contract renewal or undocumented Mexican immigrant labor would enable them to pay off their loans and improve their working and living conditions, as well as to obtain quality education for their children.

Mexican immigrant men's failure to consult their families while still requesting their acceptance and accommodation of long-term family separation across the US-Mexico border reflects the prevalence of inequality in Mexican rural towns and villages. By custom, women, children, and the elderly were not entitled to question immigrant husbands' or other male relatives' assessment of their family situation and options. Instead, Mexican women, children, and elderly people were often taken for granted. As breadwinners and heads of households, Mexican immigrant men believed they were entitled to demand their family's labor and sacrifice. Working-class men also tried to encourage their families to make sacrifices and remain behind in Mexico, since they believed that immigrating to the United States would only trap their children in far worse employment conditions than labor under the supervision of working-class families. For the most part, families assumed that their immigrant relatives knew and acted in their best interest and tried to fulfill their relatives' expectations and plans. This was especially the case for their children, who tried to excel as exemplary children without equal.

CHAPTER NINE · *Decididas y Atrevidas*
(Determined and Daring)

In Search of Answers, 1947–1964

On July 15, 1947, Grace Hermosillo was "*decidida* and *atrevida* [determined and daring]—all at once."[1] She had finally mustered the determination and daring to admit to Grace Sawyer, a social case worker at the Department of Charities of the County of Los Angeles Bureau of Public Assistance, that she had become estranged from her infant child's father, Gabriel Rodriguez. In January 1947, a few months after Grace had given birth to her baby Sylvia, Gabriel abandoned her in Los Angeles. Her Mexican American family disowned her for having had a child out of wedlock with a bracero. When Grace met Gabriel, he had been working as a bracero at one of her employer's orchards. Grace's low wages from cleaning other people's homes were not enough to provide for Sylvia's basic needs, so she sought the assistance of the US government to confirm the failure of their relationship and to secure care for their child. Gabriel's abandonment of them without leaving them so much as a note had shamed her, but she was impelled to put her pride and shame aside for Sylvia's sake.

Grace assumed that as an orphaned US citizen born to a US citizen mother, Sylvia was most likely eligible for some form of financial aid from the government, but she did not take requesting such assistance on her child's behalf lightly. It took much courage to admit to Sawyer that Gabriel did not want to help raise their child or be part of the family. Before launching a bureau investigation of Gabriel's whereabouts and intentions to determine that he had indeed abandoned them so that Sylvia could be eligible for ANC (Aid to Needy Children) benefits, Sawyer had required Grace to publicly accept and document the failure of her relationship. Signing forms in which she attested to having not heard from Gabriel or socially interacted with him for a continuous period of time was also a prerequisite for Sawyer to determine whether Sylvia was eligible for benefits. It was emotionally daunting for Grace to assert in such a formal and public fashion that they had been a couple, had had a child out of wedlock, and had become emotionally disconnected from each other—and that now she needed support to raise their child—but she understood that she had to affirm their permanent separation in order to act as a responsible parent on Sylvia's behalf.

The next step in becoming eligible was delayed because Gabriel had finished his bracero contract and, presumably, left the United States. Grace requested that Sawyer expand her investigation to Gabriel's hometown of Las Puentes in Chihuahua, Mexico,[2] but Sawyer's bureau supervisor, Arthur J. Mill, who conducted the preliminary review of the application, instructed Sawyer, on the advice of US consul H. Claremont Moses, to inform Grace that this would be too expensive. Moses told Grace she would need to request the Mexican government's assistance in locating Gabriel; then once she had found him she and Sylvia should settle in Mexico. That way, they could pursue some sort of family relationship with Gabriel.

Grace did not follow Moses's instructions. She found applying for ANC benefits to be publicly humiliating, and she was determined to request that Sawyer advocate on her and Sylvia's behalf. Grace explained that she had neither the money nor the will to pursue any sort of family relationship at Gabriel's side and in Mexico, and that as US citizens she and Sylvia deserved to have the bureau do everything within its reach and in compliance with ANC procedures to ascertain Gabriel's ability and willingness to contribute financially toward Sylvia's care. Angry, frustrated, concerned for her child, and unwilling to once again expose Sylvia or herself to Gabriel's rejection—much less in Mexico—Grace drew on her US citizenship status, as well as her knowledge that the bureau was supposed to meet her request, to pressure Sawyer to investigate their family's relationship using its networks and resources. Grace's dedication to finally obtaining information that would help her and the bureau formally determine Gabriel's personal investment to raising Sylvia emboldened her to not give up on holding the US government and Gabriel accountable for the consequences of the Bracero Program.

On July 30, 1947, US vice consul Wallace LaRue notified Moses that after successfully locating and questioning Gabriel he had learned that Gabriel doubted that he was the father and was not able to provide Grace with any financial support.[3] In his report, LaRue stated that Gabriel had volunteered to take a blood test to verify his paternity and had provided evidence of his working as a poorly paid bartender to confirm his inability to financially contribute to Sylvia's care. With this information in place, Sylvia was finally deemed eligible for ANC benefits. Nonetheless, it was emotionally devastating for Grace to learn not only that Gabriel was uninterested and unable to contribute financially to Sylvia's upbringing but that he doubted he was actually her father.

Historians have yet to consider the US government's interrogation of Mexican American and Mexican immigrant women left behind to care for their children as single mothers in the United States by their estranged bracero or undocumented Mexican immigrant boyfriends as a transnational border enforcement measure.[4] This chapter, using oral life histories, public records, and government documents to examine the US government's implementation of ANC eligibility requirements and Operation Wetback, both of which were underestimated border enforcement campaigns waged against undocumented Mexican immigrants in the United States and in the Mexican countryside, shows how these measures imposed the indignities and penalties of illegality on Mexican and Mexican American families. As a result, women of Mexican descent and varying legal statuses were often inspired to search for answers and opportunities to transition into healthier family situations.

ANC APPROACHES TO THE SUPPORT OF MEXICAN IMMIGRANT CHILDREN

Determining whether in fact the Mexican immigrant men in question could be formally deemed "absent parents" was the central concern of the ANC program. Approximately 70 percent of the ANC caseload in California dealt with the absent fathers of children whose cases were being handled by the Department of Charities of the County of Los Angeles.[5] Classifying them as "absent parents" was a way of trying to secure financial support from these men for the children in question.[6] The department, at its own discretion, occasionally recruited law enforcement to locate and interrogate these men in Mexico.

The Department of Charities of the County of Los Angeles had a long-standing mission of aiding children who it determined fully met its eligibility requirements. In 1879, the state constitution of California explicitly declared that aid would be granted to US child citizens who were either whole or half orphans or abandoned children without any mother, father, or parental guardian. In 1913, it placed an emphasis on improving the home life of children who were living in poverty even when under the custody of their parent or parents. By 1945, the emphasis had shifted to assisting children whose fathers had been continuously absent for at least three years. In 1949, this eligibility requirement was altered to require continuous absence. This change in eligibility transferred to the ANC program many children who had been receiving general relief and resulted in an increase in the state's absent-parent caseload. In 1952, the problem of nonsupport by absent parents generated amendments requiring the notification of appropriate law enforcement officers when aid was granted to a child who had not been supported by a parent for at least three months. These officers were enlisted to help the department locate absent parents when a case was being decided and to closely monitor whether the parents of children granted ANC benefits had returned to be with their children. It became law enforcement's obligation to verify that children enrolled in the ANC program were in fact abandoned and deserted by a parent throughout their program participation.[7]

Mothers applying for ANC benefits on behalf of their children were expected to be very cooperative with the Department of Charities of the County of Los Angeles's handling of their case. The department depended on women to investigate the men who had abandoned or deserted them and their children in the United States. The emphasis on locating suspected fathers to confirm their earning potential and their intention to reunite with their children placed an extraordinary burden on these women. It required them to provide essential details about the child in question, information about the presumed father's whereabouts, and confirmation that the mothers were not interested in reuniting with these men. Failure to provide such information would automatically disqualify their children from receiving ANC benefits.

Mexican immigrant mothers attempting to protect their children's interests faced aggressive questioning about the veracity of the information they provided. On May 12, 1947, Elisa Garcia was required to attest that she and Jesus Becerra, the former bracero and presumed father of her children, did not have any intention to continue their romantic or family relationship in the United States.[8] Like other Mexican immigrant women in her situation, it became her responsibility to account for her and the presumed father's attitude and action on a matter that was very personal but that, for the sake of her children, had become extraordinarily public.

On December 17, 1947, Italian American mother Sally Giacomini, who had filed an application for ANC benefits on behalf of her newborn child, wrote to the Department of Charities of the County of Los Angeles, asking officials to go to the Olympic Hotel in Tijuana, Baja California, Mexico, as well as the Hotel Rio Bravo in Juarez, Chihuahua, to locate her former bracero boyfriend.[9] After filing her case in Los Angeles, California, she sent this information by mail from Chicago. Having become demoralized and impatient with caseworkers' questions, she provided them with this information as her last attempt to determine her child's eligibility for ANC benefits. Records do not indicate whether her letter was simply filed or was used to continue the investigation of her case. Nonetheless, her case illustrates that the scrutiny of women's personal choices, most especially if they had romantic affairs with braceros or undocumented Mexican immigrant men and were parenting their children as single mothers, unfairly burdened them with much of the responsibility of finding a child's father in order to get aid and could lead them to give up entirely on obtaining it.

In 1947, the Department of Charities estimated that its implementation and enforcement of eligibility requirements—with the assistance of Mexican American and Mexican immigrant women nationwide—had resulted in an estimated 12,987 children having been granted ANC benefits.[10] Reports by the department revealed that 55 percent of absent parents were thirty-five years or younger in age, and that 68 percent of abandoned children between the ages of one and ten had been left under the care of one of their parents.[11] Regardless of the age of the child, ANC granted mothers a $130.00 monthly stipend.[12] It was expected that the women would allocate $85.00 for shelter and $8.50 for food for each child awarded such benefits. The remainder of these funds could be spent at the women's discretion.[13] Not connecting children's vulnerability to the Bracero Program, the department held firmly that neither it nor these children's mothers "could let children starve, whatever may be the faults of their parents."[14]

On March 17, 1947, Marion Wilson, a caseworker for the Tulare, California, Department of Public Welfare, opted for a humane approach to conducting an investigation of Jesus Archuleta.[15] She did not require twenty-year-old Mary Andrade to comply with the department's transnational investigation to ascertain Archuleta's ability and desire to help her raise their two-year-old son, Jessie. She understood that answering a series of personal questions about their romantic relationship to determine Jessie's eligibility for ANC benefits would be daunting to Mary. Wilson did not assume that Mary could be held solely accountable for the failure of the couple's romantic relationship or their son's welfare. Instead, she insisted that the department exhaust its resources to locate and question Jesus in the United States and Mexico. Mary was at least spared the public humiliation of having to ask US consul Stephen E. Aguirre to travel to Ciudad Juarez, Chihuahua, to complete their investigation of Jesus.

On April 3, 1947, Wilson notified Mary that Jessie was eligible for ANC benefits amounting to a $127 monthly stipend to help finance his basic needs.[16] Jesus admitted to having labored in the United States between May 18, 1944, and September 16, 1945, as a bracero and said he had married another Mexican American woman, settled with her in Ciudad Juarez, was unemployed, and was unable to contribute to Jessie's welfare.[17] He also confirmed that he did not have any intention of initiating or sustaining any personal relationship with Mary or their son. Without omitting any details, Wilson provided Mary with this information and urged her to focus on her transition into parenting Jessie on her own.

On July 11, 1947, the district director of the Los Angeles Bureau of Public Assistance, S. W. Owen, adopted a different approach by seeking to make former braceros more accountable for the emotional consequences of their poor decisions.[18] Owen collaborated with social caseworker Muriel E. Emerson and the US Consulate staff in Mexico City to investigate Francisco Rodriguez's ability to help in the financing of his three-year-old son's upbringing. The child's nineteen-year-old Mexican American mother Rosie Mendez had not heard from Francisco for over a year, and without any emotional or financial support from him or her family had applied for ANC benefits on her baby Saul's behalf. She provided Emerson with his mailing address in Mexico City, as this was the only information Francisco had shared about his experience in Mexico with her.[19]

Having met Francisco as he labored as a bracero in the strawberry fields of Oxnard, California, Rosie moved from Oxnard to Los Angeles when Francisco abandoned her. Lured by the promise of higher wages cleaning homes in this city, she anticipated that creating some distance between where they had met, dated, lived together, and begun raising their child together would be a decisive first step toward asserting the courage to confront the emotional consequences of the Bracero Program and Francisco's decisions.

Owen suspected that Rosie had already endured quite a bit of public scrutiny. Both he and Emerson agreed that Mexican American women left to raise children on their own by their former bracero or undocumented Mexican immigrant boyfriends faced shame and marginalization without much support. Owen and Emerson told the US Consulate's staff handling Rosie and Carlos's case to investigate thoroughly Francisco's employment history, earning potential, ownership of property and other assets, and family background before asking him to share and explain his ability and desire to provide for and raise Carlos as his child in the United States. Their investigation revealed that Francisco was too financially overwhelmed and unstable in Mexico to care about or contribute financially to the welfare of Carlos. Francisco already had a family of his own in Juarez and could barely meet the basic needs of his four other minor children. Working as a chef in a modest hotel, without a home or other assets to his name, and having been left to parent his children on his own when his wife abandoned him, Francisco would not be able to contribute financially to Carlos's upbringing.

Meticulously investigating the intentions and whereabouts of former braceros and undocumented Mexican immigrant men was rather exceptional in California's Department of Charities in Los Angeles County. It was standard practice for this department's supervisors and staff to expend more energy and time investigating Mexican American mothers who were requesting ANC benefits on behalf of their US-born children. Financially inexpensive and logistically convenient as a result of Mexican American women's residence in the United States in close proximity to departmental offices, questioning them was much easier than locating bracero and undocumented Mexican immigrant men in Mexico. Mexican American mothers also initiated these investigations by filing applications on behalf of their children, making it feasible to acquire and maintain careful records of their family background, personal relationships, earning potential, daily activities, and parenting. The women's investment in determining important aspects of the future of their family's welfare with the assistance of this department rendered them vulnerable to answering very personal questions for the sake of their children.

This was not the case among the men questioned. The men often claimed that they were not even the child's actual fathers, or they provided minimal information to affirm their insolvency and lack of interest in contributing to the child's financial well-being. For example, on September 19, 1960, Adolfo Marmolejo, a former bracero, merely explained that he was busy, sold old batteries, and had a small income and two children in Mexico to care for already; he would not even consider supporting or being there for his US-born son, Ismael.[20]

California's Department of Public Assistance steadily opposed providing either Mexican American women in the United States or former braceros and undocumented Mexican immigrants in Mexico with a thorough report of their findings when investigating them to determine their US-born children's eligibility for ANC benefits in the United States. So women and men received at best minimal descriptions of the outcome of these investigations. The supervisors and staff of the department were not invested in assisting the women and men in reconnecting with each other; nor were the agents interested in sharing information that would allow families to reunite in the United States. Family reunification was recommended and facilitated by the department only if couples expressed an interest in reunifying as a family for the sake of their children in Mexico and with their own money.

On May 23, 1947, twenty-year-old Estela Alarcon Fernandez learned—after California's Department of Public Assistance had investigated her estranged bracero husband, Francisco Fernandez, to determine her son Esteban's eligibility for ANC benefits—that her lover had actually passed away.[21] Having located Francisco's extended family in Ciudad Juarez, Chihuahua, Mexico, a few weeks after his passing, the department merely gave Estela a report showing his estimated decease date and the location in which he had died. US consul Stephen E. Aguirre advised that workers handling Estela's case solely express their condolences and their appreciation for his having once participated in the Bracero Program and then provide her with a copy of this report. Neither marriage nor death motivated the department to extend its efforts beyond obtaining and using these women and men's personal information for the sake of determining their children's eligibility for financial assistance. It did not hold itself responsible to help these women or men cope with their loss.

As claims for ANC benefits multiplied, the INS became increasingly concerned to ensure that Mexican immigrant men did not father children in the United States who might end up being subsidized by the government when these men lost their employment and couples split up. For example, Socorro Martinez Gutierrez was an employee at the Royal Packing Company in Soledad, California, who had initially entered the United States as a bracero but because of his exemplary employment history was being sponsored by the company for legal citizenship. The company was sponsoring his wife's one-month tourist visa as well, but because of US government anxieties about families of immigrants becoming permanently reunited in the United States the INS wanted to make sure that she would not accept any employment in the United States and that she would return immediately to Mexico upon the expiration of her tourist visa. Therefore, on September 11, 1952, Gutierrez dutifully responded to the request of his employers that he write and sign a letter, for submission to the INS, in which he attested to his good character and his earning potential and emphasized that on the strength of these he could assume complete responsibility for his wife's compliance with US immigration laws.[22]

By May 3, 1960, the number of Mexican American and Mexican immigrant mothers who had developed the courage to file applications for ANC benefits on behalf of their US-born children in California had risen to such an extent that the district attorney of the state was reported to have filed a request for special staff to handle these cases. The *Stockton Bee* reported on that date that since 1949 the number of applications for ANC benefits for children presumably born to Mexican American, Mexican immigrant, bracero, or undocumented Mexican immigrant parents had increased from 23 percent to 38 percent.[23] The cost was also described as having grown nearly tenfold. This increase in caseload and cost was also used to support increasing the prosecution of cases. Newspaper stories explained that a larger and separate staff invested in holding absent fathers accountable financially would be one way to alleviate at least some of the financial burden of providing ANC benefits to eligible children. The Department of Charities of the County of Los Angeles agreed that more funding for holding absent fathers accountable would make it feasible to conduct more extensive checking of welfare cases, reduce the number of grants for needy-children cases, discourage more persons from seeking welfare, and make it possible to collect more money from absent fathers of children receiving welfare aid.

The failure of California's Department of Charities in Los Angeles County to assist families who did not meet state residency requirements left countless children of itinerant families without access to ANC benefits. Mexican American and Mexican immigrant mothers who journeyed and labored from one US state to another in search of employment opportunities or better wages in agriculture were unable to live or work in the state for at least the required 120 days consecutively; nor would they have a home address where they could be reached throughout the investigation of their application for ANC benefits, as stipulated by the department's eligibility requirements.[24] Mothers' inability to meet these state residency requirements because of the conditions of migrant agricultural labor resulted in the automatic disqualification and, in turn, severe impoverishment of countless US child citizens throughout the state. In 1959, the Catholic Council of Working Life reported that "an estimated 2,000,000 children, women, and men worked on the Nation's farms for wages that are far below the level received by workers in non-migrant agricultural labor."[25]

On July 17, 1965, like countless Mexican American mothers laboring in agricultural labor camps throughout the United States, Maria Gonzalez had been recruited to work for the Montalvo Growers Association with her son and six daughters in the lemon orchards of Pomona, California.[26] She had started doing migrant agricultural labor in 1952 after having been abandoned by her former bracero husband, who had skipped out on his contract. This type of employment made it feasible for her and her children to work together, even though they could barely earn enough money to pay for only one meal a day. It was not a fair arrangement. Maria and her children frequently worked for two days and then, after orchards had been picked, were told to leave. During those two days they picked the equivalent of $198, but when they were supposed to receive the total sum of their wages they would routinely be paid an estimated $59. Employers like the Montalvo Growers Association would deduct fees for the rental of gloves as well as social security payments for each worker. Soon after receiving a check with these deductions, the workers were routinely laid off from these jobs. Fearful that their requesting an itemized account of deductions to their wages would ruin their chances of getting hired elsewhere, Maria and her children would move on to the next migrant agricultural labor opportunity that would employ all of them. They could not afford for any of them not to work. Being US citizens and a family did not protect these children from the exploitation of migrant agriculture labor in the United States.

On October 1, 1964, on the heels of the termination of the Bracero Program, the *Washington Post* reported that California's Department of Public Assistance was considering replacing bracero labor with that of young boys who had been deemed eligible for ANC benefits.[27] The supervisor of the department, Ernest E. Debs, explained, "We have a lot of able bodied boys on the relief program. They will not go to school or learn a trade. It seems about time to say: Either work or you will not get food." He elaborated, "Supervisor Kenneth Hahn estimated that Los Angeles County will have 330,000 unemployed youths available to take over the bracero jobs on December 31, 1964." This proposal, which was never carried out, was not specifically targeting young boys whose parents were Mexican Americans or Mexican immigrants; it was also aimed at African American boys. It stipulated that children between the ages of sixteen and eighteen years of age would earn a minimum wage of $1.25 an hour and be provided with sanitary facilities and other acceptable employment conditions. The proposal's vague terms and its replacement of adult Mexican immigrant men with children did not stir the alarm of this department but were consistent with the US government's prioritizing of the needs of US agriculture.

EFFECTS OF OPERATION WETBACK

In June 1954, the US government launched Operation Wetback, which deployed three hundred jeeps, two hundred airplanes, and thirty helicopters to detect, interrogate, and deport undocumented immigrants. Mexican Americans and Mexican immigrants bore the brunt of this operation.[28] It was estimated that 1,089,000 undocumented Mexican immigrants and countless others had gone undetected since repatriation, displacing an estimated 351,921 domestic agricultural laborers.[29] Leading up to this operation, increasing bracero and undocumented Mexican immigrant settlement in the United States led to deteriorating employment conditions among immigrant agricultural laborers. They had to plant and harvest crops for an estimated fifty cents an hour.[30] This was 45 percent less than wages paid in other unskilled employment sectors.[31] Lower wages and underemployment compelled an estimated 229,000 Mexican American girls and boys to drop out of school to work as agricultural laborers to compensate for their parents' decline in wages.[32] Similarly, an estimated 179,000 Mexican immigrant young men worked as braceros.[33] The recruitment and deployment of bracero and undocumented Mexican immigrant labor had diminished Mexican Americans' earning potential and standards of living.

Operation Wetback exacerbated existing labor competition and intraethnic tension among Mexican American, bracero, and undocumented Mexican immigrant agricultural laborers. Because of the massive influx of undocumented Mexican immigrants. border surveillance had expanded to include sites of Mexican American and Mexican immigrant interaction, and securing a Bracero Program contract had become extremely competitive and expensive. For Mexican American single mothers, renewal of ANC benefits continued to be contingent on their reassuring the Department of Charities of the County of Los Angeles that they had not reunited and would not reunite with their estranged bracero or undocumented Mexican immigrant boyfriends. Operation Wetback and news of ANC's handling of cases of Mexican American and Mexican immigrant women and their children elevated the importance of legalization through marriage and confronted Mexican American and Mexican families in the United States and Mexico with the transnational complexity of undocumented Mexican immigrant settlement in the United States. It compelled anxious and concerned Mexican American families and estranged Mexican families to investigate immigrant relatives' histories and intentions in protection of their interests.

Tired of living and laboring in the shadows, and afraid of deportation, some Mexican immigrant men did not abandon their Mexican American girlfriends but married them without consulting their families in Mexico. Such marriages made it feasible for them to pursue legal US immigration status and permanent settlement in the United States through the sponsorship of their wives. These actions were a source of emotional turmoil for families in Mexico who sought reassurance of their Mexican migrant relatives' investment in their family life in San Martin de Hidalgo and other towns and villages across the Mexican countryside.

FACING ABANDONMENT AND ESTRANGEMENT IN THE MEXICAN COUNTRYSIDE

Operation Wetback and ANC-related inquiries inspired Mexican families who had not heard from their bracero and undocumented immigrant relatives for months or years at a time to seek information from the Mexican government about those relatives' whereabouts, plans, and commitment to family obligations. Women began to question men's investments and relationships in the United States. Married women desired assurances that their husbands had not remarried or had children with other Mexican American and Mexican immigrant women in the United States. A different conversation around immigration ensued in the privacy of their homes as they struggled to define how to conduct this inquiry without tarnishing the reputations of their immigrant relatives and their families. Many feared that their inquiry would confirm the vulnerability of their marriage and Mexican immigrant relatives' recklessness, and they consulted their extended families before taking such a risk. Parents of bracero and undocumented Mexican immigrant relatives led in-depth conversations among their families to determine whether they should participate in an inquiry. Older relatives often initially cautioned against these investigations.[34] But after careful deliberation, families' decision to investigate Mexican immigrant relatives' intentions and whereabouts emerged as an integral component toward deciding how the women who were acting as heads of households would administer educational, employment, or business investments. They needed to determine whether internal migration for opportunities in skilled labor, the securing of an additional Bracero Program contract, or the undocumented immigration of other family members would be needed if they were to avoid losing their homes or dropping out of school. These families had to become flexible to protect their long-term interests with or without their Mexican migrant relatives' help.

In July 1955, throughout the Mexican countryside some women became emboldened to assert that it was in their families' interest to demand some form of accountability from the Mexican government concerning the Bracero Program's mismanagement of undocumented Mexican immigration on both sides of the US-Mexico border. These women insisted that they were not trying to control their Mexican immigrant relatives. They justified their inquiry as a call for national attention to the effects of the program, Operation Wetback, and unplanned US permanent settlement on their families' emotional and financial health. The program had at best helped pay basic business and property fees, but it had not made for a healthier quality of life. It had required them to manage businesses and homes under exploitative conditions, and it threatened to permanently separate their families.

Concerned families claimed that women's demands for investigations were consistent with women's long history of accommodating their bracero and undocumented Mexican immigrant relatives' immigration. Having documented their extended immigrant family relationships and investments for government consideration on numerous occasions, they argued that families confronting this situation were entitled to finally write individual letters to the Mexican government in support of an investigation of their own. By agreeing to make their own inquiries, concerned women understood that the true challenge was convincing other town families to publicly admit their need for the Mexican government's assistance in confronting the intimate yet national crisis that affected them through deportations, failed expectations, and unplanned permanent family separations.[35]

Receptive older women between the ages of forty and sixty often supported younger women's right and responsibility to conduct inquiries of their own. They instructed younger women, often their daughters, daughters-in-law, nieces, and sisters, in how to best address the Mexican government and investigate their immigrant relatives' status while keeping their families' reputation intact. For instance, they should write individual letters detailing their concerns without mentioning their immigrant relatives' undocumented immigrant status or speculating at all on their immigrant relatives' immigration status. They should focus on their immigrant relatives' departure date and discuss their families' overall concerns, such as the uncertainty of deportation, unplanned permanent family separation, and an increasing cost of living. The older women encouraged the younger women to request that the Mexican government launch a national effort to reconnect estranged Mexican immigrant families and to create an accessible information system detailing their immigrant relatives' employment conditions and destinations. The emphasis, they argued, should be on requesting that the Mexican government provide their immigrant relatives' contact information as well as competitive employment opportunities to which those relatives could return. These women were also were urged to express that they wanted an end to Operation Wetback. The older women justified their advice to the younger women in their families by explaining that information concerning their immigrant relatives' whereabouts would help them adapt responsibly to their immigrant relatives' immigration, handle their expenses, and meet the demands of poorly paid unskilled labor without drawing unwanted public scrutiny of their personal relationships with their immigrant relatives.[36]

Concerned Mexican immigrant families' search for answers and their demands for an end to Operation Wetback and the creation of employment opportunities comparable to contract and undocumented Mexican immigrant labor and settlement in the United States resonated as a national crisis. Between July 1954 and December 1956, countless families from Mexican rural towns and villages like San Martin de Hidalgo and throughout Mexico submitted letters of inquiry. Leading up to and throughout Operation Wetback's two years of operation, families of braceros and undocumented Mexican immigrants confronted uncertainty that compelled them to participate in a daring search for answers and change.[37]

The interaction of family representatives with other families confronting similar circumstances validated their approach and concern, confirming that the Mexican government's failure to create fair and profitable domestic employment opportunities and the US government's expansion of deportation efforts were not local but national immigration and family issues. Family representatives were convinced that they were right to draw national attention to the consequences of a poor domestic economy and the exigencies of immigration to the United States.

The indifference of the Mexican government toward these concerns confirmed how dire the situation of these families was. Families were devastated and discouraged when the Mexican government accepted their letters of inquiry but otherwise did nothing. Nonetheless, these families were determined to not give up. They asked returning and departing immigrants to inform their immigrant relatives that they needed to hear from them.[38] Increasingly younger male relatives pursued contracts or undocumented Mexican immigration. Families had no choice but to reach out to their estranged Mexican migrant relatives or to become migrants themselves. Their families desperately needed their financial support, so further immigration to the United States was unavoidable.

EXPANDING BUSINESS OPPORTUNITIES TO FORESTALL VILLAGE ABANDONMENT

After the failure of concerned families' inquiries to the Mexican government, Mexican men's pursuit of undocumented immigration and acceptance of exploitative Bracero Program conditions continued to compel their relatives left behind in the Mexican countryside to engage in internal migration or to endure exploitative family arrangements at home.[39] Nonetheless, other developments were beginning to take shape among working-class families in the Mexican countryside. Sporadic Mexican immigrant and migrant remittances continued to be foundational to town and village economies, but an unprecedented wave of unplanned, undocumented Mexican immigrant settlement in the United States compelled middle-class families to change their management of the labor of the working-class family members left behind.

Mexican immigration to the United States was draining these towns of direly needed investment, and this jeopardized middle-class interests. Far fewer Mexican immigrant families were entering loan agreements to finance their increasingly illegal departure to the United States. Instead, they were pooling their resources and depleting their extended families' hard-earned savings to finance their departure. This forced middle-class families to grow more reliant on bracero and migrant remittances.

Rural towns and villages throughout the Mexican countryside were becoming way stations for migrants venturing north from southern Mexico. Mexican men inundated town centers, resting and sleeping in alleys and parks before continuing the journey north. This made businesses in town-center marketplaces unprofitable and unmanageable and made living in close proximity to these marketplaces undesirable to middle-class families. Middle-class women and men were disturbed by their increased exposure to poor migrant men's lack of decorum. They realized that they could not recover their earning potential or the towns' livelihood by themselves.

Consequently, middle-class families became committed to breathing new life and investment into these marketplaces by, once again, targeting women and children left behind, but this time under different arrangements. Speculating that Operation Wetback had unintentionally intensified the migration of Mexican men, and determined to curb the tumultuous traffic of poor migrants invading their town marketplaces, they came together to protect their interests. They offered rural, unskilled families immigrant relatives—and especially women unable to benefit from vocational programs—opportunities to rent and operate, on affordable terms, clean and well-equipped business lots in town centers where they could pursue a trade of their choice. They were determined to integrate new participants into their enterprises on terms that protected their shared interests but still reinforced class differences. Staffing town marketplaces with these families might reinvigorate economic activity and provide some semblance of order. They hoped that these conditions would attract much-needed investment and a family-oriented clientele, and that more domestic business opportunities would reduce immigration to the United States.[40]

In San Martin de Hidalgo, families who agreed to lease and manage these lots, including children at least sixteen years of age, were required to pay an annual business lease fee. They were not allowed to gamble or engage in prostitution, and they had to donate two service hours to cleaning marketplace grounds. Any violation of these terms would result in their immediate eviction. These conditions satisfied middle-class families' anxieties concerning extended Mexican immigrant families' conduct and were compatible with the financial needs of extended Mexican immigrant families.

To persuade extended Mexican immigrant families to accept the offer, middle-class families pointed out that the United States did not accommodate Mexican immigrants' families and that *ir y venir* (coming and going to the United States) was becoming increasingly difficult and expensive.[41] Rather than invest their savings and set their sights on the United States or their Mexican immigrant relatives' return, working-class families would find it far more profitable to transition out of instability and poverty by investing in businesses of their own. Middle-class families emphasized that operating their own businesses in profitable locations and family-oriented venues was an excellent opportunity for families. They encouraged overworked, disillusioned, and financially strapped families to invest in working under yet another set of conditions while continuing to lack information concerning their Mexican immigrant relatives. Acknowledging that investing in their proposal would immediately pose an added financial burden, middle-class families stressed that in a matter of months the venture would prove worthwhile.

Beginning in August 1963, San Martin de Hidalgo's middle-class families leased an unrecorded number of marketplace lots to working-class families. Both male and female relatives signed on as the owners of these businesses. Male heads of households who were too old or physically unable to pursue bracero or undocumented immigrant labor often signed these lease agreements with their female relatives. Young men signed reluctantly, fearful that if the business failed they would not be able to migrate to a different region or to the United States in search of employment. Some women feared that their absent Mexican immigrant relatives would disapprove of their decision, but they could not wait for their approval. Feasible conditions and the participation of families confronting similar situations and doubts helped fuel their decision to pursue working in these centers without consulting absent immigrant male heads of households.

The fact that many families were agreeing to these conditions also offset women's anxiety concerning gender issues. The recruitment of other hardworking women and their families who agreed to steer clear of gambling and prostitution minimized their exposure to disreputable trades and maximized their potential to work in safe environments among families similarly invested in nurturing honorable reputations. Their ability to walk in groups to these marketplaces, to share workspaces with women and men working with their children and other supportive relatives by their side, and to cater to families and men under lawful and respectable terms also inspired women to overlook their reservations concerning these marketplaces.

Yet another motive for women to operate businesses in these marketplaces was to instill healthier self-esteem among their children. This venue's location and conditions would finally draw favorable attention to their labor and sacrifice and, in turn, elevate their public reputation. This does not mean that parents approved of children laboring like adults, but they felt that if their children worked by their side in support of revitalizing their families' earning potential they would finally earn public recognition and respect for their contribution to the town's economic rehabilitation.

Families pooled their savings and labor to purchase chairs, lamps, ovens, pantries, and tables to furnish their businesses. Entire families worked day and night to set up their lots. Then they worked long hours, operating their businesses between 7:00 a.m. and 9:00 p.m. Women, children, and men cleaned, cooked, delivered, and served customers. They operated diners, beauty salons, and restaurants and sold agricultural farming and ranching products, arts and crafts, clothing, construction materials, dry goods, produce, meat, furniture, hardware, and paper and school supplies.

Migrants no longer lounged or stayed at these centers for days at a time but restricted themselves to the orderly and respectful purchase of desired services and products. Additionally, fair lease agreement fees allowed the families who ran the businesses to provide quality products and services at affordable prices, drawing attention away from passersby and attracting a healthy clientele composed of children, women, and men from throughout surrounding towns.

Six months after making these marketplaces accessible to struggling extended Mexican immigrant families, the middle class saw them mature into clean, family-oriented, vibrant venues catering to a mix of local customers and passersby. Laboring in these businesses helped make it possible for working-class families to meet their families' basic needs under improved conditions. The families worked hard to satisfy lease agreement terms and derived a sense of pride and satisfaction in being profitable and respected entrepreneurs. Additionally, they valued creating distance between their homes and their businesses. They did not take their ability to labor in respectable and profitable family-oriented venues for granted.

Although the families were often competing with each other, they supported each other. Every morning before opening their businesses they would gather and pray for a profitable and harmonious day. They organized schedules and groups to pick up their younger children from school, discussed and remedied concerns, and coordinated fund-raisers to help pay for funerals and other emergency expenses. They also organized festivals and contests to nurture family-oriented interaction and consumption among local customers.

Not all extended Mexican immigrant families agreed to or benefited from these lease agreements. Some families could not afford to make the change from conducting business out of their homes to setting up business in the town center and paying the rent and fees. These families were already overwhelmed with financial obligations and could not consider signing another agreement. Age was also an important factor. The elderly and women with infant children abandoned by their fathers did not have adequate labor power, support networks, or money to invest.

This new plan of Mexican middle-class families still required Mexican women and children to continue to exert and focus their energy as laborers. Like internal migrants and immigrants to the United States, they had to adapt to the Mexican government's failure to create competitively fair and profitable employment opportunities. They were not entitled to make demands on business-lot owners. Instead, they were recruited into another employment network as managed unskilled entrepreneurs and laborers to prevent their future immigration, improve town economies, and accommodate their Mexican immigrant relatives' estrangement without overburdening the government.

Though many marketplace businesses flourished, these new employment opportunities did not stop women and men from pursuing bracero and undocumented immigration and settlement. Undocumented Mexican immigrant women and men continued to be apprehended in the United States, and countless others avoided deportation and settled. The incentives that local middle-class families provided could not compete with the prospect of US wages or the power of family ties. Maria Teresa Rodriguez explained, "It was difficult to stop immigrating north. With time even women took this risk. The situation demanded it."[42]

The tightening of the US-Mexico border resulted in the deportation of countless undocumented Mexican immigrants and the continued governmental management of estranged extended Mexican immigrant families throughout the United States and Mexico. Yet extended Mexican immigrant families were determined to daringly embrace their right to live and labor in support and in search of their families across the US-Mexico border.

Epilogue

*The Generative Potential of Thinking
and Acting Historically*

In chapter 7, I described the two statues erected on public patios in San Martin de Hidalgo, Jalisco, to honor the spirit of the women whose suffering, struggle, sacrifice, and agency enabled their families and their communities to grapple with the challenges of the Bracero Program. One of them is a tribute to a specific woman, Maria Guadalupe Urzua Flores, and has a plaque describing her achievements. The other honors women in general and has no plaque. There is no allusion to the historical circumstances that gave rise to *intermediarias* and awake houses and gave meaning to their daring actions. As a Chicana historian committed to writing the history of the mid-twentieth-century Mexican immigrant experience in Mexico and the United States with a concern for the women and children as well as the men, I was tempted to focus my research exclusively on the lives of women like Maria Guadalupe Urzua Flores. But I resisted because, while I do recognize the importance of her work, I wanted to trace a history of collective consciousness and resistance. In this book I have tried to show how the Bracero Program's exploitation of affective ties within Mexican families created unjust conditions and powerfully painful losses. But I also insist that the program led to powerful transformation in gender roles and relations. Even though the women who created awake houses and developed myriad other forms of action are still for the most part not recognized or celebrated publicly for the emotionally daring restorative work they undertook in support of each other and their families, they helped make a past that continues to shape the present to this day. I hope that in some small way the history I relate on these pages will not only bring to life the historical context of this town's mother-and-child statue but also focus attention on the broader historical and social transformations that it marks.

On December 31, 1964, the US and Mexican governments formally ended the Bracero Program. Its elaborate promises of progress and eventual family reunification were never kept. For more than two decades the program disrupted family and town life in Mexico, separating workers and their loved ones from each other across the US-Mexico border without adequate protections and rights. In US and Mexican towns, social life was dramatically transformed by the exploitation of the program's contract laborers, their families, and other immigrant populations. Mexican women had to take on new social roles in hopes of improving the status of their families, towns and nations. While some braceros prospered, the program mostly gave the workers and their families only a subsistence income while their labor subsidized the profits of agribusiness and promoted the interests of nation-states. To this day neither the US nor the Mexican government has ever acknowledged the emotional, financial, and physical toll of the program on bracero families.

The braceros and their families, especially the Mexican women that found themselves forced to take on new roles throughout their bracero relatives' absence, found themselves confronting the consequences of sustaining the program on their own and largely in silence. Laboring tirelessly under exploitative conditions for years on end, raising children on their own with very little money, being married to men they did not see or hear from for months to years at a time, and having their emotional, physical, and financial sacrifices and labor, which were so decisive to the implementation of the Bracero Program, unrecognized by either the US or the Mexican government convinced Mexican women that the program's promises were empty. Women's confrontations with this inhumane reality made evident to them that a program allegedly meant to advance their welfare and the fight for democracy and freedom had instead weakened their family relationships, increased their financial burdens, and threatened their well-being. Hardly anyone, let alone the US and Mexican governments, had dared to responsibly address these women, men, and children or their concerns, sacrifices, strengths, suffering, and rights as citizens, laborers, or members of families. The promises of the program had excluded their families and even been achieved at their expense. The indignities, labor, and trauma of subsidizing promises that did not benefit their families or them moved these women to think and act historically to protect their own and other immigrant families' welfare: that is, to draw on the lessons of their historical experience in ways that outlived the program.

More than seventy years after the termination of the Bracero Program, these women did not automatically welcome recognizing, recollecting, reflecting, sharing, and recording the indignities they had faced in light of the US government's continuing implementation of inhumane, cruel, and exploitative border enforcement programs like the Secure Communities Program. This program's creation of a new state of emergency mirrors the one these women faced between 1942 and 1964. It does not inspire them to abandon their guardedness when recollecting and sharing the costs of the Bracero Program with strangers or family relatives who, like me, are invested in recording, collecting, interpreting, and learning from their decisions and their resilience. But it did move them to participate in the oral life history interviews I conducted with them. A realization of the enduring emotional consequences of history emboldened these women to, at the very least, discuss some of the insecurities of family separations created by and for the convenience of the US and Mexican governments.

The current configuration of Mexican immigrant family life motivates these women to express alarm at the longevity and prevalence of what is to them an all-too-familiar and dangerous family situation. Some of them were inspired to speak out by news stories like that of April 7, 2013, published in *La Opinion*, a Spanish-language Los Angeles—based newspaper. It related the experiences of nine-year-old Mitsy Vasquez, a child repatriate, described as suffering from depression as a result of being bullied in Mexico City because of her recent arrival, US repatriate status, and poor command of the Spanish language. Mitsy had been educated in an elementary school in the United States and was not as fluent in Spanish as her new classmates in Mexico. Having to restart their life together in Mexico because of deportation was very painful for Mitsy and her family. Her parents worried that her poor emotional state would derail her education. During the last two years, she had already transferred in and out of four schools and had yet to successfully adjust to her latest school.

Mitsy and her parents had been forced to endure deportation and repatriation so that they would not become lost to each other across the US-Mexico border. During the first half of 2011, the US government's detection, detention, and deportation of undocumented Mexican immigrants resulted in the separation of an estimated forty-six thousand parents from their US-born children.[1] US Immigration and Customs Enforcement (ICE) officials and local police departments turned traffic violations and other day-to-day offenses into pathways to deportation. In Los Angeles alone, an estimated one in sixteen children is now under the custody of this city's child welfare system.[2]

The ease with which children born in the United States to undocumented Mexican immigrant parents can still be denied the right of being raised by their mothers and fathers has inspired women veterans of the Bracero Program to become more receptive to selectively sharing their recollections of their own traumatic family situations. They let me interview them in part to provoke questioning of the US and Mexican governments' definitions of "family" and "secure community," definitions that do not offer children the security of being raised by their parents. Mindful that our current debate over immigration policy largely ignores the human costs of the US and Mexican governments' enforcement of the border, these women recognize that we owe Mitsy and other children confronting similar forms of alienation our best efforts to forge perspectives, spaces, relationships, and policies that recognize that undocumented immigrants and their children are first and foremost people who have already endured much and who are most worthy of a humane existence. These women refuse to ignore that millions of today's families have been disrupted by immigration policies. Every day they are being separated: parents are being deported and children are being repatriated and left very much on their own to contend with the reconfiguration of their family life in Mexico and the United States. The costs incurred by mid-twentieth-century Mexican immigrant women and their families in Mexico and the United States have to varying degrees inspired some of these women to think and act historically, holding themselves accountable to what is occurring in the lives of people whose hard work underwrites the prosperity of others who despise them and dismiss them as public burdens in order to inspire the rest of us to hold ourselves similarly accountable.

Even though Mitsy's family situation informed some of these women's decision to recollect, share, and record the repercussions of the Bracero Program with me, they did not necessarily wish to recollect the full intensity of years of family separation. The hardships and indignities involved in subsidizing the prosperity of others inspired a myriad of responses from these women, including those in my family. Our family ties did not make this history any easier for them to share with me. Yet most of these women welcomed identifying and discussing their pride in their own resilience.

The implementation of the Bracero Program inflicted deep emotional injuries on these women and their families. Their confrontations with the US and Mexican governments' broken promises, the poor decisions of their Mexican immigrant relatives, and their own hard choices and work were difficult for them to embrace as part of their family history in the very public form of a recorded oral life history. In my pursuit of conducting, recording, collecting, and interpreting these women's oral life histories, I had to hear what they said but also sense and learn from silences. To undertake this historical research without becoming discouraged it became important for me to understand that in the best of cases these women would derive varying forms of empowerment from breaking silence regarding the anger, betrayal, disappointment, exhaustion, frustration, shame, trauma, and turmoil of having experienced the exploitation and negligence of the US and Mexican governments and in some cases their Mexican immigrant family relatives as well. The ways in which current configurations of Mexican immigrant family life mirrored those of their own families under the Bracero Program, while influential in many of these women's decision to recollect, share, and record their oral life histories with me, often did not inspire them to further explore with me the program's full effects on mid-twentieth-century Mexican immigrant family formation. Typically they grew more receptive to sharing the full extent of the costs of these empty promises only after I asked them to recollect, share, and reflect upon how they had held themselves accountable when acting in support of their families, each other, and their interests. Identifying the unique accountability and pain of dealing with count-less broken promises on their own or with very little emotional or financial support made for a connection and in turn a pathway into their recollections, allowing for documentation of the incalculable price they and their families had paid for the program.

Years of recording, collecting, interpreting, and learning from the oral life histories of these women, their families, and my own family further confirmed that there were limits to how much these women were willing to contribute their often intensely personal forms of documenting the timeless and incalculable costs of the Bracero Program for them and their families. Each oral life history made evident that these women did not hold each other or their Mexican immigrant male relatives solely or too severely accountable for the Bracero Program's costs, and that they often found it too painful to recognize that the US and Mexican governments had abandoned them to subsidize the program completely on their own. Their hesitation or reluctance to address the issue of accountability when discussing the actions of their Mexican immigrant relatives and the US and Mexican governments illuminated that the program entailed experiences that decades later women and men as parents, wives, husbands, children, and grandparents were often still too anxious, heartbro-ken, hurt, outraged, overburdened, tired, or resistant to share with anybody, whether strangers, relatives, or historians like me who, irrespective of our good intentions, connections, ties, and training, have no personal knowledge of the betrayal, exploi-tation, longing, and pain of contract labor.

In 2009, the enduring silences of bracero families inspired me to collaborate with dance choreographer Joel Valentin-Martinez to address these silences and the feelings behind them by making a humane yet frank representation of the Bracero Program family experience that would be accessible to undergraduate students and theater audiences. We focused on fleshing out the sensory qualities of the bracero family experience.[3] Our discussions of the silences in the oral life histories I had collected helped to inform his teaching of the students who choreographed and performed the dance showcase *Ask Me in the Morning Light* for theater audiences with varying levels of interest in and knowledge of the historical relationship between the Mexican immigrant experience and American life. Our collaboration resulted in an interdisciplinary portrayal of the humanity of these women and their families, and in turn, that of families unfortunately confronting similar conditions and terms in contemporary US society and elsewhere in the world.

Ask Me in the Morning Light alerted the student actors and theater audiences to the emotional and physical calibrations of the body, mind, and soul that took place in these women as they confronted the broken promises of the Bracero Program in silence. Under the direction of Valentin-Martinez, students showed how women and men shouldered resourcefully and responsibly the imperative of laboring tirelessly without any guarantees of ever seeing each other again either in Mexico or in the United States. The emotional resolve and pain of these women is palpable throughout this dance showcase performance. Collaborating with Valentin-Martinez in this way made it possible to represent the humanity of bracero families to students and theater audiences who are rarely urged to appreciate the visceral and unspoken dislocations of mid-twentieth-century Mexican immigrant family life.

Currently, I encourage students enrolled in my undergraduate courses on the Chicana/o experience at the University of California–Irvine to consider the historical continuities between their own family life and that of mid-twentieth-century Mexican immigrant families. This has also proven most helpful in inspiring these students to not settle for the silences framing the Mexican immigrant experience and to invest themselves in doing more than await or advocate for US immigration reform by signing petitions, pressuring politicians, voting, marching, and reading. Our informed discussion of the human toll of US immigration policy and labor conditions has energized students to embrace thinking and acting historically. They see a need to identify what is most problematic about the conditions of community and family life in the mid-twentieth century and its relationship to their own lives as members of families. The spirited pursuit of this perspective motivated undergraduate students like Maritza Duran to notice and ask her female relatives, especially her

US-born cousins, about why they were being automatically expected to pursue exploitative agricultural labor even after they had completed a high school education.[4] Even in 2012, enrolling in college was not promoted as a worthwhile or feasible goal for these women. Troubled not only by their parents' expectations but by her cousins' receptiveness to such employment as an opportunity, Maritza was finally able to understand the emotional strain of having to accept this labor as a given for one's future, simply because other opportunities had not been readily accessible to women as part of their family experience even when they had been born, raised, and educated in the United States.

The seamlessness of accepting exploitative agricultural labor as the only pathway toward maturing into adulthood among her female family relatives became most evident to Maritza when she and her cousin Jackie Medina were sharing photographs. Jackie's family photographs illustrated her young daughter, Darlene Medina, sitting in a cardboard crate and enjoying being fed grapes as she patiently waited for her mother to finish her shift in the fields (figure 25). That Darlene was already part of this work environment under terms that were meant to feel familiar and relaxing to her alerted Maritza to the ease with which this honorable yet often exploitative labor is introduced to children as young as Darlene as a desirable form of US employment. Maritza's love and high regard for her cousins made such realizations most painful. She learned that there is a limit to individual agency under conditions of collective social subordination. The patterns of the past continue to impose constraints on the present. Maritza's cousins' transition into adulthood follows in their parents' footsteps, and the gender and class expectations thrust upon them echo those constraining the children of braceros and undocumented Mexican immigrants of the mid-twentieth century.

It took much courage for Maritza to embrace the spirit of thinking and acting historically—reflecting on the bracero family experience, her family history, and her present experiences in McFarland, California. In this extremely conservative town steeped in agriculture and dependent on the prison complex for employment, seventy years after the Bracero Program young women—Maritza's relatives—were still not being raised to envision or pursue their own pathways into adulthood. Reflecting on Mexican immigration, agricultural labor, and immigrant family life enabled Maritza to identify and understand traces of the past in the present that demand engaged thought and action.

Maritza is among the countless students whose thinking and acting historically has led them to investigate and respond to their own and other family's experiences responsibly and resourcefully. These students' explorations make evident the

FIGURE 25.
Two-year-old Darlene Medina waiting for her mother, Jackie
Medina, as she labors in the fields of McFarland, California,
2010.

generative potential of thinking and acting historically at a moment when—as in
the time of the onset of the Bracero Program—we can get carried away by the
promise of immigration reform and distracted from the ongoing consequences of
what already is in place.

Researching and writing *Abrazando el Espíritu* has been a most heartening and
revealing journey for me. It has exposed me to the emboldening challenges of
confronting harsh contract labor and immigration laws—so much so that throughout my investigation and writing of this history I've tried to honor mid-twentieth-
century Mexican immigrant families' willingness to hold themselves accountable

and respond to the US and Mexican governments' refusal to treat them as people with feelings, promise, and rights and as members of families. I hope that this history inspires readers to grow in holding themselves accountable regarding the consequences of immigration laws and policies. Thinking and acting historically in this way can produce a humane response to a relentlessly inhumane reality.

NOTES

INTRODUCTION

1. I appreciate the comments of an anonymous reviewer for the University of California Press whose insights about the original and generative contributions of this research inform this introduction and many subsequent parts of the book.

2. Veneranda and Jesus Torres, oral life history (couple interviewed together), Wasco, CA, March 2010.

3. Ibid.

4. The book cover shows this portrait of the Torres family in Acambaro, Guanajuato, Mexico, 1962, Torres Family Personal Collection.

5. Avila Camacho, "Statement of the President."

6. Hondagneu-Sotelo, *Gendered Transitions*, 3.

7. Ibid.

8. For more in-depth information on these border enforcement measures, refer to Lytle Hernandez, *Migra!;* Ngai, *Impossible Subjects;* Pitti, *Devil in Silicon Valley;* Vargas, *Labor Rights.*

9. Handlin, *Uprooted.*

10. Jacobson, *Special Sorrows,* 5.

11. Rouse, "Making Sense of Settlement" and "Thinking through Transnationalism"; Kearney, "Local and the Global."

12. Massey et al., *Return to Aztlan,* 14.

13. Alamillo, *Making Lemonade;* M. Garcia, *World of Its Own;* Gutierrez, *Walls and Mirrors;* Lytle Hernandez, *Migra!;* Pitti, *Devil in Silicon Valley;* Cohen, *Braceros;* Vargas, *Labor Rights.*

14. Galarza, *Merchants of Labor.*

15. Durand, introduction to *Braceros,* 20.

16. Immigration and Naturalization Service, Bracero Program Labor Camp Report, August 14, 1945, Record Group 211, National Archives and Records Administration, College Park, MD.

17. Sanchez, *Becoming Mexican American,* 22.

18. Schmidt Camacho, *Migrant Imaginaries,* 286.

19. Ruiz, *From Out of the Shadows,* xvi.

20. Kelley, *Race Rebels,* 4.

21. Alanís Enciso, *Que se queden allá* and "Regreso a casa"; Bacon, *Illegal People;* Balderrama and Rodríguez, *Decade of Betrayal;* Sanchez, *Becoming Mexican American.*

22. Lipsitz, *Rainbow at Midnight,* 19.

23. Beginning in 2003 and until 2012, I conducted oral life history interviews with sixty bracero families who either were personal acquaintances or were referred to me by personal acquaintances. Each interview ranged between two to four hours in length and was conducted in the bracero family's home or in a public place like a community center or a park. At the time of the Bracero Program, most of these families had reside(d) in San Martin de Hidalgo, Guadalajara (thirty-two families), and Ameca, Jalisco (twenty-four families), but I also interviewed four families who had lived in Acambaro, Guanajuato. All of the bracero families I interviewed were working class or transitioned from middle-class to working-class status over the duration of the Bracero Program. Each interview was made up of questions addressing the emotional range and rigors of the Bracero Program.

1. BRACERO RECRUITMENT IN THE MEXICAN COUNTRYSIDE

1. Manuel Avila Camacho to town presidents in Jalisco, August 7, 1942, Governmental Correspondence, 1940–1950, Archivo Municipal, San Martin de Hidalgo, Jalisco, Mexico.

2. Avila Camacho, "Statement of the President," 8–10.

3. Manuel Avila Camacho to town presidents in Jalisco, August 9, 1942, Governmental Correspondence, 1940–1950, Archivo Municipal, San Martin de Hidalgo, Jalisco, Mexico.

4. The issue of how people in rural towns in Mexico responded and adapted to the program receives scant attention in such works as Garcia y Griego, "Importation of Mexican Contract Laborers"; Hancock, "Role of the Bracero Program"; Copp, *Wetbacks and Braceros;* Durand, *Más allá de la línea;* Calavita, *Inside the State;* Gamboa, *Mexican Labor;* Galarza, *Strangers in Our Fields, Merchants of Labor,* and *Spiders in the House;* Massey and Liang, "Long-Term Consequence"; and J. Garcia, *Operation Wetback.*

5. Avila Camacho, "Statement of the President," 8–16.

6. Ibid., 15.

7. There was only one selection center at the beginning of the program, but more were added in 1947.

8. Consuelo Alvarez's account of the forum is given in her oral life history, Ameca, Jalisco, 2003.

9. Ibid.

10. Emilia's plans were recounted by Ignacia Zarate Mandujano Rios, a family acquaintance, in her oral life history, San Martin de Hidalgo, Jalisco, 2007.

11. Ibid.

12. Information on repatriates' attitudes and actions was obtained from conversation with Desiderio Ahumanda Medina, San Martin de Hidalgo, Jalisco, Mexico, 1996.

13. Ibid.

14. Maria Elena Medina, oral life history, Tijuana, Baja California, Mexico, 2011.

15. Maria Teresa Rodriguez, oral life history, Los Angeles, 2009.

16. Francisco Rosas shared details on the efforts of his father as part of this skilled and educated class of men in his oral life history, Los Angeles, 2001.

17. Ibid.

18. Maria Teresa Rodriguez, who participated in many such conversations with family and friends, describes Carlos's aspirations in her oral life history, Los Angeles, 2009.

19. Jose Ramirez, interview by Ernesto Galarza, August 26, 1943, Interview Notes, box 17, Ernesto Galarza Collection, Special Collections, Stanford University.

20. These estimates come from oral life history interviews.

21. Artemio Guerra de Leon, oral life history, Wasco, CA, 2010.

22. Ramon Rea Rios, oral life history, San Martin de Hidalgo, Jalisco, Mexico, 2007.

23. Ibid.

24. Arturo Buendia, interview by Ernesto Galarza on August 29, 1943, Field Notes in Labor Camps, box 17, Ernesto Galarza Collection, Special Collections, Stanford University.

25. Ernesto Galarza to consular officials, Mexico City, April 13, 1943, Correspondence on Bracero Program Impact, box 18, Ernesto Galarza Collection, Special Collections, Stanford University.

26. Maria Teresa Rodriguez, oral life history, Los Angeles, 2009.

2. THE BRACERO PROGRAM AS A PERMANENT STATE OF EMERGENCY

1. Gutierrez, *Walls and Mirrors*, 134.

2. Ernesto Galarza, "Personal Writing of Ernesto Galarza," August 18, 1942, box 2, Testimony and Reports, Ernesto Galarza Collection, Special Collections, Stanford University.

3. Ibid.

4. Ibid.

5. Information about Manuel Ricardo Rosas's life and views was collected from oral life histories and archival documents provided by Francisco Rosas and Dolores Rosas in Guadalajara, Jalisco, Mexico, and Los Angeles, 1999–2008.

6. For more information on repatriation, refer to Alanís Enciso, *Que se queden allá* and "Regreso a casa"; Bacon, *Illegal People;* Balderrama and Rodríguez, *Decade of Betrayal;* Sanchez, *Becoming Mexican American.*

7. Arturo Buendia (oral life history, San Martin de Hidalgo, Jalisco, Mexico, 2005) and Gustavo Lopez (oral life history, Guadalajara, Jalisco, Mexico, 2005) were among the braceros who took part in these conversations.

8. I am thinking here of such works as Alamillo's *Making Lemonade,* Cohen's *Braceros,* Fitzgerald's *Nation of Emigrants,* Galarza's *Merchants of Labor,* J. García's *Operation Wetback,* M. Garcia's *World of Its Own,* Gutierrez's *Walls and Mirrors,* Lytle Hernandez's *Migra!,* Ngai's *Impossible Subjects,* Pitti's *Devil in Silicon Valley,* and Vargas's *Labor Rights.*

9. See, e.g., Spickard, *Almost All Aliens,* 304.

10. See Alvarez, *Power of the Zoot;* Ramirez, *Woman in the Zoot Suit.*

11. Spickard, *Almost All Aliens,* 317.

12. US Department of Labor, Children's Bureau, *Children's Bureau and Problems* [1941 and 1943]. See also McWilliams, *Report,* and a letter from Galarza to US consular officials at the US Consulate in Los Angeles, September 23, 1942, about the Children's Bureau's efforts and the emergency for children that they documented, in box 18, Ernesto Galarza Collection, Special Collections, Stanford University.

13. US Department of Labor, Children's Bureau, *Children's Bureau and Problems* [1943].

14. US Department of Labor, Children's Bureau, *Children's Bureau and Problems* [1941].

15. Ibid., 3.

16. Ibid., 5.

17. Ibid.

18. Ibid.

19. "Imported Laborers Held in Virtual Slavery," *Los Angeles Times,* November 13, 1948.

20. "El Escritorio Publico El Minutito Advertisement," Subseries G, box 10, Julian Nava Papers, Oviatt Library Special Collections and Archives, California State University, Northridge.

21. Ibid.

22. Information about Desiderio Ahumada Medina's life and photograph was obtained from an oral life history interview with his daughter, Dolores Rosas, in Los Angeles in 2008.

23. Their resourceful and responsible response to repatriation and the program earned Desiderio and Manuel a reputation as daringly thoughtful men with regard to their attitudes toward the United States. Hence, when I was conducting the research for this book, friends of Desiderio and Manuel welcomed my interviewing them for this historical investigation of their family experience. Desiderio is the father of my mother, Dolores Rosas, and, in turn, my grandfather. It was quite revealing to have all of the women and men I interviewed begin their oral life histories by expressing their profound respect for both of my grandfathers' frank and spirited assessments of what families needed and should do when facing the emergencies born out of repatriation and the Bracero Program. Actually, my mother and uncles were most invested in describing my grandfather, Desiderio, as a big dreamer and risk taker who believed that venturing to the United States should be a journey in which one would travel throughout the country to as many states as possible in search of experiences and business models that would make the wear and tear of being in the United States as a Mexican immigrant worthwhile. According to my uncles, my grandfather took pride in having defied the spirit of the US and Mexican governments' vision of the Bracero Program by visiting the United States under terms personally meaningful for their family and him. His enterprising spirit had eventually enabled them to live and thrive together in the Mexican countryside on the proceeds of a family business. Nonetheless, when reflecting on his work history, they felt most proud of my grandfather for having trained and served as a police officer in Mexico's capital. That he had prioritized undertaking a personally meaningful goal early on in his life—one that had required leaving the Mexican countryside for the city—struck them as reflective of their father's responsibly adventurous approach to life as a Mexican man. Hence, an oil-painting replica of his police academy graduation portrait adorns the living room of each of his children's family homes. After his passing and upon my undertaking of this historical research, my uncles opted for my mother to keep the original portrait of this very special moment in our family's transnational history (see figure 9). They insisted that with my research I had earned our family the honor of having this cherished portrait as part of our family home in South Central Los Angeles. The spirit of this portrait and its meaning would keep us emotionally connected across the US-Mexico border.

3. SPECIAL IMMIGRATION AND THE MANAGEMENT OF THE MEXICAN FAMILY

1. Information concerning Renato Sandoval's experience was obtained from a conversation with him in Tulare, CA, in 2003.

2. Ibid.

3. See Ernesto Galarza, "Special Immigration Field Notes," 1947, box 27, Ernesto Galarza Collection, Special Collections, Stanford University.

4. This is Galarza's assessment, found in ibid., and based on his conversations with INS officials.

5. Ibid.

6. Ernesto Galarza, "Special Immigration Field Notes," box 58, Ernesto Galarza Collection, Special Collections, Stanford University.

7. Conversation with Renato Sandoval, Tulare, CA, 2003.

8. Department of Charities, County of Los Angeles Bureau of Public Assistance, "Special" Family Fact Sheet, Record Group 84, box 4, National Archives and Records Administration, College Park, MD.

9. Ibid.

10. Ernesto Galarza, "Special Immigration Field Notes," box 21, Ernesto Galarza Collection, Special Collections, Stanford University.

11. Quote from Ngai, *Impossible Subjects,* 155. See also Calavita, *Inside the State,* 130–33.

12. Department of Charities, County of Los Angeles Bureau of Public Assistance, *Special Immigration and Immigrants, 1947–1951* (Washington, DC, 1951), quoted in Ernesto Galarza, "Report on Special Immigrants," Special Immigrant Notes and Correspondence, box 18, Ernesto Galarza Collection, Special Collections, Stanford University.

13. Ernesto Galarza, 1947, "Report on Special Immigrants," Special Immigrant Notes and Correspondence, box 18, Ernesto Galarza Collection, Special Collections, Stanford University.

14. Ibid.

15. Ibid.

16. Ibid.

17. Conversation with Rosa Rodriguez, Los Angeles, 2003.

18. Ernesto Galarza, "Special Immigration Facts," n.d., box 18, Ernesto Galarza Collection, Special Collections, Stanford University.

19. Details of local officials' standards for special-immigration moral eligibility were obtained from the oral life history of a former bracero, Ramon Rea Rios, San Martin de Hidalgo, Jalisco, Mexico, 2007.

20. Ibid.

21. These changes are described in Artemio Guerra de Leon's oral life history, Wasco, CA, 2010.

22. Catalina Ruiz, oral life history, Los Angeles, 2003.

23. Ibid.

24. Maria Elena Medina, oral life history, Tijuana, Baja California, 2004.

25. Ibid.

26. Galarza, "Special Immigration Facts."

4. GOVERNMENT CENSORSHIP OF FAMILY COMMUNICATION

1. German Santander, oral life history, Ameca Jalisco, Mexico, 2007.

2. Laurence I. Hewes Jr. to Mr. C. B. Baldwin, administrator of the Farm Security Administration, Washington, DC, October 28, 1942, Correspondence Records of Laurence I. Hewes Jr., US Consulate, Chihuahua, Mexico Files, National Archives Records Administration, College Park, MD, Record Group 211, boxes 4–11.

3. Ibid.

4. See, e.g., Alamillo, *Making Lemonade;* Cohen, *Braceros;* Fitzgerald, *Nation of Emigrants;* Galarza, *Merchants of Labor;* J. García, *Operation Wetback;* M. Garcia, *World of Its Own;* Gutierrez, *Walls and Mirrors;* Lytle Hernandez, *Migra!;* Ngai, *Impossible Subjects;* Pitti, *Devil in Silicon Valley;* and Vargas, *Labor Rights.*

5. American Consular Officer in Charge, Chihuahua, Chihuahua, Mexico, to S. Licano, Department of State, Washington, DC, July 24, 1942, Correspondence Records, US Consulate, Chihuahua, Mexico Files, National Archives Records Administration, College Park, MD, Record Group 211, boxes 4–11.

6. Ibid.

7. M. L. Stafford, US Consulate, Mexico City, to US Consulate officials in Chihuahua, Chihuahua, Mexico, December 10, 1942, alerting them to Silverstone's correspondence, in Correspondence Records of M. L. Stafford, US Consulate, Guerrero, Mexico Files, National Archives Records Administration, College Park, MD, Record Group 211, boxes 4–11.

8. Silverstone's letter is quoted in ibid.

9. M. L. Stafford to US Consulate officials in Chihuahua, Chihuahua, Mexico, November 12, 1952, alerting them to Zapien and Vega's correspondence, in Correspondence Records of M. L. Stafford, US Consulate, Mexico City, Mexico Files, National Archives Records Administration, College Park, MD, Record Group 211, boxes 4–11.

10. Ibid.

11. Ayala is apparently referring to World War II. Despite the possibilities for legal immigration that the Bracero Program offered, the scarcity of program contracts, given the vast numbers of applicants, caused many to adopt illegal means of entering the United States.

12. M. L. Stafford to US Consulate officials in Chihuahua, Chihuahua, Mexico, May 18, 1954, alerting them to Ayala and Aguilar's correspondence, in Correspondence Records of M. L. Stafford, US Consulate, Mexico City, Mexico Files, National Archives Records Administration, College Park, MD, Record Group 211, boxes 4–11.

13. US consular officials, Jalisco, to US consular officials, Mexico City, August 3, 1954, Correspondence Records, US Consulate, Jalisco, Mexico Files, National Archives Records Administration, College Park, MD, Record Group 211, boxes 4–11.

14. Churchill Murray to Luis Fernandez del Campo, August 11, 1945, Correspondence Records of Churchill Murray, US Consulate, Chihuahua, Mexico Files, National Archives Records Administration, College Park, MD, Record Group 211, boxes 4–11.

15. Ibid.

16. Churchill Murray to Maria Melchor, July 18, 1945, Correspondence Records of Churchill Murray, US Consulate, Chihuahua, Mexico Files, National Archives Records Administration, College Park, MD, Record Group 211, boxes 4–11.

17. Ibid.

18. Churchill Murray to US consular officials, Mexico City, July 18, 1945, US Consulate, Chihuahua, Mexico Files, National Archives Records Administration, College Park, MD, Record Group 211, boxes 4–11..

19. Churchill Murray to US consular officials, Mexico City, August 17, 1944, Correspondence Records of Churchill Murray, US Consulate, Chihuahua, Mexico Files, National Archives Records Administration, College Park, MD, Record Group 211, boxes 4–11.

20. Field Documents, Box 52, Ernesto Galarza Collection, Special Collections, Stanford University.

21. Ibid.

22. Ernesto Galarza, field report about braceros' correspondence with friends and relatives, Correspondence Files, box 17, Ernesto Galarza Collection, Special Collections, Stanford University.

23. Field Documents, box 52, Ernesto Galarza Collection, Special Collections, Stanford University.

24. *El Tesoro del Bracero,* Fisher Brothers Creative Printing and Stationary Company, Washington, DC, 1961, box 52, Ernesto Galarza Collection, Special Collections, Stanford University.

25. Ibid.26. Churchill Murray to Maria de Jesus Alvarez, February 21, 1945, Correspondence Records, US Consulate, Guanajuato, Mexico Files, National Archives Records Administration, College Park, MD, Record Group 211, boxes 4–11.

27. Churchill Murray to Mexican Consulate officials, February 8, 1944, Correspondence Records, US Consulate, Guanajuato, Mexico Files, National Archives Records Administration, College Park, MD, Record Group 211, boxes 4–11.

28. Maria Teresa Rodriguez (daughter of Josefina Rodriguez), oral life history, Los Angeles, 2009.

29. *Cartas a Eufemia* [Letters to Eufemia], Argel Films, 1952.

5. IN PAINFUL SILENCE

1. This story is from Hermelinda Juarez's oral life history, Guadalajara, Jalisco, Mexico, 2008.

2. "Siempre hace frio" ("It is Always Cold"), sung by Cuco Sanchez, Hispano Americana de Musica, 1956.

3. Hermelinda Juarez, oral life history, Guadalajara, Jalisco, Mexico, 2008.

4. This story is from Maria Elena Lopez's, oral life history, Ameca, Jalisco, Mexico, 2008.

5. This story was recounted by Carlos and Rosa Rodriguez's daughter Catalina Ruiz in her oral life history, Los Angeles, 2008.

6. Francisca's letter to her husband is in the Bracero Letters Collection, Special Collections, Stanford University.

7. Fidencia Abila's letter to her son is in the Bracero Letters Collection, Special Collections, Stanford University.

8. Jose Arciniega's letter to his brother is in the Bracero Letters Collection, Special Collections, Stanford University.

9. Teresa Garcia's letter to her husband, along with the enclosed letter of her daughter Rosa Lopez, is in the Bracero Letters Collection, Special Collections, Stanford University.

10. Alejandro Ortega, oral life history, Los Angeles, 2008; the song "El hijo del pueblo" ("The Rural Town's Son"), by José Alfredo Jiménez, can be heard on his CD *El hijo del pueblo* (Sony International, 1991).

11. Julio Valle, oral life history, Guadalajara, Jalisco, 2008; the song "Sufriendo a solas" ("Suffering Alone"; 1951), by Jose Angel Espinoza ("Ferrusquillo"), can be heard on his CD *En Sinaloa nací* (RCA Records, 2011).

12. Maria Teresa Rodriguez, oral life history, Los Angeles, 2009; the song "La del rebozo blanco" ("The One with the White Shawl"), by José Alfredo Jiménez, can be heard on his CD *Tesoros de colección* (Sony Music Entertainment B00136LXUG, 2007).

6. HIDDEN FROM HISTORY

1. The story recounted here comes from Esther Legaspi Delgadillo Sanchez's oral life history and the information on the photographs that she shared with me, Los Angeles, 2005 and 2013.

2. This theme receives little attention, for instance, in such works as Alamillo, *Making Lemonade;* Cohen, *Braceros;* Fitzgerald, *Nation of Emigrants;* Galarza, *Merchants of Labor;* J. García, *Operation Wetback;* M. Garcia, *World of Its Own;* Gutierrez, *Walls and Mirrors;* Lytle Hernandez, *Migra!;* Ngai, *Impossible Subjects;* Pitti, *Devil in Silicon Valley;* and Vargas, *Labor Rights.*

3. See, e.g., Escobedo, *From Coverall to Zoot Suits.*

4. Information concerning Alex Romero and Mary Romero's life history and photographs was obtained from their granddaughter Crystal Romero's oral life history, Irvine, CA, in 2012.

5. Information concerning Sara Cobla and Katie Cobla's life history and photographs was obtained from their niece Crystal Romero's oral life history, Irvine, CA, in 2012.

6. The story recounted here comes from the oral life histories of Veneranda Torres and Jesus Torres and information on the photographs that they shared with me when I interviewed them together in Wasco, CA, in 2010.

7. The story recounted here is from Artemio Guerra de Leon's oral life history, obtained when I interviewed him and his wife, Maria Graciela Garcia Guerra, together in Wasco, CA, in 2010.

8. The story recounted here is from Maria Graciela Garcia Guerra's oral life history, obtained when I interviewed her with her husband, Artemio Guerra de Leon, in Wasco, CA, in 2010.

9. The story is from Ramona Frias's oral life history, Los Angeles, 2008.

7. AWAKE HOUSES AND *MUJERES INTERMEDIARIAS*

1. The story recounted in this chapter of Ignacia Zarate Mandujano Rios's confrontation of the stresses of her bracero husband's absence and her role in forming "awake houses" is recounted in her oral life history, San Martin de Hidalgo, Jalisco, Mexico, 2007.

2. Azucena Lopez's story here is from her oral life history, Ameca, Jalisco, Mexico, 2009.

3. Veneranda Torres's story here is taken from her oral life history, Wasco, CA, 2010.

4. All subsequent page citations to this work are to the Editorial JUS (1953) edition and are given parenthetically in the text.

8. *EJEMPLAR Y SÍN IGUAL*

1. The story recounted here is taken from Andres Ramirez's oral life history, Ameca, Jalisco, Mexico, 2007.

2. José Alfredo Jiménez, "El Jinete" ("The Horseman"), from *Tesoros de Colección*, CD, Sony Music Entertainment B00136LXUG, 2007.

3. The topic of children's migration and labor is treated only tangentially in such works as Alamillo, *Making Lemonade;* Cohen, *Braceros;* Fitzgerald, *Nation of Emigrants;* Galarza, *Merchants of Labor;* J. García, *Operation Wetback;* M. Garcia, *World of Its Own;* Gutierrez, *Walls and Mirrors;* Lytle Hernandez, *Migra!;* Ngai, *Impossible Subjects;* Pitti, *Devil in Silicon Valley;* and Vargas, *Labor Rights.*

4. Los Braceros, "El Bracero Mexicano," 1944.

5. The story recounted here is from the oral life history of Maria Francisca Ordoñez Torres, Wasco, CA, 2010.

6. US Department of Labor, Children's Bureau, *State of the Department.*

7. Bayside Social Center, "Our Bay Side Social Center Report, 1948," California Printing, box 2, Manuel Ruiz Papers, Special Collections, Stanford University.

8. Works Progress Administration, *Toy Loan Program Report*.

9. "Shaved Heads for Mexicans—Are Tattoo Numbers Next?," *Los Angeles Times*, August 8, 1949.

10. "Piggy Bank Fund Sponsors Youth," *Los Angeles Times*, October 26, 1950.

11. "Pepita's Story," *Los Angeles Times*, June 3, 1963.

12. Oral life histories of Artemio Guerra de Leon, Wasco, CA, 2010, and Catalina Ruiz, Los Angeles, 2008.

13. Catalina Ruiz, oral life history, Los Angeles, 2008.

14. Ibid.

15. Ibid.

16. Maria Teresa Rodriguez, oral life history, Los Angeles, 2009.

17. Catalina Ruiz, oral life history, Los Angeles, 2002.

18. Ibid.

19. Ignacia Zarate Mandujano Rios, oral life history, San Martin de Hidalgo, Jalisco, Mexico, 2005.

20. Ibid.

21. Ibid.

22. Ramona Frias, oral life history, Los Angeles, 2005.

9. *DECIDIDAS Y ATREVIDAS*

1. Grace Hermosillo to Grace Sawyer, July 15, 1947, Correspondence Files, US Consulate, Mexico City, Mexico, National Archives Records Administration, College Park, MD, Record Group 85, box 2.

2. Grace Hermosillo to Grace Sawyer, August 30, 1947, Correspondence Files, US Consulate, Mexico City, Mexico, National Archives Records Administration, College Park, MD, Record Group 85, box 2.

3. Wallace LaRue to H. Claremont Moses, July 30, 1947, Correspondence Files, US Consulate, Mexico City, Mexico, National Archives Records Administration, College Park, MD, Record Group 85, box 2.

4. This is another topic that has received scant attention in such works on Mexican immigration as Alamillo, *Making Lemonade;* Cohen, *Braceros;* Fitzgerald, *Nation of Emigrants;* Galarza, *Merchants of Labor;* J. García, *Operation Wetback;* M. Garcia, *World of Its Own;* Gutierrez, *Walls and Mirrors;* Lytle Hernandez, *Migra!;* Ngai, *Impossible Subjects;* Pitti, *Devil in Silicon Valley;* and Vargas, *Labor Rights*.

5. Department of Charities, *History of Aid*.

6. Correspondence Files, US Consulate, Mexico City, Mexico, National Archives Records Administration, College Park, MD, Record Group 85, box 3.

7. Department of Charities, *History of Aid*, 1–2.

8. Elise Garcia to the Department of Charities of the County of Los Angeles, May 12, 1947, Correspondence Files, US Consulate, Los Angeles, California, National Archives Records Administration, College Park, MD, Record Group 85, box 5.

9. Sally Giacomini to the Department of Charities of the County of Los Angeles, December 17, 1947, Correspondence Files, US Consulate, Los Angeles, National Archives Records Administration, College Park, MD, Record Group 85, box 4.

10. Department of Charities, *Annual Report*, 23–24.

11. Ibid., 25.

12. Ibid.

13. Ibid.

14. Ibid.

15. Marion Wilson to Stephen E. Aguirre, March 21, 1947, Correspondence Files, US Consulate, California, National Archives Records Administration, College Park, Maryland, Record Group 85, box 5.

16. Marion Wilson to Mary Andrade, April 3, 1947, Correspondence Files, US Consulate, Los Angeles, National Archives Records Administration, College Park, MD, Record Group 85, box 4.

17. Ibid.

18. S. W. Owen to Consular Officials of the US Consulate in Mexico City, July 11, 1947, Correspondence Files, US Consulate, Los Angeles, National Archives Records Administration, College Park, MD, Record Group 85, box 3.

19. Muriel Emerson to S. W. Owen, July 9, 1947, Correspondence Files, US Consulate, Los Angeles, National Archives Records Administration, College Park, MD, Record Group 85, box 3.

20. Ibid.

21. Stephen E. Aguirre to Estela Alarcon Fernandez, May 23, 1947, Correspondence Files, US Consulate, Los Angeles, National Archives Records Administration, College Park, MD, Record Group 85, box 4.

22. Socorro Martinez Gutierrez to the Immigration and Naturalization Service, September 11, 1952, Correspondence Files, US Consulate, Los Angeles, National Archives Records Administration, College Park, MD, Record Group 85, box 4.

23. "D.A. Seeks Special Staff for Handling of Welfare Cases," *Stockton Bee*, May 3, 1960.

24. Muriel Emerson to Mexican Consulate officials, December 8, 1963, Correspondence Files, US Consulate, Los Angeles, California, National Archives Records Administration, College Park, MD, Record Group 85, box 5.

25. Catholic Council of Working Life, "The Migrant Agricultural Family Experience," 1959, Correspondence Files, US Consulate, Los Angeles, California, National Archives Records Administration, College Park, MD, Record Group 85, box 5.

26. The account of Maria Gonzales's working conditions and wages is in California Field Notes, box 18, Ernesto Galarza Collection, Special Collections, Stanford University.

27. "The New Workers in Our Fields," *Washington Post*, October 1, 1964.

28. For more about Operation Wetback, see Lytle Hernandez, *Migra!*

29. US Immigration and Naturalization Service, *Immigration and Naturalization.*

30. Ernesto Galarza, California Field Notes, box 18, Ernesto Galarza Collection, Special Collections, Stanford University.

31. Ibid.

32. US Farm Employment Service Agency, *National Agricultural Annual Report,* 23–25.

33. Mexican Office of Labor, *Reporte nacional,* 44.

34. Maria Esther Legaspi Delgadillo, oral life history, Los Angeles, 2009.

35. Catalina Ruiz, oral life history, Los Angeles, 2003.

36. Ibid.

37. Field Correspondence files contain copies of women's letters of inquiry, box 17, Ernesto Galarza Collection, Special Collections, Stanford University.

38. Catalina Ruiz, oral life history, Los Angeles, 2008.

39. Mexican Office of Labor, *Reporte nacional,* 45.

40. Details concerning these marketplaces obtained from Catalina Ruiz, oral life history, Los Angeles, 2005.

41. Ibid.

42. Maria Teresa Rodriguez, oral life history, Los Angeles, 2009.

EPILOGUE

1. Seth Freed Wexler, "U.S. Deports 46,000 Parents with Citizen Kids in Just Six Months," *Colorlines: News for Action,* November 3, 2011.

2. Seth Freed Wexler, "Obama: Kids Stuck in Foster Care Due to Deportation a 'Real Problem,'" *Colorlines: News for Action,* November 14, 2011.

3. This collaboration took place between dance choreographer Joel Valentin-Martinez and myself in the form of multiple conversations on the history of the Bracero Program family experience.

4. Maritza Duran, oral life history, March 2011 and February 2012, Irvine, CA, and participation in my course "Researching the Chicana/o Experience" in Spring 2010 at the University of California, Irvine.

BIBLIOGRAPHY

ARCHIVES

Archivo Municipal, San Martin de Hidalgo, Jalisco, Mexico

Bancroft Library, University of California, Berkeley

Charles E. Young Research Library and Special Collections, University of California, Los Angeles

Mandeville Special Collections Library, University of California, San Diego

National Archives and Records Administration, College Park, Maryland

Oviatt Library Special Collections and Archives, California State University, Northridge

Special Collections and University Archives, Stanford University

ORAL HISTORIES (INTERVIEWS BY AUTHOR)

Consuelo Alvarez. June 2003, Ameca, Jalisco, Mexico.

Arturo Buendia. March 2005, San Martin de Hidalgo, Jalisco, Mexico.

Maritza Duran. March 2011 and February 2012, Irvine, CA.

Ramona Frias. October 2008, Los Angeles, CA.

Maria Graciela Garcia Guerra. March 2010, Wasco, CA.

Hermelinda Juarez. July 2008, Guadalajara, Jalisco, Mexico.

Esther Legaspi Delgadillo Sanchez. March 2005 and April 2013, Los Angeles, CA.

Artemio Guerra de Leon. March 2010, Wasco, CA.

Azucena Lopez. December 2009, Ameca, Jalisco, Mexico.

Gustavo Lopez. July 2005, Guadalajara, Jalisco, Mexico.

Maria Elena Medina. June 2011, Tijuana, Baja California, Mexico.

Maria Francisca Ordoñez Torres. March 2010, Wasco, CA.

Alejandro Ortega. July 2008, Los Angeles, CA.

Andres Ramirez. July 2007, Ameca, Jalisco, Mexico.

Ramon Rea Rios. July 2007, San Martin de Hidalgo, Jalisco, Mexico.

Maria Teresa Rodriguez. October 2009, Los Angeles, CA.

Crystal Romero. January 2012, Irvine, CA.

Dolores Rosas. 1996–2012, San Martin de Hidalgo, Jalisco, Mexico.

Francisco Rosas. 2001–12, Los Angeles, CA.

Catalina Ruiz. July 2003, Los Angeles, CA.

German Santander. July 2007, Ameca, Jalisco, Mexico.

Renato Sandoval. August 2003, Tulare, CA.

Jesus Torres. March 2010, Wasco, CA.

Veneranda Torres. March 2010, Wasco, CA.

Julio Valle. July 2008, Guadalajara, Jalisco, Mexico.

Ignacia Zarate Mandujano Rios. July 2007, San Martin de Hidalgo, Jalisco, Mexico.

NEWSPAPERS

Los Angeles Times

Stockton Bee

Washington Post

OTHER SOURCES

Alamillo, Jose. *Making Lemonade Out of Lemons: Mexican American Labor and Leisure in a California Town, 1880–1960.* Urbana: University of Illinois Press, 2007.

Alanís Enciso, Fernando Saúl. *Que se queden allá: El gobierno de México y la repatriación de mexicanos en Estados Unidos (1934–1940).* Tijuana: El Colegio de la Frontera Norte, 2007.

———. "Regreso a casa: La repatriación de Mexicanos en Estados Unidos durante de Gran Depresión, el caso de San Luis Potosí, 1929–1934." *Estudios de Historia Moderna y Contemporánea de México* 29 (2005): 119–48.

Alvarez, Luis. *The Power of the Zoot: Youth Culture and Resistance during World War II.* Berkeley: University of California Press, 2008.

Avila Camacho, Manuel. "Statement of the President to the Nation." In *Mexico and the War in the Pacific*, 8–10. Mexico City: Government Printing Office, 1941.

Bacon, David. *Illegal People: How Globalization Creates Migration and Criminalizes Immigrants*. Boston: Beacon Press, 2008.

Balderrama, Francisco E., and Raymond Rodríguez. *Decade of Betrayal: Mexican Repatriation in the 1930s*. Albuquerque: University of New Mexico Press, 1995.

Calavita, Kitty. *Inside the State: The Bracero Program, Immigration, and the I.N.S.* New York: Routledge Press, 1992.

Cohen, Deborah. *Braceros*. Chapel Hill: University of North Carolina Press, 2009.

Copp, Nelson Gage. *Wetbacks and Braceros: Mexican Migrant Laborers and American Immigration Policy, 1930–1960*. San Francisco: R and E Research, 1981.

Castaño, Rosa de. *Braceros [Mojados, Wetbacks]: Teatro y cine Mexicanos, en cuatro escenas o actos*. Aguilar: Editorial JUS, 1953.

Department of Charities of the County of Los Angeles. *Annual Report*. Washington, DC, 1947. Copy in Florence Richardson Wyckoff Papers, carton 23, Bancroft Library, Special Collections, University of California, Berkeley.

———. *The History of Aid to Needy Children Handbook*. Washington, DC, 1957. Copy in Florence Richardson Wyckoff Papers, carton 23, Bancroft Library, Special Collections, University of California, Berkeley.

Durand, Jorge. Introduction to *Braceros: Las miradas mexicanas y estadounidense: Antología (1945–64)*, edited by Jorge Durand. Zacatecas: Miguel Ángel Porrúa, 2007.

———. *Más allá de la línea: Patrones migratorios entre Mexico y Estados Unidos*. Mexico, D.F.: Consejo Nacional para la Cultura y Artes, 1992.

Escobedo, Elizabeth. *From Coveralls to Zoot Suits: The Lives of Mexican American Women on the World War II Home Front*. Chapel Hill: University of North Carolina Press, 2013.

Espiritu, Yen Le. *Home Bound: Filipino American Lives across Cultures, Communities, and Countries*. Berkeley: University of California Press, 2004.

Fitzgerald, David. *A Nation of Emigrants: How Mexico Manages Its Migration*. Berkeley: University of California Press, 2009.

Galarza, Ernesto. *Merchants of Labor: The Mexican Bracero Story, an Account of the Managed Migration of Mexican Farm Workers in California, 1942–1960*. Charlotte, NC: McNally and Loftin, 1964.

———. *Spiders in the House and Workers in the Fields*. South Bend, IN: University of Notre Dame Press, 1970.

————. *Strangers in Our Fields: Based on a Report Regarding the Compliance with the Contractual, Legal, and Civil Rights of Mexican Agricultural Contract Labor in the United States.* 2nd ed. Washington, DC: US Section, Joint United States-Mexico Trade Union Committee, 1956.

Gamboa, Erasmo. *Mexican Labor and World War II: Braceros in the Pacific Northwest, 1942–47.* Austin: University of Texas Press, 1990.

Garcia, Juan Ramon. *Operation Wetback: The Mass Deportation of Mexican Undocumented Workers in 1954.* Westport, CT: Greenwood Press, 1980.

Garcia, Matt. *A World of Its Own: Race, Labor, and Citrus in the Making of Greater Los Angeles, 1900–1970.* Chapel Hill: University of North Carolina Press, 2003.

Garcia y Griego, Manuel. "The Importation of Mexican Contract Laborers to the United States, 1942–1964: Antecedents, Operation, and Legacy." Working Papers in US-Mexican Studies, University of California, San Diego, 1980.

Gutierrez, David G. *Walls and Mirrors: Mexican Americans, Mexican Immigrants, and the Politics of Ethnicity.* Berkeley: University of California Press, 1995.

Hancock, Richard. "The Role of the Bracero in the Economic and Cultural Dynamics of Mexico: A Case Study of Chihuahua." 1959. Reprint, Stanford, CA: Hispanic American Society, 1981.

Handlin, Oscar. *The Uprooted.* 2nd ed. Boston: Little, Brown, 1990.

Hondagneu-Sotelo, Pierrette. *Gendered Transitions: Mexican Experiences of Immigration.* Berkeley: University of California Press, 1994.

Jacobson, Matthew Frye. *Special Sorrows: The Diasporic Imagination of Irish, Polish, and Jewish Immigrants in the United States.* Cambridge, MA: Harvard University Press, 1995.

Kearney, Michael. "The Local and the Global: The Anthropology of Globalization and Transnationalism." *Annual Review of Anthropology* 24 (1995): 549.

Kelley, Robin D. G. *Race Rebels: Culture, Politics, and the Black Working Class.* New York: Free Press, 1994.

Lipsitz, George. *Rainbow at Midnight: Labor and Culture in the 1940s.* Champaign: University of Illinois Press, 1994.

Lytle Hernandez, Kelly. *Migra! The History of the US Border Patrol.* Berkeley: University of California Press, 2010.

Massey, Douglas, Rafael Alarcon, Jorge Durand, and Humberto Gonzalez. *Return to Aztlan: The Social Process of International Migration from Western Mexico.* Berkeley: University of California Press, 1990.

McWilliams, Carey. *Report on the Importation of Negro Labor to California.* Washington, DC: US Division of Immigration and Housing, 1942. Copy in box 1, Carey McWilliams Papers, University of California Special Collections.

Massey, Douglas, and Zai Liang. "The Long-Term Consequence of a Temporary Worker Program: The US Bracero Experience." *Population Research and Policy Review* 8, no. 3: 1989: 199–226.

Mexican Office of Labor. *El reporte nacional del Programa Laboral Mexicano (Bracero), 1954* [Mexican Farm Labor Program National Report, 1954]. Mexico, D.F.: Publicaciones de Empleos Agriculturales, 1954.

Molina, Natalia. *Fit to Be Citizens: Public Health and Race in Los Angeles, 1879–1939.* Berkeley: University of California Press, 2006.

Ngai, Mae M. *Impossible Subjects: Illegal Aliens and the Making of Modern America.* Princeton, NJ: Princeton University Press, 2004.

Pitti, Stephen. *The Devil in Silicon Valley: Northern California, Race, and Mexican Americans.* Princeton, NJ: Princeton University Press, 2003.

Ramirez, Catherine. *The Woman in the Zoot Suit: Gender, Nationalism, and Cultural Politics of Memory.* Durham, NC: Duke University Press, 2009.

Rouse, Roger. "Making Sense of Settlement: Class Transformation, Cultural Struggle, and Transnationalism among Mexican Migrants to the United States." *Annals of the New York Academy of Sciences* 645 (1992): 25–52.

————. "Thinking through Transnationalism: Notes on the Cultural Politics in the Contemporary United States." *Public Culture* 7, no. 2 (Winter 1995): 353–402.

Ruiz, Vicki L. *From Out of the Shadows: Mexican Women in Twentieth-Century America.* Oxford: Oxford University Press, 1998.

Sanchez, George J. *Becoming Mexican American: Ethnicity, Culture, and Identity in Chicano Los Angeles, 1900–1945.* New York: Oxford University Press, 1993.

Schmidt Camacho, Alicia. *Migrant Imaginaries: Latino Cultural Politics in the US-Mexico Borderlands.* New York: New York University Press, 2008.

Spickard, Paul. *Almost All Aliens: Immigration, Race, and Colonialism in American History and Identity.* Oxford: Routledge Press, 2007.

US Department of Labor. Children's Bureau. *The Children's Bureau and Problems of the Spanish Speaking Minority Groups, Report Files, 1941.* Washington, DC: Government Printing Office, 1941. Copy in box 18, Ernesto Galarza Collection, Special Collections, Stanford University.

US Department of Labor. Children's Bureau. *The Children's Bureau and Problems of the Spanish Speaking Minority Groups, Report Files, 1943.* Washington, DC: Government Printing Office, 1943. Copy in box 18, Ernesto Galarza Collection, Special Collections, Stanford University.

————. *The State of the Department of Labor Child Bureau Report, 1948.* Washington, DC: Government Printing Office, 1948. Copy in box 27, Ernesto Galarza Collection, Special Collections, Stanford University.

US Farm Employment Service Agency. *National Agricultural Annual Report, 1954.* Sacramento: Farm Employment Service Agency Publications, 1954.

US Immigration and Naturalization Service. *Immigration and Naturalization, 1960–1970.* Washington, DC: Government Printing Office, 1970.

Vargas, Zaragosa. *Labor Rights Are Civil Rights: Mexican American Workers in Twentieth-Century America.* Princeton, NJ: Princeton University Press, 2004.

Works Progress Administration. *Toy Loan Program Report.* Washington, DC, 1949. Copy in box 2, Manuel Ruiz Papers, Special Collections, Stanford University.

FILM

Cartas a Eufemia (*Letters to Eufemia*), Argel Films, 1952.

MUSICAL RECORDINGS

"El bracero mexicano" ["The Mexican Bracero"]. By Los Braceros. 1944.

"El hijo del pueblo" ["The Rural Town's Son"]. By José Alfredo Jiménez. From *El hijo del pueblo,* CD, Sony International, 1991.

"El jinete" ["The Horseman"]. By José Alfredo Jiménez. From *Tesoros de colección,* CD, Sony Music Entertainment B00136LXUG, 2007.

"La del rebozo blanco" ["The One with the White Shawl"]. By José Alfredo Jiménez. From *Tesoros de colección,* CD, Sony Music Entertainment B00136LXUG, 2007.

"Pal' Norte" ["To the North"]. By Calle 13. From *Residente o Visitante,* CD, 2007.

"Siempre hace frio" ["It is Always Cold"]. By Cuco Sanchez. Hispano Americana de Musica, 1956.

"Sufriendo a solas" ["Suffering Alone"] [1951]. By Jose Angel Espinoza ("Ferrusquillo"). From *En Sinaloa nací,* CD, RCA Records, 2011.

INDEX

Pages references in italics indicate illustrations. "The program" refers to the Bracero Program.

Avila Camacho, Manuel, 5, 19–24, 27, 33–34, 36, 191, 193
awake houses and *intermediarias*, 15, 147–84; and accountability (see *Braceros: Mojados*); an awake classroom, 157–58; Azucena Lopez, 158–64; Castaño's *Braceros: Mojados*, 149, 172–84; communication with braceros encouraged, 151; emotional support-seeking encouraged, 151–52; expansion of an awake house, 168–72; and gender expectations, 151, 159, 165–67, 169; goals of *intermediarias*, 148–49; and husbands' lack of communication, 170–71; Ignacia Zarate Mandujano Rios, 148–58; Maria Guadalupe Urzua Flores, 184; overview of, 147–50, 183–84, 215; purpose of awake houses, 148–49; record keeping by the women, 150–51; and sharing with children, 151; and sharing with parents/siblings, 152–54, 158–66, 168; and support by parents, 154–57, 165–68; Veneranda Torres, 164–72; and vocational education, 154–55
Ayala, Enrique, 91, 231n11

Barn Hill Ranch (San Antonio), 188
Bayside Social Center of California, 188–89
beauty salons, 80
Becerra, Jesus, 200
birria (spicy meat entrée), 79
Bowen, John, 66–67, 69
"El Bracero Mexicano," 187
Bracero Program (Emergency Farm Labor Program): contract guarantees/provisions, 20–21; contracting process for, 161–62; cyclical nature of, 8; dehumanization/segregation by, 7, 12, 36–37, 161–62; documenting costs/pain of, 218–20;

failures of, overview of, 3–4, 216; idealization of, 14, 28, 37; inauguration of, 5; Mexican immigration to United States managed via, 5–7, 11; number of men in, 7; purpose of, 1; recognition of exploitation/indignities endured under, 216–17; revenue from, 13; scholarship on, 1, 6; selection centers for, 12, 22, 227n7; termination of, 88, 216; transnational families created by, 1–2, 5–9, 12–13; transportation costs for braceros, 22; travel restrictions for braceros, 69–70, 72; wages under, 20–21; women's confrontation of (see awake houses and *intermediarias*); workers' rights under, 7. See also recruitment for the program
Bracero Program as a permanent state of emergency, 40–65; idealization of the program, 14; and letters to braceros, importance of, 48–49; parents' support of braceros, 42–46; and patriotism, 40–41; and repatriation of injured workers, 44; and repatriation problems, 59–62; silencing braceros, 40–42; and the Sleepy Lagoon incident, 57–58; a transnational family history (Rosas case study), 46–57, 47, 50–51, 53–54; US child citizens, 58–62
Los Braceros, 187
Braceros: Mojados (Castaño), 149, 172–84
Buendia, Arturo, 37, 228n7

caldo de birria (*birria* stew), 79
California: immigrant families' alienation, flexibility, and resilience in, 11; labor camps in, 12, 66 (see also Tulare)
Cartas a Eufemia (Letters to Eufemia), 98–99
casa despierta. See awake houses and *intermediarias*

Casillas, Dolores, 109–10
Castaño, Rosa de: *Braceros: Mojados*, 149, 172–84; *El Coyote*, 173
Catholic Council of Working Life, 205
censorship of families' correspondence, 14–15, 85–99; as blocking family sources of information, 90–92; *Cartas a Eufemia* (Letters to Eufemia), 98–99; censoring children, 93–94; as dividing couples, 88–90; documenting potential illegal immigrants via, 94–95; goals of, 86–87, 93–94; overview of, 85–88; presented as a wartime measure, 98; questions about US and Mexican governments' accountability for, 97–98; *The Treasure of the Bracero*, 95–97; as unpublicized, 86, 98–99; as withholding crucial/tragic news, 92–93
Chihuahua (Mexico), 87–88
child citizens, US, 58–62, 197–206, 217–18
childhood's loss, 15, 185–96; abuse of children, 188; children's migration/labor in search of their fathers, 186; exemplary children without equal, 186–92, 196; girls as laborers, 188; local programs for bracero children in Mexico, 191–96; overview of, 185–87; and the toy loan program, 189
Children's Bureau (US Department of Labor), 58–62, 188
The Children's Bureau and Problems of the Spanish Speaking Minority Groups, 59–62
Clark, Tom, 189–90
class stratification, 10, 23, 27. *See also* under San Martin de Hidalgo
Cobla, Katie and Sara, 124, *125*
contract labor. *See* Bracero Program
El Coyote (Castaño), 173

Delgadillo Sanchez, Esther Legaspi, *115*, *119–20*

Department of Charities (County of Los Angeles Bureau of Public Assistance), 197–203, 205, 207
Department of Public Welfare (Tulare, California), 201
Diaz, Jose, 57–58
dress shops, 80
Duran, Maritza, 220–21

Emergency Farm Labor Program. *See* Bracero Program
Emerson, Muriel E., 202
El Escritorio Publico el Minutito ("The Quick Minute" Notary Public), 62–63
exemplary children without equal, 186–92, 196

femininity, traditional, 25
Fernandez, Estela Alarcon, 204
Fernandez, Francisco, 204
Fisher Brothers Creative Printing and Stationary Company, 96
Flores, Juana G., 94
Flores, Maria Guadalupe Urzua, 184, 215
Frias, Ramona, 140–42, *141*
Frias, Salvador, 140–42, *142*

Galarza, Ernesto, 10, 40–41, 73–74
Garcia, Elisa, 200
Garcia, Teresa, 108
Garcia, Vicenta F., 94
Giacomini, Sally, 200–201
Gonzalez, Francisca Negrete, 106
Gonzalez, Maria, 205–6
Gonzalez Garcia, Juan, 106
grower associations, 21, 58, 205–6
Guadalajara, 39, 226n23
Guerra, Maria Graciela Garcia, 131–39, *134, 136–37, 139*
Guerra de Leon, Artemio, 36–37, 131–33, *132, 135–36, 136, 138–39, 139*
guest worker initiative. *See* Bracero Program

business lots leased in, 211–14; middle-class business opportunities for working-class families in, 211–14; middle-class families' programs for/ employment of bracero children in, 191–95; middle-class families recruited in, 24–25; middle-class women in, 26; recruitment fees in, 22; special-immigrant status in, 76–81; statues honoring townswomen of, 183–84, 215–16; transnationalization of, 10–12; vocational education of women in, 154–55; working-class braceros financed by middle-class families in, 22, 24, 27, 31; working conditions for bracero families in, 37–38

Santa Cruz (Arizona), 60

Santander, Estefania, 85–86

Santander, German, 85–86

Sawyer, Grace, 197–98

Schmidt Camacho, Alicia, 13

Secure Communities Program, 217

sevillana (shawl worn over women's head and shoulders), 156

Silverstone, Sonya M., 88–89

Sleepy Lagoon incident, 57–58

songs: role in long-distance relationships, 100–101, 103–4, 108–10; sung by exemplary children without equal, 187

Sonora (Mexico), 20

special immigration, 14, 66–81; braceros' reaction to, 69, 73; and bracero violence, 75; exploitiveness of, 72–73, 81; introduction of the policy, 68; mobility and managing braceros in the United States, 68–70, 72–76; moral eligibility for, 68, 73, 77–78; morality and managing families in Mexico, 76–81; movement of families to the United States, 70–72; opposition to, 73; overview of, 66–68; selection centers for the program, 71; status/

contracts of special immigrants, 67–71, 73–77; termination of, 81

Stockton Bee, 204–5

"Suffering Alone," 109

Swing, Joseph M., 68

thinking historically. *See* acting and thinking historically

Torres, Jesus, 3–4, 124–30

Torres, Maria Francisca Ordoñez, 3, 124–26, 128, 188

Torres, Veneranda, 2–3, 124–31, *126–27*, *164–72*

Torres Vigil, Antonio, 92

town hall meetings, as gendered/ family-oriented, 25

toy loan program, 189

transnational family process: border enforcement/deportation's impact on, 7–8; a family history (Rosas case study), 46–57, *47, 50–51, 53–54;* as gendered, 6; under the program, 1–2, 5–9, 12–13

The Treasure of the Bracero, 95–97

Tulare (California), 66–67, 69–70, 72–73, 75, 201

undocumented Mexican immigration, 15, 197–214; and abandonment/estrangement in Mexican countryside, 207–10; absent parents' accountability, 199–201, 205; ANC support of immigrant children, 197–207; bracero-on-bracero crime, 75; deportation of immigrants, 214, 217; forestalling village abandonment, 210–14; labor shortage due to emigration, 35–36; legacy of, 221; Mexican public notary office's assistance to migrants, 62–63; Operation Wetback's effects on, 199, 206–7, 209–11; opposition to, 12; overview of, 197–99; repatriated US citizen children, 59–62. *See also* Operation Wetback

AMERICAN CROSSROADS

Edited by Earl Lewis, George Lipsitz, George Sánchez,
Dana Takagi, Laura Briggs, and Nikhil Pal Singh